American Buddhism as a Way of Life

SUNY series in Buddhism and American Culture

John Whalen-Bridge and Gary Storhoff, editors

American Buddhism as a Way of Life

Edited by
Gary Storhoff
and
John Whalen-Bridge

Published by State University of New York Press, Albany

For information, contact State University of New York Press, Albany, NY
www.sunypress.edu

Production by Diane Ganeles
Marketing by Michael Campochiaro

Library of Congress Cataloging-in-Publication Data

American Buddhism as a way of life / edited by Gary Storhoff and John
Whalen-Bridge.
     p. cm. — (SUNY series in Buddhism and American culture)
   Includes bibliographical references and index.
   ISBN 978-1-4384-3093-5 (hardcover : alk. paper)
   ISBN 978-1-4384-3094-2 (pbk. : alk. paper)
   1. Buddhism—United States.   2. Buddhism and culture—United States.
I. Storhoff, Gary.   II. Whalen-Bridge, John.

   BQ732.A44 2010
   294.30973—dc22   2009033231

10 9 8 7 6 5 4 3 2 1

Gary Storhoff dedicates his work on this volume
to his brother, Steve Storhoff.

John Whalen-Bridge dedicates his work on this volume
to his father, Josiah Bridge.

Contents

In Memoriam, Roger Corless (1938–2007)

David L. Dupree

Meeting Roger some fifteen years ago at an Alcoholics Anonymous meeting was the beginning of a major friendship. Little did I know that he was such a highly respected scholar. However, as he would remind me, he did Professor very well. Roger was born on Mercyside, England in 1938, and was brought up in the Church of England, but he told his mother at twelve that he was a Buddhist of ages past. She and his father, taking little note of this assertion, watched him earn a Bachelor of Divinity at Kings College, University of London, and a PhD at the University of Wisconsin.

Roger's as-yet-to-be-published final contribution is a novel he called *Where Do We Go From Here? Buddhism, Christianity, and the Next Step*. I hope to have it published within the next year and will certainly announce it on THE CORLESS website, along with other links about this remarkable man. THE CORLESS is a nonprofit foundation that provides scholarships to graduate students studying interfaith dialogue.

Roger became a part of my family, encouraging me to adopt my son when I hesitated, including me in some of his adventures as I did him mine, and generally being the older brother I never had but had always wanted. As he lay passing at 1:45 a.m. on January 12, 2007, I thought many things. But he did not look unhappy.

Foreword

Thomas A. Tweed

"Hold back the edges of your gowns, Ladies, we are going through hell." That's how William Carlos Williams introduced American readers to Allen Ginsberg's 1956 volume, *Howl and Other Poems*.[1] That was an appropriate herald for Ginsberg's poetic rant, but readers of this collection of scholarly essays, *American Buddhism as a Way of Life*, require a different sort of introduction. Few of you are wearing gowns—or so I assume. Not all of you are Ladies. And the editors, Gary Storhoff and John Whalen-Bridge, are not leading you to hell— or so they hope. At the same time—you should be warned—you're also not headed to a distant Pure Land, a land of bliss removed from the messy realities of everyday life.

Some of the essays profile the transmitters and popularizers of Buddhism in the United States, like D. T. Suzuki and Alan Watts, but even in those portraits the everyday is always near, as when Ellen Pearlman recalls dining with D. T. Suzuki's former secretary and remembers holding Ginsberg's hand on his death bed. Other authors ascend to doctrinal heights to consider complex Buddhist ideas—like no-self, dependent co-origination, and nonduality—but they always move back to the ordinary: to work out an engaged Buddhism, to imagine our obligations as we face the living, the dying, and the unborn. From an enlightened perspective, the world of suffering is identical to the world of bliss—in Buddhist terms, *samsara* is *nirvana*. Suffering, however, seems real enough. And the contributors don't flinch as they offer historical, sociological, and ethical analyses of the personal and collective suffering that Americans have faced, from agonizing decisions about abortion and euthanasia to brutal encounters with homophobia and racism.

But the Buddhists described in these essays are not solitary travelers. They journey together toward the here and now, as part of the *sangha*. And they invite you along. They ponder Buddhist life in the home and beyond those domestic spaces—in Rochester Zen Center's garden and a Nisei Buddhist temple in Hawai'i. As with those Japanese Buddhists, however, the gaze also seems focused on the wider national landscape. For it's in the political, social, and cultural landscape of America, not some distant hell or heaven, that these U.S. Buddhists have made their way.

So hold back the edges of your gowns, Ladies, we're staying right here in the messy bliss of the everyday.

Notes

1. Allen Ginsberg, *Howl and Other Poems* (San Francisco: City Lights Books, 1956).

Introduction

American Buddhism as a Way of Life

Gary Storhoff and John Whalen-Bridge

There is an orientalism in the most restless pioneer, and the farthest west is but the farthest east.

—Henry David Thoreau, *A Week on the Concord and Merrimack Rivers*

Go forth on your journey, for the benefit of the many, for the joy of the many, out of compassion for the world, for the welfare, for the benefit and joy of mankind.

—Shakyamuni Buddha, *Vinaya* I, 21

America today is one of the most vital Buddhist countries in the world.

—Rick Fields, *How the Swans Came to the Lake*

Because of the focus of media, celebrity converts, popular film, and the popularity of the Dalai Lama, most Americans would find it difficult to overlook the prominence of Buddhism in American culture today, even though fewer than 1 percent of Americans are Buddhists.[1] It is clear that non-Western religions, especially Buddhism, are transforming the American religious perspective. Buddhism has expanded through a wide spectrum of American culture, including literature, art, psychology, film, and other religious traditions. Our first volume in this series on American Buddhism, *The Emergence of Buddhist American Literature*, demonstrated the profound influence of this very decidedly immigrant faith in American culture since the beginning of the twentieth century; the essays in that volume revealed the pervasive influence of Buddhism in contemporary American literature as well. Indeed, *The Emergence of Buddhist American Literature* represents the most complete treatment to date of Buddhism in American literature, including discussions of seminal writers of High Modernism such as Ernest Fenollosa and Ezra Pound; innovative treatment of the Beats such as Allen Ginsberg and Jack Kerouac; and—perhaps groundbreaking for contemporary studies of American Buddhism—analyses of Buddhist principles in literary works by contemporary writers of color, such as Maxine Hong Kingston, Lan Cao, and Charles Johnson.

American Buddhism as a Way of Life continues the series on Buddhism culture by examining in wide-ranging essays how Buddhism has been transmitted to America spiritually and materially in the late twentieth and early twenty-first centuries. Rather than focus in this volume on cultural practices such as literature, however, we have decided to emphasize how American Buddhism has indeed become a "way of life"—to paraphrase Pierre Hadot, whose title *Philosophy as a Way of Life* inspired our own: American Buddhism is, to draw on Hadot's eloquence, "a way of life, both in its exercise and effort to achieve wisdom, and in its goal, wisdom itself. For real wisdom does not merely cause us to know: it makes us 'be' in a different way."[2] Americans typically search for new religious expression, as public opinion surveys repeatedly show. Released in February 2008, the U.S. Religious Landscape Survey conducted by the Pew Forum demonstrates conclusively the strength of American religion;[3] however, the Americans surveyed very much desire, using Hadot's formulation, to " 'be' in a different way" from the living styles offered by conventional religions: According to the Pew Report, 44 percent of the Americans surveyed have left their original religious home for another—Buddhism being one of those new residences.[4]

Yet Buddhism's appeal to contemporary American society is ambiguous and sometimes contradictory: Where does a fashionable and trendy practice of Buddhism end, and where does a serious, committed, and devotional focus on Buddhism begin? In a visit to the local bookstore, one can purchase such titles as *Zen and the Art of Poker* or (perhaps aiming at a more ambitious audience) *Zen and the Art of Anything*. Also, this ancient religion has predictably invaded the Internet; for example, MSN.com offers a site called the Zen Guide to American Cities, describing primarily vegetarian restaurants, sushi takeouts, health food stores, and massage centers. Part of the success of *The Matrix* films were their presumed basis in Buddhist epistemological principles. To many Americans, Buddhism has become the primary gateway to a meaningful life, an all-encompassing "Way."

To a great degree, then, Buddhism may have been superficially absorbed by segments of American popular culture, and the problem of deciding what is "serious" and what is a passing New Age fad may detract from the importance of the fact that at least a million Americans have indeed borrowed liberally from a wide variety of ancient Buddhist traditions, usually in a genuine effort to seek a new, more satisfying "way of life." It goes without saying that American culture has historically no clear institutional parallel to Buddhism, since the introduction of Buddhism to America has depended upon immigrants: The Buddhist influeneek is especially striking when we consider the cultural divide that has been traversed. Unlike Asia, America has no millennia-old categories of tradition, myth, and lore that center on Buddhist spiritual and meditative traditions. As the English immigrant Alan Watts writes in his introduction to *The Way of Zen*: "Zen Buddhism is a way and a view of life which does not belong to any of the formal categories of modern Western thought."[5]

On the surface it would seem that the prevailing worldview of the United States is antithetical to a Buddhist vision of reality—with its emphasis on no-self (*anatman*), emptiness (*sunyata*), and dependent origination (*pratityasamutpada*). This tension between Buddhist thought and an American culture emphasizing individualism and self-reliance has long been noted and debated. For instance Richard Hughes Seager, in his discussion of the introduction of Buddhism in The World's Parliament of Religions in Chicago in 1893, asks, "Could the teachings of Buddha about the nonexistence of the self be reconciled with American individualism? Could a tradition emphasizing contemplation thrive in a culture known for its extroversion and activism?"[6]

In spite of its cultural alterity, Buddhism has thrived in America, perhaps partly because many American Buddhists have developed a kind of reciprocity with their faith: as Buddhism changes them, they have changed the faith itself. Historically Buddhism has evolved wherever it has spread, responding as a vital and dynamic religion to local customs and emotional needs. It would be unreasonable to expect forms of Japanese, Tibetan, or Chinese Buddhism—all of which have a millennial lineage in specific cultural environments—to satisfy perfectly the needs of contemporary American Buddhists. And although the understanding of Buddhism is often characterized by appropriation and misunderstanding, an orientalism usually combined with genuine sincerity, it is fair to say with James William Coleman in *The New Buddhism* that "Western Buddhism is no longer in its infancy, but neither has it reached mature adulthood. Fresh, innovative, and diverse, it still shows a good deal of adolescent awkwardness as well. But like most adolescents, it is easy to see the seeds from which its character is growing and its differences from the parents that gave it birth."[7]

The contributors of *American Buddhism as a Way of Life* avoid the "mysterious Orient" perspective that has been apparent in the "adolescent awkwardness" Coleman describes, but instead they enthusiastically engage with the various ways Buddhism has become implicated in American culture. As the eleven studies in this volume indicate, the range of social concerns motivating serious American Buddhists to public service and political activism include various areas of community experience and suffering: race, human rights, gender relations and sexual orientation, hospice living and end-of-life decisions, the workplace and marketplace. As Christopher S. Queen writes, "The direction of contemporary Buddhism, like that of other ancient faith traditions, has been deeply influenced both by the magnitude of social suffering in the world today, and by the globalization of cultural values and perspectives we associated with the Western cultural tradition, especially the notions of human rights, economic justice, political due process, and social progress."[8]

Buddhists of all sorts revere the Triple Gem of *Buddha, Dharma,* and *Sangha,* and this volume has taken an organizational cue from the central categories of Buddhism. *Buddha* signifies the effects of the teacher, and the first section of essays in this volume is about teachers. Part 1, *Buddha*: The Teacher as Immigrant, discusses two major influences of Buddhism in twentieth-century America: D. T. Suzuki and Alan Watts. David L. Smith's chapter on Watts focuses on Watts's "authenticity" as a teacher of Buddhist philosophy: Does Watts deserve an exalted position as a Buddhist thinker and American disseminator? Part of the problem of Watts's career, as Smith explains, is that Watts organized his beliefs on paradoxes. Watts himself denied his commitment to Buddhist practice even as he practiced Buddhism, and he insisted that he had nothing to teach, even as his followers made him a source of Buddhist teachings. In Smith's nuanced analysis of the paradoxical nature of Watts's career, Watts approached Buddhism in a complex, eclectic, though thoroughly modest way. Smith shows that Watts's ambivalence in defining himself as a Buddhist and his disavowal of the role of Teacher were both central to his Buddhist principles, which he derived from the paradoxes of both Eastern philosophy and the modern general systems theory of the double-bind. Smith's chapter carefully recuperates Watts's reputation while also explaining why Buddhism—as taught by Watts—was so popular among Americans.

Part 1 also includes two chapters devoted to D. T. Suzuki, another seminal teacher of American Buddhism. Carl T. Jackson surveys Suzuki's entire career, wrestling with the controversy first raised by Brian Victoria and other students of Buddhism: To what extent was Suzuki an advocate of the Japanese military aggression during World War II? Was Suzuki a Nihonist? Jackson presents a balanced account of this controversy, but the reader must encounter the evidence suggesting that Suzuki was at least an implicit sympathizer of Nihonism. Jackson argues that Victoria and other critics may not be accurate in their more extreme arguments insisting on Suzuki's guilt. The next chapter, "My Lunch with Mihoko" by Ellen Pearlman, presents a spirited defense of Suzuki with a personal narrative of her visit to Japan and her lunch with Mihoko Okamura, Suzuki's secretary during the last fifteen years of his life. Ms. Okamura, of course, is predictably fierce in her defense of her former employer, and whether or not readers are persuaded by Mihoko's apologetics, they will enjoy the charm and verve of Pearlman's account of her visit to Japan and her encounter with one of the last living members of what Pearlman calls the "first wave" of Buddhism's transmission to America during the 1950s.

Dharma examines the doctrines taught by the historical Buddha and also those developed by later Buddhist traditions; Part 2 of this volume is concerned with doctrinal discussions. *Dharma*: Doctrine, Belief, and Practice in America deals with how Buddhism has been naturalized into ethics and philosophy in modern and postmodern American culture. This section seeks to show how Buddhism's rich tradition of thought on ethics can be employed to address painful and contentious issues that are currently confronting American society; the chapters treat varied topics such as bioethics, racial identity formation, feminism, gay rights, and postmodernist theory. Each chapter demonstrates the way Buddhism extends beyond its own origins, so its ethics may therefore be understood within the context of its contemporary practice. This part is theoretically based, but it also proposes concrete and pragmatic actions a Buddhist might choose to take in American public life. The first chapter in part 2 is Michael Brannigan's "What Can Buddhist No-Self Contribute to North

American Bioethics?" Brannigan acknowledges the seeming contradiction between the American emphasis on individualism as it applies to patient rights, especially as these rights pertain to crucial end-of-life decision-making for the patient and his or her family. During such critical times, Brannigan proposes, Buddhism may provide emotional relief and a spiritual refuge for patients and families who must make difficult decisions. Furthermore, he argues that a consideration of the core Buddhist teaching, specifically the doctrines of no-self (*anatman*) and dependent origination (*pratityasamutpada*), within the context of patient rights, may lead to major reassessments of American bioethics. Understanding these doctrines may, Brannigan asserts, result in diminished pain and greater compassion for patients, their families, and the caregivers caught between them. Brannigan's speculative chapter searches deeply into health care and ethics in America.

If Brannigan's essay explains how Buddhism may clarify or expand viable ethical alternatives for end-of-life decisions in America, Rita M. Gross's chapter demonstrates how an equally complex issue, abortion, may be reconceived using Buddhist ethics as a moral framework for the debate. In her chapter, "A Contemporary North American Buddhist Discussion of Abortion," Gross explains how confusion over language in the abortion debate—where "pro-choice" proponents are usually defined as "pro-abortion"—obviates rational thinking. Instead, she recommends the Buddhist virtues of mindfulness and compassion as linguistic resources. Like Brannigan, Gross argues that the doctrine of dependent origination would help clarify the ethical dimensions of the abortion issue, and also that introducing a clearer definition of "life" might help reduce the intense emotions of anger and guilt associated with the abortion debate. Gross's chapter shows that feminism in contemporary American politics is not inconsistent with fundamental Buddhist doctrine.

Judy D. Whipps's chapter, "Touched by Suffering: American Pragmatism and Engaged Buddhism," builds on Gross's chapter by demonstrating that Buddhist principles of compassion and mindfulness have never been entirely alien to American social action. In her discussion of Buddhism, Jane Addams, and the founding of Hull House, Whipps challenges the present-day reader to embrace Buddhist principles, as he or she imagines how best to engage with contemporary political problems and to evaluate the power of Buddhism in dealing with those in prisons, shelters, hospices, and on the streets. Although Buddhism is often considered a quietist religion, Whipps shows how the Engaged Buddhism movement, begun by the Vietnamese Buddhist Thich Nhat Hanh, has philosophical connections with early twentieth-century American pragmatists such as Jane Addams. Whipps also discovers in the increased practice of ordained Buddhist women a political impact on American political and social practice. Whipps's pragmatic and historical discussion of Buddhism and ethics is balanced by the next highly theoretical discussion of identity and the American self in relation to Buddhism. John Kitterman's "Identity Theft: Simulating *Nirvana* in Postmodern America," which develops postmodern theory, specifically the work of Slavoj Žižek, to interrogate the nature of the "real" in American society from a Buddhist perspective. Kitterman returns the reader to the question of how Buddhism can possibly survive in postmodern American culture. To what extent, Kitterman asks, can Buddhism thrive in a nation that simultaneously seeks the "real" with passion while simultaneously avoiding the "real" through simulation?

Sangha has a range of meanings, either referring to the monks and nuns who renounce worldly life to take up the Buddhist way exclusively, or denoting in a much more inclusive manner the community of Buddhist practitioners, whether robed or not. Part 3 of this volume has to do with the social dimensions of American Buddhism. The volume's third part is entitled *Sangha:* Who Is an American Buddhist? It begins with the perennial questions in American Buddhist studies: Who is an American Buddhist? What constitutes the Buddhist life in America? These questions have given scholars of American Buddhism much to think about. In fact, Peter N. Gregory likens answering these questions to the famous Buddhist parable of blind men attempting to describe an elephant: As each man touches a different part of the elephant, a different description of the animal is given—the point being that the subject (who is a Buddhist?) is almost too large to comprehend.[9] Robert Wuthnow and Wendy Cadge have recently taken a very different perspective to this question. Instead of what they term "the strictness hypothesis" of simply counting Buddhists—a controversial project—they recommend "a broader argument about institutional embeddedness"; that is, they attempt to assess Buddhism's great appeal to contemporary Americans and the reasons for it. They write, "Americans' receptivity to Buddhism requires paying attention to the institutions in which Buddhists and Buddhist teachings are embedded."[10] It is in the spirit of Wuthnow and Cadge's essay that the authors of this volume proceed.

"Buddhism," it could be said, is giving way to "Buddhisms": Given the plurality of practices and beliefs, the authors must reformulate definitions and descriptions. One of the foremost experts on the question, Charles S. Prebish begins part 3 by presenting a general introduction to spiritual kinship in Buddhism in relation to family life. This discussion leads to his speculations about the "ideal" family life in Buddhism, whether of American converts or of immigrant Asians. Because American society brings together the various traditions of Buddhism into a close proximity that was not historically common in Asia, Prebish's chapter is especially valuable for its exploration of how children are instructed in Buddhism—a study curiously neglected in earlier scholarship. His discussion of the family-oriented Buddhist, then, charts a new direction in Buddhist studies.

Part 3 continues with Lori Pierce's discussion of Japanese American religious identity in the early-to-mid twentieth century. Pierce's chapter, "Buddha Loves Me This I Know: Nisei Buddhists in Christian America, 1889–1942," combines Prebish's insights on the instruction of Buddhists to their children and the difficulties of reconciling Buddhist belief with an anti-Asian culture at the advent of World War II. As Pierce shows, second-generation Japanese Americans (Nisei) created a new American identity that was based on coordinating the Japanese values of their immigrant parents (Issei) with American cultural and social values such as individualism and freedom of choice. Despite the enormous pressure to reject Japanese values, Pierce shows, the majority of the Nisei remained true to their Buddhist faith. Pierce also connects the myriad philosophical and personal connections that supported American Buddhism in the early twentieth century.

If Pierce's chapter deals with the oppression of Japanese Americans in Hawai'i after Pearl Harbor, Roger Corless forcefully asks what American Buddhists can learn from the gay liberation movement. "Analogue Consciousness Isn't Just for Faeries" argues for social engagement by American Buddhists, showing how Buddhism itself could be modified by the principles of the gay pride movement in America. Unfortunately, Roger died as this volume was coming to press, so that he was never able to develop and expand his thoughts on queer theory and Buddhism; nevertheless, this essay is one of his last published works, one he hoped would inspire controversy, speculation, and critical thinking. For Corless, Buddhism as it is traditionally practiced is frequently based on a dualistic worldview, despite the claim that Buddhism is nondualistic. Corless reveals in his provocative analysis Buddhism's potentially world-denying feature, and the often subtle homophobia concealed in Buddhist practice. As an alternative to this often obscured dualistic practice in Buddhism, Corless recommends Harry Hay's concept of the "analogue" or "subject-SUBJECT consciousness," which would allow Buddhism *and* Christianity to accept nonduality in practice, not just theory. Corless intended his chapter to be speculative rather than definitive; perhaps the best memoriam to him would be to consider his argument and respond to the issues in as lively a manner as "Analogue Consciousness" does.

We hope readers will find *American Buddhism as a Way of Life* to be an anthology of diverse and beautiful flowers, and so the volume concludes with an essay on gardening—one which emphasizes the growing centrality of Buddhism in American material and spiritual life. Jeff Wilson's "'A Dharma of Place': Evolving Aesthetics and Cultivating Community in an American Zen Garden," examines how two very different traditions of Asian Zen spiritualism and American materialism cross-pollinate in the making of the Rochester Zen Center garden. Wilson's essay shows that the garden's design expresses an intention to move the Zen practitioner from his or her own personal perspective toward the consciousness of being part of a group. The construction of the center itself thereby reflects the aesthetics and values that the Buddhist community celebrates—interdependent mutuality. Our volume on American identity and Buddhist culture, then, brings together eleven wide-ranging discussions of the intercultural engagement of two seemingly dichotomous worldviews. The contributors to this collection explore this relationship in a manner established in previous scholarship, but also with an enthusiasm for the contemporary synergy created by the potential fusion of American and Buddhist visions.

Notes

1. Martin Baumann, in "The Dharma Has Come West: A Survey of Recent Studies and Sources," online at http://www.urbandharma.org/udharma/survey.html, writes that in the mid-1990s there were three to four million Buddhists in the United States.

2. Pierre Hadot, *Philosophy as a Way of Life: Spiritual Exercises from Socrates to Foucault*, ed. Arnold I. Davidson, trans. Michael Chase (Oxford: Blackwell, 1995), 265.

3. Pew Forum on Religion & Public Life, "U.S. Religious Landscape Survey," www.religions.pewforum.org/reports. Survey published 25 February 2008 (accessed 21 April 2008).

4. The survey reveals that .7% of those surveyed identify themselves as Buddhist, though as most commentators agree, the actual number of Buddhists is exceptionally difficult to ascertain. See, for example, Peter N. Gregory, "Describing the Elephant: Buddhism in America," *Religion and American Culture: A Journal of Interpretation* 11:2 (2001): 233–63. None of our contributors attempt to establish the number of Buddhists in America.

5. Alan Watts, *The Way of Zen* (New York: Vintage Books, 1957), 3.

6. Richard Hughes Seager, *Buddhism in America* (New York: Columbia University Press, 1999), 37.

7. James William Coleman, *The New Buddhism: The Western Transformation of an Ancient Tradition* (Oxford: Oxford University Press, 2001), 217–18.

8. Christopher S. Queen, ed., *Engaged Buddhism in the West* (Boston: Wisdom Publications, 2000), 23.

9. Gregory, "Describing the Elephant," 233–34.

10. Robert Wuthnow and Wendy Cadge, "Buddhists and Buddhism in the United States: The Scope of Influence," *Journal for the Scientific Study of Religion* 43:3 (2004): 363–80.

Part I

Buddha: The Teacher as Immigrant

1

The Authenticity of Alan Watts

David L. Smith

Alan Watts (1915–1973) was one of the most influential teachers of Buddhism in mid-twentieth-century America, although he was neither a Buddhist nor, to his own way of thinking, a teacher. Whatever he became, he made his way by evading conventional categories. Early on, as a student at a highly conventional English preparatory school, he distinguished himself by declaring himself a Buddhist. Later, in America, he invented his own vocation as a freelance lecturer, broadcaster, and author of books on comparative philosophy in general and Zen Buddhism in particular. Throughout his adult life, however, Watts refused to call himself a Buddhist, arguing in fact that it would be un-Buddhist of him to do so.[1] He participated regularly in no Buddhist community or practice, and apart from a brief association with Sokei-an in New York, he studied with no Buddhist teachers. His "tastes" in religion, as he liked to put it, lay rather "between Mahayana Buddhism and Taoism, with a certain leaning towards Vedanta and Catholicism."[2] More a connoisseur of religious ideas than a committed participant, Watts was accordingly reluctant to represent himself as a teacher of any of the traditions he loved. He preferred to think of himself as a gadfly or "philosophical entertainer."[3] He had nothing to offer anyone, he held, that they did not already know.

Watts nevertheless had a substantive message. Its core, consistently reiterated throughout his career, was a remarkably fresh and cogent version of religious nondualism. Generally speaking, nondualism is a philosophical position, or more precisely a mode of skeptical

13

argument, that radically undermines the categories of subject and object, self and environment, and cause and effect according to which conventional views of our selves and our place in the world are structured. Nondualism is a spiritual teaching, in turn, because the adoption of a nondualist viewpoint can have consequences that are felt to be saving or liberating. To dissolve the distinction between the experiencing self and the experienced world can have the effect of untying knots that render ordinary life painful and problematic. Nondual thought and spirituality, then, figure prominently in a number of religious traditions, most notably Advaita Vedanta, Madhyamaka Buddhism, and philosophical Taoism.[4]

Not coincidentally, it was precisely these religious schools that interested Watts. Moreover, to his credit as an original thinker but to the detriment of his reputation as a scholar, it was only insofar as these traditions exemplified the logic of nondualism that he was interested in them. Commentators over the years have faulted Watts for this selective, highly individual approach to religious traditions. Often they simply point to the title of his autobiography, *In My Own Way*, as sufficient cause to dismiss him.[5] As I hope to show, however, this line of criticism reflects a basic misunderstanding of Watts's intellectual project, which had less to do with scholarly reconstruction than with the creation of something new. It is true that Watts's typical strategy throughout his career was to discuss the ideas that excited him in the context of the religions in which he had discovered them—piggybacking on found poetry, so to speak. Thus, he drew extensively on Madhyamaka for its argumentation, Taoism for its poetry, Hinduism for mind-boggling cosmic dramaturgy, and Zen for practical wisdom. He even wrote books that are ostensibly about Zen, Taoism, and Vedanta.[6] However, Watts never claimed to be the kind of scholar who represents a subject whole and on its own terms. As he put it in *The Way of Zen* (1957), his goal was to speak from neither the standpoint of Zen nor that of conventional scholarship, but from a third perspective that triangulated between them.[7] Taoism and Zen were important to him, that is, because they were vehicles of nondualism, and therefore pointers to that independent third thing. Nondualism was important to him, in turn, not because it was Buddhist or Chinese, but because it seemed to authenticate itself through its power to illuminate circumstances closer to home—the foibles of Western society and the wonder of being alive.

Watts's distinctive version of nondualism seems to have grown out of his own experience of the paradoxes of the spiritual quest. A conversation he reports from 1937 is paradigmatic. Inspired by the writings of Krishnamurti, Watts was straining desperately at the time to realize perfect concentration on the present moment. His girlfriend, however, pulled the rug out from under his effort with an offhand comment: " 'Why try to concentrate on it? What else *is* there to be aware of . . . ? The present is just a constant flow, like the Tao, and there's simply no way of getting out of it.' "[8] This deft piece of spiritual jujitsu left Watts feeling suddenly freed from all the traps he had been struggling to escape. It became, in effect, his model for how to deal with the human spiritual predicament.

The epigraph to a book he published in the same year stated the point concisely: "To seek after the Tao is like turning round in circles to see one's own eyes. Those who understand this walk straight on."[9] Human beings long for wholeness and meaning, that is, and they typically seek it as if it lay elsewhere. Watts's discovery, however, was that the wholeness sought is already implicit in our condition. There is no essential difference between the life we desire and the life we live. A larger, more mysterious reality than our conscious selves is already the seer of our seeing, the agent of our actions, our real nature. We may not be able to observe It, but we *are* It. Watts was thus convinced that the sense of alienation that gives rise to the desire to become whole should be relatively easy to overcome, if only we could get past the stubborn illusion that we are anything other than whole in the first place. A second epigraph to that early book completes the thought: "it is only when you seek [the Tao] that you lose it." We will become ourselves when we stop *trying* to become ourselves.

Watts was never sure how to characterize this insight, which he took to be at once the heart of all wisdom literature, the key to human freedom and sanity, and as common as grass. To call it "mystical" or "spiritual" seemed too otherworldly, for the awareness and its object were perfectly natural. "Cosmic consciousness" likewise had "the unpoetic flavor of occultist jargon."[10] *Satori, moksha,* enlightenment, and grace were all appropriate in their ways, he believed, but came trailing too much doctrinal baggage from their respective traditions. The insight was independent of any religious system, and so it provided a critical perspective on all of them. As he found in his mature works, it could be discussed as readily in the language of science as that of theology.[11]

Accordingly, Watts's approach to all traditional religious forms was indeed highly individual and selective, and in refusing the Buddhist label, he was only being honest. There is another sense, however, in which the same qualities of individualism, eclecticism, and universalism that made him impatient with conventional schools of the *dharma* relate Watts to an important Buddhist lineage of a different kind: the international movement characterized by Donald Lopez as "modern Buddhism."[12] As Lopez and others tell the story, over the last century and a half, scholars, seekers, and religious reformers in both the orientalist West and the nationalist East have colluded in the development of a form of Buddhism that understands itself to transcend particular historical styles, creeds, and modes of worship.[13] It is a Buddhism shaped by distinctively modern values of rationalism, egalitarianism, universalism, and individualism, which nevertheless understands itself to represent the original, uncorrupted insights of the historical Buddha—a pure and timeless truth unmixed with ritual and doctrinal accretions. Watts learned Buddhism from the modernizers, especially from the early writings of D. T. Suzuki. His own work, in turn, exemplified the basic themes of the movement in its selective preference for the intellectual, nondualist elements of Buddhism as distinct from its developed traditions of ritual, belief, and practice. Watts valued Buddhism, in fact, precisely because it seemed to him to have an intellectual, practical core that was separable from its ritual and doctrinal husk; it was preeminently, as he liked to say, "the religion of no-religion."[14] Thus, Watts could only be the sort of Buddhist he wanted to be by refusing to be a Buddhist, just as he could only be the sort of teacher he wanted to be by denying that he had anything to teach.

Watts is best understood, then, as a spokesman for the supposedly timeless truth of nondualism rather than as a Buddhist—and yet as someone closely aligned with a particular kind of Buddhism for all that. Likewise, he was more an artist of the written and spoken word than a scholar, and more a trickster than a teacher—and yet an unusually effective teacher in consequence. His books, lectures, and radio broadcasts reached hundreds of thousands. Even some of his harshest detractors acknowledge his role as an awakener or precursor to a spiritual or scholarly engagement with Buddhism. Edward Conze, for example, writing in the 1970s, noted that "most of my American students first became interested in Buddhism through Alan Watts. It is true that they had to unlearn most of what they had learnt. It is equally true that he put out the net that caught them in the first place."[15] Although the current climate of academic opinion makes most readers reluctant to admit that they ever took him seriously, his after-image and influence have been remarkably persistent. This chapter aims, then, to bring Watts in out of the cold by drawing attention back to the heart of his intellectual project. First, it outlines Watts's life and career with an eye to his associations with other modern Buddhist teachers; second, it attempts a summary of the central themes of his thought to demonstrate their essential coherence; third, it surveys some of the ways he applied his ideas in cultural and religious spheres; and finally, it assesses his continued relevance as a religious thinker in his own right.

Life and Career

Watts was born in Chislehurst, a suburb of London, in 1915. As he remembered it, his otherwise unremarkable middle-class home was filled with oriental art. His mother taught at a school for the children of Anglican missionaries, and many copies of classic Chinese and Japanese landscape paintings had come to her as gifts from students. Watts recalled being fascinated, even as a child, by an elusive quality in those paintings, especially apparent to him in their treatment of flowers and grass. "There was something about the treatment that struck me as astonishing, even though the subject matter was extremely ordinary. . . . I had to find out what the strange element in those bamboos and grasses was."[16] This interest, in turn, fatefully influenced Watts's choice of a means of adolescent rebellion. As a scholarship student at King's School, Canterbury, away from home and painfully class-conscious, Watts crafted a distinctive identity for himself out of the literature of turn-of-the-century orientalism. As he tells it, a friend of the family with a well-stocked library

> lent me Edmond Holmes's masterly book, *The Creed of Buddha*, which happened to contain a yellow pamphlet, written by a certain Christmas Humphreys, about Buddhism, and the work of the Buddhist Lodge in London. I was also reading Lafcadio Hearn's *Gleanings in Buddha-Fields*, where I found an essay on *nirvana* which gave me such a convincingly different view of the universe from the one I had inherited that I turned my back on all I had been taught to believe as authority. That did it. I wrote to the Buddhist Lodge, became a member . . . , and shortly sought out Christmas Humphreys.[17]

After sabotaging his one chance to win a scholarship to Oxford by freakishly choosing to write his qualifying exams in the style of Nietzsche,[18] Watts had little to fall back on besides this affiliation with the Buddhist Lodge. With the continued support of his family, Watts left formal education behind to try his luck in the cultural ferment of London in the 1930s. He read diligently in the fields of religion, philosophy, and psychology, as he continued to do throughout his life. He published widely in the small journals of esoteric religion and visionary politics that flourished at the time, and in 1936, he became the editor of the Lodge's theosophically flavored journal, *Buddhism in England*.[19] Through Christmas Humphreys, Watts also came into contact with people and books that crucially shaped his future course. One of these was Fredric Spiegelberg, a comparative philosopher and enthusiast for the writings of Sri Aurobindo who first introduced Watts to the concept of a "religion of non-religion,"[20] and who later, in America, helped to place Watts in the only academic post he ever held. Even more consequentially, Humphreys encouraged Watts's interest in the early writings of D. T. Suzuki, whose ideas Watts found so congenial that he wrote his own first book, *The Spirit of Zen* (1935), in an attempt to put Suzuki's thoughts into more lucid prose.

In Watts's reworking of Suzuki, however, one also sees the distinctive features of his own thought beginning to emerge. Suzuki's presentation of Zen emphasized a number of broadly romantic themes: iconoclasm, irrationalism, experience over belief, and religious insight as a return to the ordinary—all ideas that were also dear to Watts. Watts's characteristic nondualism is apparent, however, in the way he subtly veers away from Suzuki's presentation of *satori* as the essence of Zen. Suzuki, at least in the early *Essays*, characterized *satori* as a goal or attainment, a "fiery baptism" to be achieved by means of a distinctive course of practice and discipline.[21] In so doing, Suzuki relied uncritically on the metaphor of religion as a path or quest with a transformative experience as its goal. Watts, by contrast, was drawn to a more paradoxical side of Zen teaching, alluded to by Suzuki but unstressed, according to which path and goal are one, and thus according to which enlightenment consists in the realization that there is really nothing to be achieved. Zen insight, to this way of thinking, was less the object of a quest than an open secret, hidden in plain sight.[22] According to Watts in *The Spirit of Zen*:

> it is really a paradox to speak of the secret of Zen, and in spite of all the apparently abstruse or ridiculous answers of the Zen masters to the urgent questionings of their disciples, nothing is being hidden from us. The truth is that Zen is so hard to understand, just because it is so obvious, and we miss it time and time again because we are looking

for something obscure; with our eyes on the horizon we do not see what lies at our feet.[23]

The point was to become Watts's constant theme: the self and the world, the self and its potential wholeness, are always already nondual. The very idea that the lost and lonely self is something that needs to be saved, cured, or eliminated, he insisted, is based on an illusion—the illusion that we could ever have been anything other than whole, anything other than what we are. *The Spirit of Zen* gropes toward this point in its conclusion:

> to chase after Zen is like chasing one's own shadow, and all the time one is running away from the sun. When at last it is realized that the shadow can never be caught, there is a sudden "turning about," ... and in the light of the sun the dualism of self and its shadow vanishes; whereat man perceives that what he was chasing was only the unreal image of the one true Self—of That which he ever was, is and shall be.[24]

The imagery of sun and shadow is still too dualistic for the purpose, and to my knowledge Watts never used it again.[25] Nevertheless, the underlying idea of the nonduality of the everyday self and the self to be attained is one that he spent the rest of his life refining and applying.

In 1937, the intellectually flourishing but impecunious Watts met and fell in love with a young American heiress, Eleanor Everett, whose mother, Ruth Fuller Everett—later Ruth Fuller Sasaki—had visited the Buddhist Lodge one evening to report on her studies of Zen in Japan. Alan and Eleanor married and moved to New York in 1938, where Ruth paid the rent on their Manhattan apartment. Ruth also provided Watts with access to a wide circle of American friends, including the Jungian wing of the New York psychoanalytic community and local Buddhists. One of these Buddhists was the independent Japanese Zen teacher Sokei-an-Sasaki, with whom Watts briefly undertook koan study. Watts soon left formal training, but when Ruth and Sokei-an took up residence together in a neighboring apartment, Watts seized the opportunity to "study with Sokei-an without his knowing it," observing "a Zen master in his personal everyday life."[26] It was during this period, too, that Watts first tried his hand at earning money as a lecturer and seminar leader, attracting his first audience through a mailing to Ruth's Jungian social network. The book he published in 1940, *The Meaning of Happiness*, was a product of this milieu, attempting to define a territory where depth psychology and "Oriental wisdom" overlap.

Watts was not content with his modest success as a freelance intellectual, however. Anxious to stand on his own feet financially as well as intellectually, he decided to have a go at the one professional track that seemed open to a well-spoken, mannerly young Englishman with a strong interest in things religious: namely, the Episcopal priesthood. Given his earlier revolution in worldviews, the move may seem hypocritical, but it was not. (Opportunistic, perhaps, but not hypocritical.) Watts's religious universalism inclined him to believe that the "highest" insights of any religion could be found in all, and his Jungian interests inclined him to affirm "the tremendous power of the Church's symbols to excite the unconscious depths of the soul."[27] It was Watts's sincere hope, then, that Christian theology and liturgical symbolism, properly understood, could be a fit vehicle for the insights that meant most to him. Convincing himself of that fit became his unhappy intellectual task over the next eight years.

Although he lacked a university degree, Watts was admitted to Seabury-Western seminary outside of Chicago on the evidence of his published writings. In 1944, he was ordained and given a job as university chaplain at Northwestern University in Evanston. He took up the work with sincere if not entirely orthodox intentions. The liturgical displays he organized were lavishly theatrical; the discussion groups he ran for students were popular and ultimately notorious. He diligently argued for the coherence of Christianity and the purest insights of nondualist religion in books such as *Behold the Spirit* (1947) and *The Supreme Identity* (1950). The strain of the effort to fit himself into a Christian mold was apparent, however, in both the relatively murky prose of these works and the mess he was making of his personal life. In 1950, both his marriage to Eleanor and his career as a "paradox priest" came to an end.[28] Like Ralph Waldo Emerson, whose career and message as a purveyor of radical religion in America parallels Watts's in many respects, Watts resigned from the church, abandoned his livelihood, and leapt into the unknown.

Luckily, he soon hit a safety net in the form of a small grant from the Bollingen Foundation, secured for him with the help of Joseph Campbell. Campbell also arranged for Watts, together with his new wife, Dorothy, to live in a farmhouse outside of Poughkeepsie, New York, for six months. There, facing an unpredictable future in a country that was still strange to him, Watts wrote the book in which he first found his own distinctive voice, *The Wisdom of Insecurity* (1951). This was also the book in which Watts began to utilize insights from some of the formative intellectual movements of the postwar era: especially the newly minted "cybernetics" of Norbert Weiner,[29] general systems theory, and gestalt psychology. These, as we shall see, became the backbone of his mature thought.

During his stay in rural New York, Watts reestablished contact with Fredric Spiegelberg, then teaching at Stanford, who fortuitously offered Watts a job with the unaccredited school he was just then organizing in San Francisco, the American Academy of Asian Studies. Intended to prepare businessmen and government officials for travel in the East, the academy actually became a catalyst and network hub for the San Francisco literary renaissance of the 1950s. Thus, Watts's work with the academy over the next six years, first as a teacher and ultimately as its chief administrator, gave him a perch in the San Francisco Bay Area at a crucial time in its cultural development. During this period, Watts made contact with the circle of early Beat writers, whose Buddhist interests intrigued him and some of whom he positively admired, particularly Gary Snyder.[30] The essay he wrote in response to the uniquely American Buddhism of the Beats, "Beat Zen, Square Zen, and Zen" (1958), is a classic statement of the "modern Buddhist" attempt to distinguish the essence of Buddhism from both its traditionalist and popular forms. Also at this time, Watts began ongoing conversations with several Buddhist teachers who were then beginning their careers in the Bay Area: Lama Govinda in Berkeley and, the priests at the Soto Zen Temple in San Francisco, soon to include Shunryu Suzuki. Finally, it was during these years that Watts began his long association with Pacifica Radio. His weekly broadcast talks were a powerful medium for carrying his voice and thought to thousands of listeners over the years.

Then, in 1957, Watts decided to cut loose once again, first from his job at the academy and soon from his second marriage, in order to dedicate himself to writing, lecturing, and experimental living. The books he produced in rapid succession over the next eight years, from *Nature, Man, and Woman* (1958) through *The Book: On the Taboo Against Knowing Who You Are* (1966), constitute his finest and most characteristic achievements. Throughout this period and until his death in 1973, Watts also lectured actively on the college circuit, on radio and television, and in subscription seminars held on his houseboat in Sausalito. His reputation and popularity grew with the rise of the counterculture. He was an instrumental participant in such iconic events as the San Francisco Be-In in 1967, the first seminars of the Esalen

Institute, and the founding of the Zen Mountain Center at Tassajara Springs. Increasingly, however, in his final years he coasted on well-worn thoughts, and his personal life went into a steep decline. Alcohol had always been Watts's besetting sin, but toward the end it took over his life. Although he never lost his talent for coherent, largely extemporaneous verbal performance, his death, when it came, was due to the complications of alcoholism.

His end raises interesting questions about the strength of his spiritual insight in the face of the psychic demons that eventually dragged him down. Perhaps he failed to take to heart the advice he gave himself at age twenty-four: "You have to come to terms with the gods before you can ignore them."[31] Or perhaps—to treat the matter as lightly as he might have wished—sainthood was simply another category that Watts successfully evaded. In any case, it is his thought rather than his life that constitutes his genuine legacy, and to this we now turn.

The Field, the Double-Bind, and Play

As noted above, Watts is best understood not as a flawed representative of Eastern religious traditions but as the exponent of a distinctively modern nondualist spirituality that deserves to be understood on its own terms. In what follows, the main themes of Watts's mature thought will be summarized by reference to three images or structural concepts that recur throughout his many books and recorded lectures: the field, the double-bind, and play. These images were used by Watts to explicate, respectively, the nature of reality, the fundamental problem of human consciousness, and the life made possible by its solution.

The first and most important term in Watts's exposition of nondualism is the field. Watts found support for a nondual account of the human condition in several mid-twentieth-century intellectual movements. These included gestalt psychology, general systems theory, cybernetics, and ecology. What is common to these movements is the idea that there is no subject or unit of analysis that can be understood apart from its external relations, because in any given system the subject and its environment are mutually defined. Organism and environment, figure and ground, part and whole, and subject and object thus need to be understood as aspects of the larger fields or systems that constitute them. Gestalt psychology, according to Watts, gives the fundamental account of this interrelationship: "What we perceive . . . is never a figure alone but a figure/ground relationship.

The primary unit of perception is therefore neither the thing (figure) nor the space (ground) in which it appears; it is the field or relationship of the two."[32] The behavior of agents in an environment is described, in turn, by general systems theory to a similar effect: "The structure and behavior of any system is only partially accounted for by analysis and description of the smaller units that allegedly 'comprise' it. For what any of the units is and does depends upon its place in and its relation to the system as a whole."[33]

Watts's principal use of the concept of the field was to develop a picture of human identity as inextricably interrelated with the environment. If the universe is most properly understood as a field of mutually enabling transactions rather than as a collection of independent parts, then it is a mistake to see the self as something either isolated or independent. If the field is the primary reality, that is, the common idea of the self as what Watts sometimes called a "skin encapsulated ego" is incoherent.[34] Rather, what we call "I" is most properly seen as a function of the whole. We habitually analyze the field into components—into something that acts and something acted upon. But "the world outside your skin is just as much you as the world inside."[35] In truth, there is only the self-organizing, self-regulating activity of the whole. The word "I" has about the same status, then, as the word "it" in the phrase "it is raining."[36] The self is something the field as a whole is doing. Its reification is a matter of grammatical convenience.

A view of the self according to which "the line between myself and what happens to me is dissolved"[37] naturally raises the question of freedom and determinism, which Watts handles rather elegantly. We are "determined," he allows, in the sense that what we are is wholly embedded in the network of circumstances; but we are also free in the sense that what we are is of a piece with the radical contingency of the whole. "Certainly the will is free, but it is not the 'I' [i.e., the isolated ego] that wills."[38] If the real "I" is a function of the whole, that is, it also partakes of the strength and intelligence of the whole; it is at once the windblown leaf and the wind that blows. To find oneself is thus to find oneself "not *in* a world, but *as* a world which is neither compulsive nor capricious."[39]

So what goes wrong? If the idea of the "skin encapsulated ego" is indeed incoherent, why has it been so persistent? In responding to this question, Watts makes sophisticated use of information theory and cybernetic systems models to account for a characteristic glitch in human consciousness. General systems theory understands the world not as a static configuration of figure and ground, but as a constant flow of information—a communications network governed by feed-back between subsystems.[40] Systems of communication, in turn, have characteristic diseases. They can generate misinformation along with information, and their regulatory mechanisms can become unbalanced, as when a positive feedback system gets into an infinite loop and begins to "howl."[41]

In human experience, the principal sort of error that arises in our interaction with the environment is something that Watts, following Gregory Bateson, called the double-bind. Generally speaking, a double-bind arises when an agent encounters contradictory instructions for behavior, and at the same time is prevented from realizing or dealing with the paradox.[42] Watts's favorite cases involve the particular sort of paradox that arises when one is commanded to do something voluntarily. For example, one is told that one must love one's parents, or that "thou shalt love the Lord thy God." For this love to be genuine, it must be spontaneous and uncoerced. To act on the commandment, however, is to act unspontaneously. The paradox is thus clear and inescapable: to acknowledge that one is under a commandment to love is to be unable to fulfill it. A psychic feedback loop ensues, and the resulting howl is painful.

Double-binds arise in connection with many aspects of human life (the commands to "be yourself" and "relax" being two of Watts's favorite examples), but the underlying cause of them all is our view of ourselves as independent egos. As already noted, according to Watts, the ego concept is an error—a reified fragment of the universal field. Nevertheless, it is an error that arises in a perfectly reasonable way, and Watts outlines several explanations for why it occurs. One is social, based on the idea that the regulation of a social network is facilitated when individual units of society take responsibility for controlling their own actions. We evolve self-awareness and the idea of independent agency, that is, in order police ourselves for the overall benefit of the group. Another possible explanation begins with the human capacity for language, and with the kind of focused awareness of particulars that language makes possible. The same capacity that allows us to name things—to discriminate patterns from the field—also allows us to isolate our*selves* from the field, becoming objects of our own observation. Self-awareness thus arises as a side effect or unintended consequence of language.[43]

Thus, there are good functional and even sociobiological reasons why the ego concept arises. The problem, however, is that once the concept is introduced, it tends to take over the whole field of mental activity like an invasive weed. The capacity for conscious attention, for example, gives us impressive abilities to analyze, manipulate, and control the environment. It has made humanity's four-thousand-year experiment with civilization possible, which is fine as far as it goes. However, this power to focus has a tendency to become addictive. We become so fascinated by it ("like chickens hypnotized with their beaks to a chalk line," he quips)[44] that we forget that there are other ways of relating to the world. The "spotlight vision" that enables discriminating awareness has distracted us from our more inclusive capacity for "floodlight vision"—the immediate, unreflective "organic intelligence" that constitutes our primary preconscious relation with the world and that "enables us to regulate the incredible complexity of our bodies without thinking at all."[45]

The ego's function of social control or self-monitoring likewise tends to get out of hand, resulting in a sort of primordial double-bind. The very idea that we must control or observe ourselves encodes a basic contradiction. For if I am to watch myself, where is this "I" that I should be watching apart from the I that watches? How can a subject become an object to itself without ceasing to be a subject?[46] In the classic metaphors of nondualism, the eye cannot see itself; the hand cannot grasp itself. That the self is ungraspable and beyond our control, however, is something we are deeply reluctant to admit. To acknowledge that the self is not substantial or that it cannot be observed negates the only self and world we know and gives up the game society asks us to play. The more clearly we see the self's contingency, the more we struggle to deny it. And so the vicious circle of anxiety on behalf of our illusory ego relentlessly turns, generating ever more elaborate schemes to control the uncontrollable and establish the unreal. As we will see in the next section, most of Watts's extensive culture criticism—his diagnosis of civilization's mania for control and its alienation from the sensuous immediacy of the world—unfolds from this analysis of the predicament of the ego.

This diagnosis of the problem of consciousness led Watts to his understanding of the cure. The way to untie the double-bind, he suggests, is simply to acknowledge the encompassing reality of the field, and thus to realize the impossibility of what the ego has set itself to do. This brings us back, in turn, to Watts's fundamental insight into the nonduality of path and goal. The problem of consciousness will not be solved by a quest for some new position, he insists, but only by waking up to the reality of the place in which we already stand. The truth is not elsewhere. It consists, rather, in being alive to the interrelatedness of all things in the field. Nothing is added to our situation by this realization, he writes, and nothing is really restored.

"[T]he point is not . . . that it would be good to return to our original integrity with nature. The point is that it is simply impossible to get away from it."[47] "[A]s long as I am trying to grasp IT, I am implying that IT is not really myself."[48] The nonduality of self and world, that is, is simply what has always been the case. Accordingly, coming to understand that this is so is not really an achievement, for "there is no way to where we are."[49] Realization comes immediately, as a simple return to sanity, or not at all.

Watts's ingenious but endlessly provocative account of the nature of religious discipline follows from these same principles. The real purpose of intensive religious practice, he argued in *Psychotherapy East & West* (1961), is not to lead one along a path to new knowledge or a new birth. Rather, it is to trick one into the realization that there is nothing beyond the given that one needs. To trigger this insight, according to Watts, religious disciplines typically trap the student in a kind of therapeutic double-bind: "you must stop thinking"; "you must overcome all desire"; "you must act unselfishly." All these commands are impossible to fulfill intentionally because their deliberate pursuit involves the very thing one is trying to overcome: I *want* to end desire, or I *intend* to stop thinking. The only way out of the teacher's trap, then, is to realize that the whole way of thinking that got you into it was an illusion. You started down the path because you believed you were far from the truth. Having walked into the trap, however, the only way you will find the freedom or wholeness you originally sought is by giving up the quest. You only reach your goal, that is, by giving up your increasingly futile effort to reach it. Religion's ultimate lesson, then, is that it has nothing to teach. Or as Wittgenstein put it, "the solution of the problem of life is seen in the vanishing of the problem."[50]

Watts comes very close here to the claim that discipline and effort in religion are unnecessary and even wrongheaded. He has been criticized accordingly for failure to do justice to the transformative dimension of religion and to the feelings of alienation that are often the mainspring of religious life. There is a crucial difference, it is said, between the mere knowledge that one is interrelated with the universe and the experiential realization of wholeness. Effort is required to bridge the gap between notional knowledge and experience. Therefore a philosophy that dismisses all yearning as misguided is not likely to sustain one through the change.[51]

This criticism has undeniable practical force, but there is also reason in Watts's reply. Human alienation is real enough, he allows, but its structure is such that its cure is more likely to be found through an instantaneous insight than through years of laborious training. If the problem of self-knowledge really is like that of an eye trying to see itself, no amount of effort is going to get us closer to the goal. The abandonment of false notions of who we are and what we are doing may not be the whole of the matter, but it is a great deal. Thus, as Watts wrote in his autobiography,

> I was always being accused of being a lazy fellow who had the absurd idea that transcendence of egocentricity could be achieved (by whom?) without long years of effort and discipline. You would immediately feel one with all nature, and with the universe itself, if you could understand that there is no "you" as the hard-core thinker of thoughts, feeler of feelings, and senser of sensations, and that because your body is something in the physical world, that world is not "external" to you. . . . This has nothing to do with making an effort or not making an effort; it is simply a matter of intelligence.[52]

Of course, the simplicity of this realization is also infinitely hard to achieve—impossible to "achieve," in fact, for "there is no way to where we are." Also, of course, the "intelligence" to which Watts attributes the power to change is not the abstract conceptual mind, but the intelligence we share with the cosmos—the self-organizing genius by which we live, move, and have our being. Intelligence is what we already have and foolishly think we need to realize. Coming to it, then, is at once the most obvious and most subtle of arts.

In any case, Watts has a characteristic description of the result: "to be released from the . . . double-bind is to see that life is at root playing."[53] Play is an activity whose end is in itself, and this is precisely Watts's point. For one who realizes that "there is no 'you' as the hard-core thinker of thoughts, feeler of feelings, and senser of sensation," life is an activity whose end is in itself, whose value is intrinsic rather than instrumental. "It is a dance, and when you are dancing you are not intent on getting anywhere. You go round and round, but not under the illusion that you are pursuing something, or fleeing from the jaws of hell."[54] Ordinary deluded awareness undertakes the business of life as a job, a struggle, whereas enlightened awareness undertakes that same business as play—as a kind of stage business necessary only to get on with the show.

Enlightened awareness, that is, does not change our fundamental position in the world at all. In the classic formulas of nondualism, *nirvana* is *samsara*; Zen is your everyday life. The game goes on as it always has, with the world expressing itself as self and the self as world. Nevertheless, says Watts, to realize what has always been the case can bring about a dramatic shift in affect:

> Your body is no longer a corpse which the ego has to animate and lug around. There is a feeling of the ground holding you up, and of hills lifting you when you climb them. Air breathes itself in and out of your lungs, and instead of looking and listening, light and sound come to you on their own. Eyes see and ears hear as wind blows and water flows. All space becomes your mind. Time carries you along like a river, but never flows out of the present: the more it goes, the more it stays, and you no longer have to fight or kill it.[55]

Realization thus brings freedom—not freedom in the impossible sense of independence from the web of causation but in the ecstatic mode of play. We realize that our every push is also a pull, that self and world are ideal dancing partners, caught up in a whirl in which leader and follower are one.

Play thus represents the abandonment of the purposive quest for meaning, and the discovery of a deeper sort of meaningfulness—or more properly, meaning*less*ness; "the wonder of natural nonsense"[56]— in the abandonment of the quest. Things still are as they are, but one comes to feel their value precisely in their being as they are—in pure aesthetic attention. The world achieves the condition of music in the realization that "life isn't going anywhere, because it is already *there*."[57] And so we go on, still in the world but out of the trap.

Watts's Culture Criticism

These ideas define the point of view from which Watts spoke throughout the major phase of his career. His purpose in speaking, however, was never simply to expound a philosophy but to apply his ideas in a useful way to the tasks of personal and cultural transformation, culture criticism, and the practical appropriation of religious ideas. Watts believed, that is, that many of the problems of "modern Western man" were due to the same fundamental errors of thought that the nondual analysis addressed. Of course, Watts was hardly original in proposing "the wisdom of the East" as a cure for Western ills. At his best, though, Watts realized that the perspective from which he spoke was neither that of the East or the West, but a "third" point of view—that of nondualism itself—which the modern convergence of worlds had brought into focus.[58] In any case, Watts applied this analysis therapeutically to a wide range of topics. We will touch on only a few of them here.

A typical lecture or chapter by Watts begins with a rehearsal of his basic nondualist account of our predicament and possibilities, and proceeds to apply this line of thought to one or more of his pet concerns. Some of these were weighty problems like death anxiety, rapacious consumerism, and the ecological crisis. Others were relatively trivial lifestyle issues: bad food, uncomfortable clothing, and inattentive sex. Shallow or deep, however, Watts believed that all these maladies had a common cause: namely, the Western view of the self as separate from nature, and our consequent alienation from sensuous immediacy with the world. Because of our exclusive addiction to conscious attention, that is, we live in a state of abstraction. Self-reflexive awareness is always one step removed from immediacy. Thus, insofar as we identify ourselves with the self-reflexive side of our minds, we do not live in the world or in the moment, but in our thoughts. Uncomfortably aware of this alienation, we make efforts to complete ourselves, to bring the world closer. However, because of our objectifying habits of thought, the things and experiences with which we try to make up for our lack are themselves objectified, isolated, and unreal. We cannot cure our condition by means of a symptom of the disease. And so our pursuit of satisfaction is endless.

This line of thought culminated in Watts's observation, most fully explored in *Nature, Man, and Woman* (1958), that the supposed "materialism" of the West is not genuine materialism at all, but is rather a measure of the extent to which we have forgotten our actual material embeddedness in the world. A person who races from one act of consumption to another is not a person who loves the material world, but one who finds no satisfaction in it. The cause of this dissatisfaction, as outlined above, is our self-identification with the detached ego. But nondual awareness returns us to a sense of our actual position in the web of interrelationship. It roots us in our material, bodily conditions and makes us more attentive to them. Enlightened persons, then, will be not only more compassionate stewards of the earth, but also better lovers, better cooks, and more tasteful interior decorators. This juxtaposition of sweeping profundities with banalities about the proper conduct of domestic life is typical of Watts's late culture criticism. The evils that he hoped enlightenment would cure included not only war and environmental degradation but tight shoes and Wonder Bread. It is sometimes hard to tell which of these causes was closest to his heart.[59]

In any case, Watts saw all the instances of restlessness and grasping in our culture—from nuclear proliferation to the suburban rat race—as symptoms of a single madness that could be addressed through a single spiritual insight. The fundamental error that Watts pointed to was the illusion of the independent self and the consequent view that a relationship with the world is something that has to be acquired. In this, Watts's views were similar to the classic Buddhist analysis of the root causes of human suffering in an erroneous view of self-nature. His ways of applying this insight, in turn, are a clear precedent for the work of contemporary Buddhist culture critics like David Loy.[60]

A more diffuse expression of Western restlessness that Watts frequently addressed was death anxiety or the problem of suffering. His principal aim in this discussion was to show how the fear of death was an error, similar to the mistake we make about our own identity. We cling to life, he said, because we see pain and death as evil, but the concept of evil itself is no more that a product of dualistic habits of thought. God and the devil are mutually generating fictions. This he demonstrated to his own satisfaction in such works as *Myth and Ritual in Christianity* (1953) and *The Two Hands of God* (1963), half-believing that intellectual insight alone would be enough to make the whole syndrome dissolve like an unquiet dream. On a deeper level, however, Watts recognized that human suffering could not be so easily conjured away. Watts, that is, was too humane to ignore the moral weight suffering has for conventional consciousness, even while he was too much of an idealist to fully believe in it. Thus, his explicit statements on the matter tended to leap directly to the perspective of enlightenment, affirming that from the ultimate viewpoint, the network of reality is a harmonious whole. Our feelings of disharmony, by implication, are products of ignorance. Pain is born of nothing more than the "cramp of consciousness"—of our stubborn determination to cling to the illusion of separateness. An open attitude to experience, he sometimes said, could actually turn pain to pleasure, or at least into something that has no moral valance.[61]

If Watts the theorist was awfully quick to wave suffering away, however, Watts the artist occasionally managed a more nuanced account. Consider, for example, an image he develops in a late essay, "The Water," published in *Cloud-Hidden, Whereabouts Unknown* (1974). At the start of the essay, Watts watches the ocean and contemplates the joys and sorrows of the food chain, "the tortuous process of life continuing by the painful transformation of one form or body into another."[62] Apropos of this time, he notices a gull pecking at a crab in a tide pool. At first, his imagination takes the part of the crab: "the crab shrinks from the walls of its shell which is resounding to the tap, tap, tap of the gull's beak. Who's that knocking at my door?" The gull, in turn, becomes a metaphor for the threat posed by the cosmos to our separate identity—death itself pounding at the shell of our carefully defended world, "beating against all the boundaries of space and consciousness."[63] The horror of life, invoked here in miniature, is real. At the same time, Watts knows that this is simply the way the world is. Life, after all, is food. Moreover, he understands that the fear he attributes to the crab is most likely a projection of a distinctively human attitude—a result of our own deluded desire to cling to separateness. Thus, Watts finds himself at an impasse between pity and wonder, unable to reconcile what he feels with what he knows. Finally, however, in the essay's last sentence, an ecstatic perspective dawns that transforms his view of the situation while denying none of the world's sorrow: "And, oh yes, I have just discovered that that knocking on the walls of all space and consciousness is my own heart beating."[64] This astonishing turn, whereby the cosmic threat of death is identified with the beating of one's own heart, perfectly replicates the opening to life that Watts presents elsewhere as the result of non-dual awareness. The realization that "you are It"—that the seemingly hostile and external power of the universe is a function of your own being—somehow enables both freedom and compassion, embracing both our complicity in the ways of the world and our painful love of all that passes. The problem of suffering blooms, if it does not dissolve, into this eternal surprise.

A more specific area of Watts's culture criticism that is worth a closer look, if only because it has played a role in shaping his subsequent reputation, is his view of psychedelic drugs. Watts had participated in controlled medical studies of LSD as early as 1959. Like Aldous Huxley, his experiences with psychedelics resonated powerfully with his knowledge of classical mysticism and with his own previous insights. In fact, Watts's description of his experiences with LSD in *The Joyous Cosmology* (1962) is simply a more florid version of the accounts he gives elsewhere of coming to understand the world as a nondual field. His attitude toward the drug, accordingly, was guardedly positive. A psychedelic experience could indeed be a catalyst for an insight into the basic truth of nondualism. But in this it was actually nothing special. Like religion, at base, drugs had nothing to teach us that we do not already know. Also like religion, however, drugs could easily become a crutch or a distraction if one relied on them too heavily as a means. Thus, while Watts refused to condemn drug use, and was therefore sometimes seen as an advocate, his message on psychedelics was cautionary. As in his earlier attempt to transcend the alternatives of "beat Zen" and "square Zen," Watts's writings on psychedelics sought a middle path between prohibition, or what he presciently described as the madness of a war on drugs, and unbridled advocacy, as it was soon to unfold in the career of his friend Timothy Leary. Watts's position, we might say, was in the counterculture but not of it.

Watts's most controversial application of nondualism, however, remains his interpretive use of it as a key to oriental religions. Nondualism, he believed, represented the core teaching of the religions that interested him most: Mahayana Buddhism, Taoism, Vedanta, and even Catholic Christianity. When Watts's subject was Buddhism, then, his own account of nondualism—formed as it was through a conversation with Buddhist texts over the years—gave him a wide range of analogies to apply to its central teachings. His concept of the field, for example, was a tool for explicating the fundamental Madhyamaka doctrine of dependent origination (*pratityasamutpada*). He used his ideas about the double-bind, in turn, to understand the distinctive style and strategy of Zen. As interpretive tools, these notions are not bad, and they have been applied in more detail by others.[65] Like any attempt to isolate a religion's "core," however, Watts's approach can be criticized for its reductivism. Judgments of the adequacy and accuracy of his treatment will vary, depending on one's purpose. If that purpose is to describe Buddhism as traditional Buddhists practice it, then it must be admitted that there is much that Watts leaves out and much that he distorts.[66]

Nevertheless, as noted above, there is a form of Buddhism that Watts effectively illuminates and to which his own work arguably belongs: namely, the lineage of "modern Buddhism." Indeed, the same traits that distance Watts from conventional forms of Buddhism ally him with the work of the modernizers. For example, Watts exemplifies modern Buddhism's attempt to find common ground between Oriental tradition and modern Western sensibilities. For Watts, as for many Buddhist modernizers, this meant interpreting Buddhism in ways that were scrupulously naturalistic, or at least non-supernaturalistic. Thus, in *Psychotherapy East & West*, Watts states that while his aim was to explicate the "so-called mystical consciousness," he also wants to be clear that this involves "nothing either supernatural or metaphysical in the usual sense. It has nothing to do with a perception of something else than the physical world. On the contrary, it is the clear perception of this world as a field."[67] Much like Stephen Batchelor today, that is, Watts advocated a "Buddhism without beliefs." How far such a modernizing reform can go before it stops being Buddhist is, of course, a matter of dispute.

A related concern of "modern Buddhism" has always been to demonstrate the coherence of Buddhism with Western science. This theme was taken up by both Eastern and Western apologists for Buddhism in the nineteenth century and continues in today's sophisticated explorations of the common interests of Buddhist psychology and contemporary neuroscience.[68] In this connection, Watts's reliance on cybernetics and general systems theory for some of his central interpretive concepts is not only pertinent but prescient. It is striking, in fact, thirty-five years after his death and more than forty years after he did his best work, how well Watts's account of the self holds up in relation to views that have become commonplace among contemporary cognitive scientists. Watts, for example, anticipated Daniel Dennett's critique of the "Cartesian Theatre"—our attachment to the idea that there must be an "I" ultimately responsible for thinking our thoughts and feeling our feelings, and our reluctance to think that there could be action without an actor.[69] More profoundly, he anticipated Dennett's account of the ego as a function of language, a "narrative self" constructed through interior monologue to create a sense of persistence through time,[70] as well as Dennett's recent discussions of how a significant concept of freedom is compatible with the insight that "we are something the world is doing."[71] All these philosophical positions are, of course, arguable, but the very fact that they remain worth arguing about should indicate Watts's value as a contemporary conversation partner. His work, indeed, is an object lesson in how contemporary cognitive science can provide both a fresh approach to the comparison of religious systems and a productive context for religious reflection in its own right.[72]

Conclusion

To sum up Watts's contributions to Buddhism in America, we must grant that from the point of view of traditional or orthodox Buddhist lineages, he was a marginal figure at best. To paraphrase Conze, he was more a catalyst than a catechist. With respect to "modern Buddhism," he may be judged an important contributor or fellow traveler, but even here he stands apart from all but the most radical modernizers in his willingness to let go of over-beliefs and faith-claims in favor of what he took to be the *dharma*'s practical and scientifically plausible core.

The guardians of the Way—Buddhist and scholarly alike—therefore have good reason to question Watts's authenticity. His many grateful readers and admirers have equal reason to affirm, however, that authenticity, as an intrinsic quality, is where you find it. Watts's nondualist vision of the spiritual path was vividly expressed, cogently developed, and adhered to with remarkable persistence throughout his career. That his life and thought were frequently "wayward" in many respects may be taken as simply the hazard inherent in his cardinal strength: his stubborn but good-humored refusal to allow any tradition to distract him from his own central insight. In his autobiography, Watts assessed this aspect of his character as "wayward, which is surely towards the way."[73] This may overstate the case. Surely, a Buddhism that resists the pun out of hand is a Buddhism that has lost its essential suppleness, not to say its soul.

Therefore, we end with a brief tribute to the authenticity of Alan Watts. He was, first of all, an effective teacher of religious nondualism and an authentic artist in the realm of ideas. He had an incisive, if sometimes glib, ability to formulate issues simply and memorably; a style that struck a seemingly effortless balance between conversational immediacy and intellectual rigor; and a voice in both his writing and speaking that was a fine-tuned instrument for coaxing an audience into astonishment. His prose, in its simultaneous precision and playfulness, is a perfect complement to his message, exemplifying what Wallace Stevens once called the office of the true poet: to represent "the mind in the act of defending us against itself."[74] Beyond this, though, there is also the authenticity Watts achieved through his refusal of models, as a thinker with the courage of his waywardness. As Gary Snyder put the case in his valedictory poem, "For Alan Watts," Watts was an effective guide precisely because his vision so often led him off the path.

> Many guides would have us travel
> Single file, like mules in a pack-train;
> And never leave the trail.
> Alan taught us to move forward like the breeze;
> Tasting the berries—greeting the blue jays—
> Learning and loving the whole terrain.[75]

Buddhism's ability to incorporate wayward insights—to hold its forms lightly in relation to its deeper understanding—is surely a source of its strength, just as Watts's faithfulness to his own lights is unquestionably one of his. Whatever the limits of his theory and practice, then, Watts's claim on us remains strong. As the authentic voice of an important option in modern Western spirituality, as a seminal figure in the development of a distinctively modern understanding of Buddhism, and as an authentic master of expository prose, Watts deserves and richly repays our attention.

Notes

1. For example, see Alan Watts, *The Way of Zen* (New York: Pantheon, 1957), xii; and Alan Watts, *Buddhism: The Religion of No-Religion. The Edited Transcripts*, ed. Mark Watts (Boston: Tuttle Publishing, 1995), 8 and 40.

2. Alan Watts, *In My Own Way: An Autobiography* (New York: Vintage Books, 1973), 73.

3. Watts, *In My Own Way*, 252.

4. See David Loy, *Nonduality: A Study in Comparative Philosophy* (Amherst, NY: Humanity Books, 1998).

5. If Watts has any place at all in the field of religious studies today, it is in what might be called its negative canon. Scholars still occasionally define themselves over against him, using him as a cautionary example of just how wrong modern appropriations of Buddhism can be. For example, see Charles S. Prebish, *Luminous Passage: The Practice and Study of Buddhism in America* (Berkeley: University of California Press, 1999), 13. For attempts to turn the title of his autobiography against him, see Dale S. Wright, *Philosophical Meditations on Zen Buddhism* (Cambridge: Cambridge University Press, 1998), 127; and Louis Nordstrom and Richard Pilgrim, "The Wayward Mysticism of Alan Watts," *Philosophy East and West* 33:3 (1980): 382.

6. For example, *The Way of Zen* presents a kind of overview of the history and cultural backgrounds of Zen. It is his most "academic" or conventionally expository book, although it clearly states a more constructive philosophical agenda in its introduction. Alan Watts, *Tao: The Watercourse Way* (New York: Pantheon, 1975) takes Taoism as its subject. More obliquely, Alan Watts, *The Book: On the Taboo Against Knowing Who You Are* (New York: Vintage Books, 1989) purports to offer a version of Vedanta, but a more straightforward discussion of the subject is in Alan Watts, *The Supreme Identity* (New York: Pantheon, 1950).

7. Watts, *The Way of Zen*, xi–xii.

8. Watts, *In My Own Way*, 152–53.

9. Alan Watts, *The Legacy of Asia and Western Man: A Study of the Middle Way* (Chicago: University of Chicago Press, 1938), xviii.

10. Alan Watts, *"This Is IT" and Other Essays On Zen and Spiritual Experience* (New York: Vintage Books, 1973), 17.

11. In the end, Watts preferred to designate the insight and its object by the term "It"—the ultimate placeholder. By minimizing content, he sought to stay true to the essential quality of the insight as surprise. See Watts, "*This Is IT*," 22.

12. See the editor's introductory essay to Donald Lopez, ed., *A Modern Buddhist Bible: Essential Readings from East and West* (Boston: Beacon Press, 2002), vii–xii, esp. xxxix.

13. In addition to Lopez, see especially David L. McMahan, *The Making of Buddhist Modernism* (New York: Oxford University Press, 2008).

14. Watts, *Buddhism*, 37.

15. Edward Conze, quoted in the principal editor's introduction to Alan Watts, *The Early Writings of Alan Watts: The British Years, 1931–1938*, ed. John Snelling, with Mark Watts and Dennis T. Sibley (Berkeley, CA: Celestial Arts, 1987), 11.

16. Watts, *Buddhism*, 37.

17. Watts, *In My Own Way*, 84.

18. Monica Furlong, *Zen Effects: The Life of Alan Watts* (Woodstock, VT: Skylight Paths Publishing, 2001), 40. This excellent study and Watts, *In My Own Way*, are the principal sources for the biographical details that follow.

19. For Watts's writings during this period, see Watts, *The Early Writings*, primarily for his contributions to *Buddhism in England*; and Alan Watts, *Seeds of Genius: The Early Writings of Alan Watts*, ed. Mark Watts, with John Snelling, (Rockport, MA: Element Books, 1998) for his contributions to *The Modern Mystic* and *The Eleventh Hour*.

20. Watts, *In My Own Way*, 133.

21. D. T. Suzuki, *Essays in Zen Buddhism: First Series* (New York: Grove Press, 1961), 229–66, esp. 246.

22. See the discussion of secrecy in religion in David L. Smith, " 'The Sphinx Must Solve Her Own Riddle': Emerson, Secrecy, and the Self-Reflexive Method," *Journal of the American Academy of Religion* 71:4: 838–44.

23. Alan Watts, *The Spirit of Zen: A Way of Life, Work, and Art in the Far East*, 3rd edition (New York: Grove Press, 1960), 46.

24. Watts, *Spirit of Zen*, 123.

25. Alan Watts, *The Meaning of Happiness: The Quest for Freedom of the Spirit in Modern Psychology and the Wisdom of the East* (New York: Perennial Library, 1970), xix; and Watts, *The Way of Zen*, 201, are both echoes of this passage. However, these later versions significantly omit the dualistic reference to the sun, which implies that the source of identity lies elsewhere.

26. Watts, *In My Own Way*, 165.

27. See Watts, *Legacy of Asia*, 41. This idea gets its fullest expression in Alan Watts, *Myth and Ritual in Christianity* (Boston: Beacon Press, 1968), written after Watts had left the church.

28. Watts, *In My Own Way*, 213.

29. See Alan Watts, *The Wisdom of Insecurity: A Message for an Age of Anxiety* (New York: Pantheon, 1951), 69, n. 1.

30. Watts appears in Kerouac's *Dharma Bums* as Arthur Wane, a formal, loquacious intellectual among the hipsters. Of Gary Snyder, Watts wrote memorably that "he *is* just what I have been trying to *say*. . . . A universe which has manifested Gary Snyder could never be called a failure" (Watts, *In My Own Way*, 309.)

31. Watts, *Seeds of Genius*, 139. The weight of his unresolved psychic burdens is also indicated by his comment to a friend that he could not stop drinking because "I don't like myself when I am sober" (Quoted by Al Chung-liang Huang in the afterword to Watts, *Tao*, 125).

32. Alan Watts, *The Two Hands of God: The Myths of Polarity* (New York: Collier Books, 1969), 19.

33. Alan Watts, *Beyond Theology: The Art of Godmanship* (New York: Vintage Books, 1973), 219.

34. Alan Watts, *Psychotherapy East and West* (New York: Ballantine Books, 1969), 24. Actually, Watts's use of the phrase, which has subsequently become something of a cliché in the "new consciousness" literature, was rare. He preferred variants of the more colloquial "ego in a bag of skin" (see Watts, *The Book*, 8). The stuffier formulation, however, was promulgated with attribution to Watts by Timothy Leary (in *The Psychedelic Experience*) and more recently by Deepak Chopra (e.g., in *Aging Body, Timeless Mind*).

35. Watts, *The Book*, 125.

36. Alan Watts, *Nature, Man and Woman* (New York: Vintage Books, 1991), 6.

37. Watts, *The Book*, 124.

38. Watts, *Legacy of Asia*, 18.

39. Watts, *The Book*, 124.

40. See Joanna Macy, *Mutual Causality in Buddhism and General Systems Theory* (Albany: State University of New York Press, 1991).

41. Watts, *Psychotherapy*, 97.

42. Watts, *Psychotherapy*, 52.

43. Watts, *The Book*, 53–85.

44. Watts, *Nature*, 7.

45. See Watts, *Nature*, 62–63; and Watts, *Way of Zen*, 8.

46. Watts, *Nature*, 42.

47. Watts, *Nature*, 21.

48. Watts, *The Book*, 151.

49. Watts, *Nature*, 116.

50. Ludwig Wittgenstein, *Tractatus Logico-Philosophicus*, trans. D. F. Pears and B. F. McGuinness (London: Routledge & Kegan Paul, 1961), 149.

51. See Nordstrom and Pilgrim, "The Wayward Mysticism," 381–401.

52. Watts, *In My Own Way*, 290.

53. Watts, *The Book*, 127.

54. Watts, *Wisdom of Insecurity*, 116.

55. Watts, *The Book*, 125.

56. Watts, *Nature*, 124.

57. Watts, *Psychotherapy*, 210.

58. Watts, *Way of Zen*, xii.

59. For examples of Watts on domestic reform, see especially the articles collected in Alan Watts, *Does It Matter: Essays on Man's Relation to Materiality* (New York: Vintage Books, 1971).

60. See David Loy, *A Buddhist History of the West: Studies in Lack* (Albany: State University of New York Press, 2002); and *The Great Awakening: A Buddhist Social Theory* (Boston: Wisdom Publications, 2003).

61. See Watts, *Nature*, 97–113.

62. Alan Watts, *Cloud-Hidden, Whereabouts Unknown: A Mountain Journal* (New York: Vintage Books, 1974), 5.

63. Watts, *Cloud-Hidden*, 6.

64. Watts, *Cloud-Hidden*, 11.

65. See especially Macy, *Mutual Causality*. A view similar to Watts's of the therapeutic function of Zen training is developed by Richard DeMartino in D. T. Suzuki, Erich Fromm, and Richard DeMartino, *Zen Buddhism and Psychoanalysis* (New York: Harper & Row, 1960), 142–71.

66. On the tendency toward Romantic distortion in modern Western versions of Buddhism generally, see Dale S. Wright, *Philosophical Meditations on Zen Buddhism* (Cambridge: Cambridge University Press, 1998).

67. Watts, *Psychotherapy*, 58.

68. For example, see Francisco J. Varela, Evan Thompson, and Eleanor Rosch, *The Embodied Mind: Cognitive Science and Human Experience* (Cambridge, MA: MIT Press, 1993); and B. Alan Wallace, *Buddhism and Science: Breaking New Ground* (New York: Columbia University Press, 2003).

69. Daniel C. Dennett, *Consciousness Explained* (Boston: Little, Brown and Company, 1991), 107ff; and Watts, *The Book*, 54–55.

70. Dennett, *Consciousness*, 416ff; and Watts, *Way of Zen*, 47.

71. Daniel C. Dennett, *Freedom Evolves* (New York: Viking Penguin, 2003); and Watts, *Nature*, 7.

72. The logic of nondualism can unquestionably be found cross-culturally in religion—not universally but frequently. The classic error of perennialism is to claim that it, or something like it, is the essence of religion generally. It is clearly not that. However, nondualism may nevertheless be seen as an important item on the roster of "family resemblances" that characterize religious systems. Moreover, it is an item on that list that comes far closer to what many today mean by "spirituality" than do most of religion's other common features (e.g., ritual, spirit beliefs, the social authority of narratives). The persistence of nondual modes of thought thus warrants study in its own right, care being taken not to overextend our claims for it or to mistake the part for the whole.

73. Watts, *In My Own Way*, ix.

74. Wallace Stevens, *Opus Posthumous* (New York: Alfred A. Knopf, 1972), 174.

75. Gary Snyder, *Left Out in the Rain: New Poems 1947–1985* (San Francisco: North Point Press, 1986), 123.

2

D. T. Suzuki, "Suzuki Zen," and the American Reception of Zen Buddhism

Carl T. Jackson

Perhaps no single individual has had greater influence on the introduction of an Asian religious tradition in America than Daisetz Teitaro Suzuki, the Japanese Buddhist scholar whose very long life spanned the period from the early years of Japan's Meiji Restoration through the American counterculture of the 1960s. Almost single-handedly, he made Zen Buddhism, previously unknown to Americans, a focus of interest. For prominent intellectuals, religionists, and creative artists as diverse as Alan Watts, Erich Fromm, Thomas Merton, and John Cage, as well as numerous American Zen enthusiasts, the Japanese scholar was accepted as the final authority on the Zen experience. Hailed in 1956 by historian Lynn White as a seminal intellectual figure whose impact on future generations in the West would be remembered as a watershed event, Suzuki has more recently come under sharp criticisms. Scholars such as Bernard Faure and Robert Sharf charge that in his desire to reach a Western audience, the Japanese writer greatly altered Zen's teachings, creating a Westernized "Suzuki Zen" that has misrepresented the traditional Zen message.[1] In the present essay an attempt will be made to evaluate Suzuki's career, presentation of Zen to Americans, and the arguments of his critics. Special attention will be focused upon the formative years he spent in America between 1897 and 1908, which, I suggest, exercised a decisive influence on his success as a transmitter of Zen to the West.

Born in 1870, only three years after the Meiji Restoration committed Japan to modernization, Teitaro Suzuki grew up in an impoverished samurai family in Kanazawa on the western coast of Japan. Suzuki's father died when the boy was only six, leaving his widow and five children in dire economic circumstances. Despite mounting difficulties, young Suzuki continued his education until he was seventeen, when the family's financial problems forced him to drop out of school. Fortunately, his studies had given him sufficient acquaintance with English that he was able to find employment as an English teacher, a crucial linguistic acquisition in view of his subsequent career as an interpreter of Zen to the West. However, his mastery of the language must have remained very limited: He recalled many years later that the English he had taught as a young man "was very strange—so strange that later when I first went to America nobody understood anything I said."[2] Thanks to the financial backing of a brother, he was able to continue his education at Waseda University and Tokyo's Imperial University. In view of his later international reputation as a scholar, it seems surprising that he never completed his college studies; his only degree was an honorary doctorate bestowed upon him at the age of sixty-three by Kyoto's Otani University.

Suzuki's first exposure to Zen Buddhism began quite early, as his family observed Zen practices. Troubled by the early death of his father and the family's financial problems, at one point he sought out the priest of a small Rinzai Zen temple in his home city of Kanazawa. Apparently the experience proved disappointing. "Like many Zen priests in country temples in those days," Suzuki would later recall, "he did not know very much."[3] Soon after his move to Tokyo to continue his studies at the Imperial University, he made the thirty-mile trip to Kamakura, where he became a follower of Kosen Imagita, the abbot of the important Rinzai Zen temple Engakuji; and, following Kosen's death, became a disciple of Kosen's replacement, Shaku Soen (also known in the West as Soyen Shaku and Shaku Soyen), who would become a major influence on Suzuki's life.[4] During the later nineteenth century Buddhism was going through a very difficult time in Japan, assailed by sharp attacks on all sides while being forced to accept the Meiji government's expropriation of its income-producing properties as the nation moved toward modernization. Caught between Shintoists and nationalists on one side and Western-oriented reformers on the other, Buddhist leaders responded by attempting to redefine the Buddha's message as a "new Buddhism," emphasizing a more universal, more scientific approach.[5] Soen played a leading role in the creation of this "new Buddhism," participating in an 1890 conference of Buddhist leaders in Japan that sought to unify the tradition's different groups, which culminated in the compilation of a document entitled "The Essentials of Buddhist Teachings—All Sects." As a disciple of Soen, Suzuki was clearly influenced by the more cosmopolitan, universal conception of Buddhism embraced by his teacher.

Though his writings would come to be regarded by most Americans as the definitive statement of Zen Buddhism, it should be noted that Suzuki remained a Buddhist layman always, never completing the formal training necessary to become a Zen priest. He did pursue Zen enlightenment for several years under the guidance of Soen and claimed in his 1964 memoir that, just before his departure for America in 1897, he had finally achieved a breakthrough.[6] At this time Soen gave his young disciple the name Daisetz, usually translated as "Great Simplicity." (Suzuki would later inform Western admirers that, in fact, his name should be rendered as "Great Stupidity.")

Meanwhile, developments in faraway America were about to intrude, which would dramatically transform Suzuki's life. The precipitating event was the World Parliament of Religions, held in conjunction with the 1893 Chicago World's Fair, where representatives of the world's major religions were invited to present their teachings. An unprecedented gathering, the Parliament attracted a number of Asian religious spokesmen, including the charismatic Swami Vivekananda, who spoke for Hinduism at the congress, and the Singhalese Anagarika Dharmapala, who championed Buddhism. Suzuki's spiritual mentor, Soen Shaku, attended as a member of the Japanese Buddhist delegation, and his paper "The Law of Cause and Effect, as Taught by Buddha" was read to the assembled audience.[7] During the Parliament's sessions Soen became acquainted with Paul Carus, the German American philosopher and editor of *The Open Court*, who had developed an interest in Buddhism. They became friends. When Carus subsequently prepared a compilation of the Buddha's major teachings, *The Gospel of Buddhism*, he sent a copy of the book to Soen in Japan, who instructed his disciple to prepare a Japanese translation. Carus then set out to translate the Tao Te Ching and asked Soen to suggest someone who could assist him with the translations. In response, Soen recommended Suzuki. Soen revealed to the *Open Court* editor that his young protégé had been so "greatly inspired" by Carus's works that he strongly desired "to go abroad" to study under Carus's "personal guidance."[8] As a result, in 1897 at the age of twenty-seven, Suzuki made the long journey to La Salle, Illinois, then a small mining town outside Chicago, where he would remain for the next eleven years.

If Soen Shaku served as Suzuki's spiritual guide, Paul Carus became his intellectual mentor, who in some ways influenced Suzuki's future career and writings even more profoundly than his Japanese teacher. With a PhD from a German university, Carus had impressive credentials to introduce his Japanese assistant to the profundities of Western philosophy. In addition to his fairly extensive writings on Buddhism and Asian thought, Carus served as editor of *The Open Court* and *The Monist*, important philosophical journals at the turn of the century. As Carus's assistant, Suzuki performed a wide variety of tasks, though he devoted most of his time to assisting Carus with his Asian translations and carrying out editorial tasks connected with the publication of *The Open Court* and *The Monist*. As a result of these duties, his mastery of English rapidly improved—a fluency that would prove crucial in his future career as an interpreter of Zen to the West.[9]

One of the two men's earliest collaborations was a translation of the Tao Te Ching. Suzuki laboriously translated word-for-word from Chinese into English, which Carus then put into his own words, after comparing his assistant's version with available European translations. In 1906 they prepared translations of two other Daoist works, published as *T'ai-Shang Kan-Ying P'ien* and *Yin Chin Wen*, and then undertook a translation of the Analects of Confucius. During these years in La Salle Suzuki also translated a number of Carus's other writings into Japanese, including a pamphlet on Chinese philosophy and several Buddhist short stories.[10] Happily, Suzuki found time for his own research and writing as well. Over his eleven years as Carus's assistant, the young Japanese published his first scholarly reviews and articles in English, including brief pieces on Confucius and Buddhism in *The Open Court* and more extended essays on Asvaghosa, the first Buddhist Council, and early Chinese philosophy in *The Monist*.[11] Finally, during these crucial formative years Suzuki also published his first two scholarly books in English, a translation of Asvaghosa's *Discourse on the Awakening of Faith in the Mahayana* (1900) and his pioneering *Outlines of Mahayana Buddhism* (1907).

Suzuki's extended sojourn in America was critical in shaping his future career as a Zen transmitter to the West in several ways. First and perhaps most important, it gave him the necessary skills—a familiarity with Western philosophic conceptions, command of English, and editorial experience—needed to reach Western readers. His publication of some thirty books in English, which sold widely among

Western readers, emphasize how well he learned from the American apprenticeship. Second, the eleven years under Carus's tutelage greatly furthered his education as a future scholar. With the rise of research universities in the later nineteenth century, aspiring scholars were forced to spend years in graduate school honing their research and writing skills. Suzuki, who stopped short of a bachelor's degree, acquired the basic skills under Carus's direction at the office of the Open Court Publishing Company. Trained in one of Germany's ranking universities and holding a doctorate in philosophy, Carus was superbly equipped to initiate the young Japanese into the complexities of Western scholarship and philosophical analysis.

The evidence of Carus's influence on Suzuki may be detected in the close similarities between the two men's approach to scholarship. Like Carus, Suzuki combined scholarship and advocacy, with both men going well beyond disinterested analysis in their promotion of personal philosophic and religious positions. Suzuki's emphasis on Buddhism's compatibility with modern science closely paralleled Carus's insistence on the compatibility of science and religion. And it is surely no coincidence that when Suzuki subsequently founded the *Eastern Buddhist* as a vehicle for the promotion of Buddhist scholarship, its format and contents mirrored that of *The Open Court* and *The Monist*. Like Carus's journals, the *Eastern Buddhist* offered its readers popular as well as scholarly articles and emphasized both English translations and philosophical expositions of Asian religious works.[12] Without the extended apprenticeship under Carus, Suzuki might still have made his mark as a Buddhist scholar; but it seems unlikely that he would have become one of the twentieth century's most influential proponents of Asian thought.

Suzuki left America to return to Japan in 1908 at the age of thirty-eight, where he would remain for the next forty years with the exception of occasional trips abroad. During his return to Japan, he stopped off in Europe for several months to copy Buddhist manuscripts at the Bibliotheque Nationale and for two months at the Swedenborg Society in London, where he undertook a Japanese translation of the Swedish mystic Emanuel Swedenborg's *Heaven and Hell*. Though usually passed over, Swedenborgianism obviously exerted considerable attraction for Suzuki at this time, another indication perhaps of the impact of his years with Carus. He seems to have become aware of Swedenborg while assisting Carus through contact with Albert Edmunds, a Swedenborgian and Buddhist scholar who frequently contributed to *The Open Court* and *The Monist*. As is well known, the Swedish philosopher's thought was an important influence on a number of nineteenth-century American thinkers, including Ralph Waldo Emerson and the elder Henry James, father of psychologist William James. At the Swedenborg Society's invitation, Suzuki returned to England a second time in 1912 to translate three other Swedenborgian works into Japanese—*The Divine Love and the Divine Wisdom*, *The New Jerusalem*, and *The Divine Providence*—and he subsequently published an introduction to the Swedish mystic's thought, *Swedenborugu*, for Japanese readers. Perhaps because he subsequently realized that many of his American and European readers would be uneasy about Swedenborgianism, Suzuki almost never mentioned the Swedish philosopher again in later years.[13]

Suzuki's life and career may be usefully divided into three periods: the years from 1870 to 1908, the time of preparation and his American apprenticeship; the period from 1909 to 1949, which he spent largely in Japan teaching and engaged in scholarship; and the final years from 1950 to 1966, when he resumed contact with the West and achieved international fame. After his return to Japan in 1909, Suzuki filled a series of teaching positions before accepting a 1921 appointment as professor of Buddhist philosophy at Otani University, where he would spend much of the remainder of his life. He never allowed his teaching duties to divert him from scholarship, and indeed, in the decades after his return to his homeland, published volume after volume on Buddhism, Zen, and traditional Japanese culture. With his wife Beatrice Erskine Lane, he also founded and co-edited *The Eastern Buddhist* in 1921. The landmark volumes that would establish his reputation and fame in the West now appeared in rapid succession: the first volume of his *Essays in Zen Buddhism* (1927), his *Studies in the Lankavatara Sutra* (1930), and the second and third volumes of the *Essays in Zen Buddhism* (1933 and 1934), followed by *The Training of the Zen Buddhist Monk* (1934), *An Introduction to Zen Buddhism* (1934), the *Manual of Zen Buddhism* (1935), and *Zen Buddhism and Its Influence on Japanese Culture* (1938). Composed in English, these volumes once again demonstrated his acquired fluency in the language. The works became bibles to eager American Zen students after World War II.[14]

During the interwar years Suzuki for the most part lived the quiet life of a scholar. Thanks to his books and rising international reputation, he played host to a steady stream of Western visitors interested in Buddhism, including Charles Eliot, James Bissett Pratt, L. Adams Beck, Dwight Goddard, Kenneth Saunders, and Ruth Fuller. In 1936 he returned to the West for the first time in over two decades to participate in a World Congress of Faiths organized by Sir Francis

Younghusband in London. During this visit, Suzuki met and entered into a lifelong friendship with Christmas Humphreys, who became one of the West's most active promoters of Buddhism.[15] While abroad the Japanese scholar lectured at universities in Great Britain and the United States before returning home to Japan in 1937, as the dark clouds of World War II were rising. Though his books were attracting increasing attention in the West, the numbing events of World War II would delay Suzuki's wider Western impact until after 1945.

The coming of World War II and the ascendancy of militarism in Japan placed Suzuki in a precarious position. The fact that he had spent over a decade in the United States, married an American woman, and published extensively in a Western language, undoubtedly raised the suspicions of Japan's militarists. At a time of extreme nationalist feeling when all things Western were frowned upon, it is not surprising that his publications in English largely ceased after 1938, to be replaced by a flood of Japanese publications. Led by Brian Victoria, some recent scholars have raised disturbing questions concerning the degree to which Suzuki, as well as members of the so-called Kyoto School led by Suzuki's close friend and philosopher Nishida Kitarō, supported the Japanese war effort during World War II. Critics note that Suzuki's spiritual mentor Soen Shaku had hailed Japanese victories in the Sino-Japanese and Russo-Japanese wars; that, beginning in 1935, Suzuki's writings increasingly emphasized *nihonjinron*, the innate spirituality and distinctiveness of Japanese culture; and that during the war years and after Suzuki never denounced Japan's attacks on its neighbors. Meanwhile, in such writings as *Zen Buddhism and Its Influence on Japanese Culture*, published in 1938, he emphasized the close connection between Zen and the warrior ethic of Bushido, which critics have pointed to as the basis for "war Zen" or "soldier Zen." Suzuki wrote: "The soldierly quality, with its mysticism and aloofness from world affairs, appeals to the will-power. Zen in this respect walks hand in hand with the spirit of Bushido."[16]

While critics such as Victoria have clearly raised important questions about Suzuki's position, defenders have stepped forward to counter the charges. Drawing upon materials not included in the Japanese scholar's *Complete Works*, Kirita Kiyohide argues that Suzuki never accepted the concept of an absolute state and early in his career questioned the role of the imperial family in magazine articles and personal correspondence. According to Kirita, Suzuki clearly disapproved of the recklessness and parochialism of the militarists and always remained isolated from Japanese politics, with no connection to the militarists. Moreover, in the years after the war he had urged his Japanese compatriots to reject state Shintoism and worship of the state. Revisiting the issue in 2001 with a focus on the ethical implications of the Buddhist response to the war, Christopher Ives argues that the critics have not and cannot demonstrate a real linkage between writings emphasizing what he calls the "Zen-bushido connection" and the actions of Japanese soldiers and kamikaze pilots in the actual war zone. Ives concludes that the flowering of Japanese militarism before and during the war years had complex, multiple roots.[17]

What conclusion may be drawn? At the very least it seems clear that Suzuki chose to go along with, or at least not to resist, his nation's war efforts. This hardly seems surprising for the time: Most intellectuals in Western as well as Asian societies—with some notable exceptions—supported the war aims of their respective governments. The tendency to link his views to those of the Kyoto School philosophers seems overextended; though a close friend of Nishida's, he cannot be held responsible for his friend's or the other members of the Kyoto School's views. And the fact that he emphasized the Zen-Bushido connection in some passages of his scholarly writings hardly qualifies him as a flag-waving militarist or a major contributor to the Japanese war effort. At most, his scholarly writings would have provided very limited encouragement to the Japanese military, who would rarely have read his works. In retrospect, one might wish that Suzuki had resisted the militarists; instead, he chose to wait out the war, retreating to his study to concentrate upon scholarship and writing.

It could be argued that Suzuki's return to the United States in 1951 as a lecturer on Buddhist philosophy at Columbia University ignited the American Zen boom of the 1950s and 1960s. Amazingly, the venerable Japanese author was already eighty-one when he began his lectures at Columbia. Stimulated by the Beat movement's celebration of Zen—led by Jack Kerouac, Allen Ginsberg, and Gary Snyder—young people across the country began to turn to Zen Buddhism and to Suzuki's books as never before. Overnight, the Japanese octogenarian found himself a celebrity who was constantly sought out by curiosity-seekers as well as by prominent writers, theologians, and psychologists. Born five years after the close of the American Civil War, astonishingly, Suzuki became something of a spiritual hero to many young people in the 1950s and 1960s. Winthrop Sargeant's admiring profile in *The New Yorker* in 1957 suggests Suzuki's iconic status. Describing the unique impression made by the Japanese scholar, who regularly lectured on Friday afternoons at Columbia, Sargeant wrote:

Despite his great antiquity—he is eighty-seven—he has the slim, restless figure of a man a quarter of his age. He is clean-shaven, his hair is closely clipped, and he is almost invariably dressed in the neat American sports jacket and slacks that might be worn by any Columbia undergraduate. The only thing about him that suggests philosophical grandeur is a pair of ferocious eyebrows, which project from his forehead like the eyebrows of the angry demons who guard the entrances of Buddhist temples in Japan.[18]

Over the following years Suzuki attracted a distinguished audience to his Columbia lectures, where he continued to teach until 1957. At one time or another his listeners included neo-Freudian psychologists Erich Fromm and Karen Horney, modernist composer John Cage, and philosopher Huston Smith, among others. Philip Kapleau, who subsequently underwent Zen training at a temple in Japan and became one of America's best-known, native-born teachers of Zen, also attended. While Suzuki's lectures charmed those able to attend his classes, most enthusiasts had to rely on his books for acquaintance with Zen. Opportunely, the 1950s paperback revolution occurred at just the right time, making his books available to a popular audience at very low cost. Though he also wrote extensively on Mahayana and Shin Buddhism, the works that captured the American public's imagination were unquestionably the books on Zen. Serious students perused the three-volume *Essays in Zen Buddhism*, but most readers undoubtedly preferred his more popular expositions such as *An Introduction to Zen Buddhism*, a concise summary of barely one hundred pages. Other works that attracted a wide audience included his *Manual of Zen Buddhism* and *Zen and Japanese Culture*. Many readers (including the author) gained their first exposure to Suzuki's writings through such popular anthologies as William Barrett's *Zen Buddhism* (1956) and Bernard Phillips's *The Essentials of Zen* (1962), which offered selections from the Japanese Zennist's vast body of writings.[19]

If Suzuki presented the essentials of Zen Buddhism with an authority and lucidity unmatched by any other scholar in his time, it is clear that he also brought his own special understanding and interpretation to the task, which later commentators began to refer to as "Suzuki Zen." Several elements may be said to distinguish his presentation of Zen. First off, the emphasis throughout his writings reflected his Rinzai Zen background and preferences. Reading Suzuki, one might never have realized that, historically, Zen in Japan included not only the Rinzai school but also Soto and Obaku Zen. Rinzai's emphasis upon the role of riddles or koans and the sudden achievement of spiritual enlightenment or satori contrast sharply with Soto Zen's emphasis upon prolonged sitting or zazen and the belief that illumination develops gradually. Thanks to Suzuki's influence, Zen for most Americans *was* Rinzai Zen. The Rinzai emphasis on nonsensical answers and paradox obviously appealed to many Westerners in the post-World War II era who were also drawn to existentialism and Freudianism. (If the Rinzai tradition dominated American Zen in the 1950s and 1960s, in recent decades Soto Zen has achieved a growing American acceptance, led by such Japanese teachers as Shunryu Suzuki, founder of the San Francisco Zen Center, and Hakuyu Taizan Maezumi, who founded the Zen Center of Los Angeles.)

Secondly, in his presentation of Zen, Suzuki emphasized inner experience rather than rituals, doctrines, or institutional practices. Writing in *An Introduction to Zen Buddhism*, Suzuki insisted that "Personal experience, therefore, is everything in Zen. No ideas are intelligible to those who have no backing of experience." In this respect, he distanced himself from the institutionalized practices of Zen temples in Japan. Ultimately, he viewed the inner Zen experience as universal, as the spirit or essence underpinning all religions. "Zen professes itself to be the spirit of Buddhism, but in fact it is the spirit of all religions and philosophies," he wrote.[20] When he did bother to notice Zen's institutional form, he criticized its narrowness and sectarianism. By downplaying the rituals of institutional Zen while stressing Zen's emphasis on experience and its universality, he obviously widened Zen's appeal for Americans.

Thirdly, as presented in Suzuki's writings, Zen offered an activist viewpoint that called for engagement with the world, again an emphasis largely missing in the traditional Zen of Japan. He found the rationale for such an interpretation in the Zen monastery rule "No work, no eating," noting that the daily life of a Zen monk required a continuous round of cleaning, cooking, and farming. At one point he even referred to the Zen ideal as a "gospel of work."[21] On another occasion he went so far as to describe the Zen approach as a "radical empiricism," an interesting choice of words that linked the ancient Japanese tradition to the modern philosophical positions of American pragmatists William James and John Dewey. If the ultimate Zen goal remained individual realization, "Suzuki Zen" did not ignore the responsibility for social action. Writing in 1951, the Japanese scholar suggested that Zen was as "socially-minded" as "any other religion," though its spirit had been "manifested differently." He proclaimed that the Zen monastery was not meant "to be a hiding place from the worries of the world."[22]

Finally, despite his insistence on Zen's irrationality and nonlogical nature, "Suzuki Zen" presented the Zen experience as a coherent and all-embracing perspective on reality—in effect, as a philosophy. I say this while recognizing that throughout his writings he again and again asserted that Zen Buddhism was neither a philosophy nor a religion and while acknowledging his repeated objections to all efforts to present the Zen experience as an intellectual system. However, even as he denounced philosophizing as a futile exercise, his books present a philosophic interpretation of Zen. (There is an obvious analogy to Freud: though the founder of psychoanalysis emphasized the role of the irrational throughout his writings, he was surely no irrationalist.) As a Zen Buddhist, Suzuki must have appreciated the paradox involved. In writing so many books attempting to explain Zen, he obviously violated one of Zen's most fundamental assumptions; and, indeed, he sometimes described his numerous publications as "my sins." Though steadfastly denying that he was a philosopher, his writings on Zen clearly offer a philosophic presentation of Zen.[23] Knowing his background, one should not be surprised by this philosophic bent. After all, his American mentor had been trained as a philosopher, while his close friend Nishida Kitarō ranks as Japan's greatest twentieth-century philosopher. Significantly, many of Suzuki's articles appeared in important philosophical journals such as *The Open Court*, *The Monist*, and *Philosophy East and West*.

The final years of Suzuki's life from 1950 until his death in 1966 were years of astonishing activity and widening international fame. In addition to his high-profile lectures at Columbia University, he became a regular participant at the Eranos Conferences in Ascona, Switzerland, which brought together some of the world's most eminent scholars, theologians, and psychologists. He also took part in the Third and Fourth East-West Philosophers' Conferences held in Hawai'i in 1959 and 1964 and in a 1957 conference on Zen and psychoanalysis organized by Erich Fromm in Cuernavaca, Mexico. In his eighties, he continued to publish new works almost yearly, including his *Studies in Zen* (1955), *Zen and Japanese Buddhism* (1958), *Mysticism: Christian and Buddhist* (1957), and *Zen Buddhism and Psychoanalysis* (1960), the latter two revealing his desire to link Buddhist tradition and Western thought. Though perhaps a surprising choice for an elderly Japanese man in his eighties, during these later years New York City became his home away from home. Curiously for such a noisy and bustling center, one of the city's attractions was that it provided a quiet refuge where he could do his work; in Japan he was constantly besieged by a stream of visitors.

A full examination of Suzuki's amazingly prolific career as a writer and scholar would require many more pages than are available here. However, three generalizations concerning his Zen writings and their role as a source of the modern West's understanding of Zen stand out. First, though almost automatically identified with Zen, it is striking that he did not really begin to focus on Zen Buddhism until the 1927 appearance of the first volume of his *Essays in Zen Buddhism*, when he was already fifty-seven years old. (He did publish a brief, unnoticed piece on Zen in the 1906–1907 volume of the *Journal of the Pali Text Society*.) In the West at least the tendency has been to ignore his extensive non-Zen writings. In fact, nearly all of his early publications, including numerous contributions in *The Open Court* and *The Monist* and his first scholarly book, *Outlines of Mahayana Buddhism*, focused upon Mahayana Buddhism and Buddhism generally—not on Zen Buddhism. It may be that in his desire to reach a wider Western audience he found it best in the beginning to emphasize Buddhism's broad message rather than its sectarian differences. In later years he paid increasing attention to Jodo Shinshu or Shin Buddhism, an interest encouraged by his long association with Otani University, a Jodo Shinshu institution.[24] To put it differently, early and late Suzuki focused much attention on both Mahayana and Shin Buddhism; Zen Buddhism was never his sole interest.

Secondly, despite his Western reputation as a great scholar whose publications offer the authoritative presentation of Zen Buddhism, his writings clearly reveal a spirit of advocacy. Influenced by his teacher Shaku Soen as well as Meiji-era Buddhist thinking, he came to his studies of Buddhism not as a disinterested scholar, but as a believing Buddhist committed to the defense and exposition of the Buddha's way as a spiritual choice. Though he certainly deserves his reputation as a great scholar whose translations and scholarly publications continue to provide illumination, we a must always remember that the ultimate goal of his scholarship was not knowledge for knowledge's sake, but the presentation of Buddhism and Zen Buddhism as religious choices. This stance may, of course, be viewed as positive, depending upon one's perspective. If his personal Buddhist commitments may be cited by critics as a distorting influence, the fact that he was a practicing Buddhist would only have increased the authority of his writings for others.

Thirdly, it is clear that much of Suzuki's success in the West stemmed from his ability to simplify Zen for a general audience. In the best sense of the word, he was a popularizer. In his writings he regularly passed over complexities, eliminated technical terms, and offered well-chosen stories to make his points. By largely ignoring the differences in the historical forms of Buddhism while emphasizing its core teaching, he made it much easier for Westerners to understand and embrace the Buddhist message. And by blurring the differences between Theravada and Mahayana Buddhism and between the Ch'an Buddhism of China and the Zen Buddhism of Japan, he also made Buddhism seem much more unified and more universal than the facts justified.

In concluding, we may turn finally to the contemporary scholarly evaluation of Suzuki's published works on Zen Buddhism. Hailed by a generation of Western readers as the world's greatest authority, what are contemporary scholars saying? The answer seems to be that, while his works are still frequently cited, his interpretation of Zen has come under severe attack. While the intensity of this criticism has greatly increased in recent years, it should be noted that the questioning goes back at least to the 1950s. One of the earliest critics, Chinese historian Hu Shih charged in 1953 that by ignoring Zen's historical roots, Suzuki was greatly distorting its lineage and teachings. Objecting to Suzuki's contention in the second volume of his *Essays in Zen Buddhism* that Zen was "above space-time relations" and "even above historical facts," Hu Shih insisted on the importance of recognizing Zen's roots in the Ch'an Buddhism of China. Obviously stung by Hu Shih's attack, Suzuki responded with uncharacteristic harshness that Zen needed to be "understood from the inside" rather than from the outside as in Hu Shih's approach.[25] In the 1960s other critics, led by R. J. Zwi Werblowsky and Ernst Benz, complained that Suzuki's writings were diluting and psychologizing Zen's teachings, encouraging a widespread misunderstanding among Westerners.[26]

The criticisms have greatly increased since the 1980s as a revisionist view has become dominant. The emerging consensus seems to be that the Zen Buddhism that D. T. Suzuki presented in his many books represents a modern, Western-influenced Zen that broke sharply with the traditional Zen of Japan. Presenting arguments too complex to summarize here, the two leaders in this reevaluation, Bernard Faure and Robert Sharf, have produced meticulously documented critiques that argue that the Japanese Zennist has, in effect, reconceptualized Zen, greatly distorting its traditional teachings. In his *Chan Insights and Oversights*, Faure suggests that, like his close friend Nishida Kitarō, Suzuki had both adopted and reversed Western Orientalist assumptions. In their description of Zen they had effectively "inverted" the

image created by earlier Christian missionaries, replacing the hostile
Christian view by an idealized image of Japanese culture and Zen.
Insisting that the importance of Suzuki's work has been greatly exag-
gerated, Faure attacks Suzuki's Rinzai sectarianism, his tendency to
emphasize mysticism as a common foundation for Zen and Christianity, and his nativist tendencies. Faure concludes that Suzuki's interpretation was very much colored by his isolation from his own people
and marginality in Japanese culture. Leaving Japan for the United
States as a young man, his thought revealed "his confrontation with
Western values," including Christianity, psychoanalysis, and existentialism—all of which had profoundly distorted his Zen view.[27]

In his important essay, "The Zen of Japanese Nationalism," published in the *History of Religions* in the same year as Faure's *Chan
Buddhism*, Robert Sharf added his voice to those critical of Suzuki's
reinterpretation of Zen. Beginning with the influence of Meiji-era
Buddhism, Sharf documents the degree to which Suzuki's view of
Zen was transformed by his personal experiences. The most important influences were his early years in the United States, the influence
of the Western conception of "direct" experience through William
James, and his attraction to nativist and *nihonjinron* ideas of Japanese
"innate spirituality." Like Faure, Sharf concludes that the common
feature of "virtually all" Japanese writers responsible for the modern
Western interest in Zen, and certainly Suzuki, was their "relatively
marginal status within the Japanese Zen establishment."[28]

Perhaps the criticisms have now gone far enough, with a need
to strike a better balance. While the findings of scholars such as Faure
and Sharf unquestionably demonstrate how much the Japanese scholar
reinterpreted traditional Zen teachings, they do not diminish Suzuki's
immense importance as a transmitter of Zen and Asian thought to the
West. Indeed, his very success in recasting Zen Buddhism as a modern, universal, yet quintessential expression of Japanese culture made
it possible for Zen to reach Western intellectuals and seekers who
would not otherwise have found such an exotic tradition attractive.
Clearly, as many have noted, Buddhism must become an American
Buddhism to put down roots, and the same is true for Zen Buddhism.
Through the centuries the adherents in all religious traditions have
frequently disagreed concerning the permissible limits in the adaptation of the core teaching to new conditions. The tension between past
and present, between tradition and change have been present always.
For most Americans, traditional Japanese Zen, or even the Meiji-era
Zen that sought to adapt itself to modern conditions, would have
seemed too foreign for acceptance. In the future, Suzuki's historical

reputation will rest less on the "correctness" of his interpretation of Zen than on his critical role as its transmitter to the West. In the midst of a needed reevaluation of his role as an interpreter of Zen, we should not lose sight of his extraordinary contributions as an influ-ence in introducing Americans and the West to Zen Buddhism.

Notes

1. Lynn White, Jr., ed., *Frontiers of Knowledge in the Study of Man* (New York: Harper, 1956), 304–05; Bernard Faure, *Chan Insights and Oversights: An Epistemological Critique of the Chan Tradition* (Princeton: Princeton University Press, 1993), especially chap. 2, "The Rise of Zen Orientalism"; and Robert Sharf, "The Zen of Japanese Nationalism," *History of Religions* 33 (August 1993): 1–43.

2. Daisetz T. Suzuki, "Early Memories," *The Middle Way* 39 (November 1964): 101–08. Quote on p.103. In a long career as a writer that began in his twenties and extended into his nineties, the Japanese scholar rarely spoke of his own life. For other biographical sources, see the Suzuki Memorial Issue, published after his death in *The Eastern Buddhist*, N.S., 2 (August 1967), which includes memories and testimonials by friends and associates. Masao Abe, ed., *A Zen Life: D. T. Suzuki Remembered* (New York: Weatherhill, 1986) reprints eight pieces from the memorial issue, along with additional contributions including Suzuki's "An Autobiographical Account" on pp. 13–26. Biographical materials in Japanese are included in the ongoing multivolume *Suzuki Daisetz Zenshu (The Complete Works of D. T. Suzuki)* (Tokyo: Iwanami Shotem, 1968–). Also see Margaret H. Dornish's dissertation, "Joshu's Bridge: D. T. Suzuki's Message and Mission. The Early Years, 1897–1927" (PhD diss., Claremont Graduate School, 1969), which remains helpful, and A. Irwin Switzer's brief sketch, *D. T. Suzuki: A Biography*, ed. John Snelling (London: The Buddhist Society, 1985).

3. Suzuki, "Early Memories,"101.

4. See Shokin Furuta, "Shaku Soen: The Footsteps of a Modern Japanese Zen Master," *Philosophical Studies of Japan* 8 (1967): 67–91.

5. See James E. Ketelaar's excellent *Of Heretics and Martyrs in Meiji Japan: Buddhism and Its Persecution* (Princeton: Princeton University Press, 1990).

6. Suzuki, "Early Memories," 107. He describes his spiritual struggles during this period on pp. 105–08.

7. For the role of Asian delegates at the Parliament, see chap. 13, "The Parliament of Religions: The Closing of One Era and the Opening of Another," in Carl T. Jackson, *The Oriental Religions and American Thought: Nineteenth-Century Explorations* (Westport: Greenwood Press, 1981), 243–61 and Richard H. Seager, *The World's Parliament of Religions: The East/West Encounter, Chicago, 1893* (Bloomington: Indiana University Press, 1995). Also see Judith Snodgrass, *Presenting Japanese Buddhism to the West: Orientalism, Occidentalism,*

and the Columbian Exposition (Chapel Hill: University of North Carolina Press, 2003), which provides a more detailed analysis of the Japanese Buddhist participation at the Parliament.

8. Quoted in Larry A. Fader, "The Philosophically Significant Western Understandings of D. T. Suzuki's Interpretation of Zen and Their Influence on Occidental Culture Examined Critically in Relation to Suzuki's Thought as Contained in his English-Language Writings" (PhD diss., Temple University, 1976), 37. Fader's dissertation remains useful. For Suzuki's account of his association with Carus, see his "A Glimpse of Paul Carus," in Joseph Kitagawa, ed., *Modern Trends in World Religions—Paul Carus Memorial Symposium* (La Salle: Open Court Press, 1959), ix–xiv. Harold Henderson questions Suzuki's recollection that he had originally come to the United States at Carus's invitation, arguing that in fact he came at his own request with the desire to study philosophy with Carus. See Henderson, *Catalyst for Controversy: Paul Carus of Open Court* (Carbondale: South Illinois University Press, 1993), 101.

9. For this formative period in Suzuki's life, see Suzuki, "Early Memories," 101–08 and Shojun Bando, "D. T. Suzuki's Early Life in La Salle," *The Eastern Buddhist* N.S., 2 (August 1967): 137–46.

10. For a more detailed examination of Carus's interest in Asian thought and association with Suzuki, see the author's "The Meeting of East and West: The Case of Paul Carus," *Journal of the History of Ideas* 29 (January–March 1968): 73–92.

11. See D. T. Suzuki, "Confucius," *The Open Court* 13 (November 1899): 644–49; "The Breadth of Buddhism," *The Open Court* 14 (January 1900): 51–53; "Acvaghosha, the First Advocate of the Mahayana Buddhism," *The Monist* 10 (January 1900): 216–45; "The First Buddhist Council," *The Monist* 14 (January 1904): 253–82; and "A Brief History of Early Chinese Philosophy," *The Monist* 17 (July 1907): 415–50, continued in ibid., 18 (April 1908): 242–85 and ibid. 18 (October 1908): 481–509.

12. Indeed, Suzuki's original intention was to publish two magazines with exactly the same difference in emphasis as Carus's, one a monthly "to be devoted to a popular exposition of Buddhism" and the other, a quarterly, "in which more scholarly articles" would be published. See Editorial, *The Eastern Buddhist* 11 (January–February, March–April 1922): 387.

13. For Suzuki's involvement with Swedenborg, see Andrew Bernstein's introduction to D. T. Suzuki, *Swedenborg: Buddha of the North* (West Chester: Swedenborg Foundation, 1996), 5–12. The volume provides a translation of Suzuki's *Swedenborugu* and other Swedenborgian writings from the Japanese, as well as several essays analyzing his indebtedness to Swedenborgianism.

14. For a listing of his most important book and pamphlet publications, see the bibliography in Masao Abe, *A Zen Life*, 235–46.

15. See Christmas Humphreys, "Buddhism in England 1920–1980: A Personal Study in Dharma," *The Middle Way* 55 (February 1981): 153–64 and *Both Sides of the Circle: The Autobiography of Christmas Humphreys* (London: George Allen & Unwin, 1978).

16. Cited in Brian A. Victoria, *Zen at War* (New York: Weatherhill, 1997), 106, a key work. For an excellent collection of essays that addresses the issue with reference to the Kyoto School, see James W. Heisig and John C. Maraldo, eds., *Rude Awakenings: Zen, the Kyoto School, and the Question of Nationalism* (Honolulu: University of Hawai'i Press, 1994). Also see Sharf, "The Zen of Japanese Nationalism," and Graham Parkes's "The Putative Fascism of the Kyoto School and the Political Correctness of the Modern Academy," *Philosophy East and West* 47 (July 1997): 305–36.

17. See Kirita Kiyohide, "D. T. Suzuki on Society and the State," in Heisig and Maraldo, *Rude Awakenings*, 52–74 and Christopher Ives, "Protect the Dharma, Protect the Country: Buddhist War Responsibility and Social Ethics," *The Eastern Buddhist* N.S., 33:2 (2001): 15–34.

18. See Winthrop Sargeant's charming portrait, "Great Simplicity," *The New Yorker* 33 (August 31, 1957): 34–36ff. Quote on p. 36.

19. William Barrett, ed., *Zen Buddhism: Selected Writings of D. T. Suzuki* (Garden City: Doubleday, 1956) and Bernard Phillips, ed., *The Essentials of Zen Buddhism: An Anthology of the Writings of Daisetz T. Suzuki* (New York: E.P. Dutton, 1962).

20. D. T. Suzuki, *An Introduction to Zen Buddhism* (New York: Grove Press, 1964), 33, 44.

21. D. T. Suzuki, *Essays in Zen Buddhism. First Series* (London: Luzac, 1927), 303.

22. D. T. Suzuki, "The Philosophy of Zen," *Philosophy East and West* 1 (July 1951): 14.

23. On this point, see Hiroshi Sakamoto, "D. T. Suzuki as a Philosopher," *The Eastern Buddhist* N.S., 11 (Oct. 1978): 33–42, who argues that though "not a philosopher" in the formal sense, Suzuki developed a distinctive "system of philosophy of his own."

24. See his *Collected Writings on Shin Buddhism* (Kyoto: Shinshu Otaniha, 1973). Galen Amstutz discusses Suzuki's Shin interests in "Modern Cultural Nationalism and English Writing on Buddhism: The Case of D. T. Suzuki and Shin Buddhism," *Japanese Religions* 22 (July1997): 65–86.

25. See Hu Shih, "Ch'an (Zen) Buddhism in China: Its History and Method," *Philosophy East and West* 3 (April 1953): 3–24 and D. T. Suzuki, "Zen: A Reply to Hu Shih," ibid., 25–46. Quote on p.26. The reverberations caused by Hu Shih's article continued for years after, with Arthur Waley proposing a middle position in "History and Religion," *Philosophy East and West* 5 (April 1955): 75–78. James D. Sellmann revisited the controversy as recently as 1995 in his "A Belated Response to Hu Shih and D. T. Suzuki," *Philosophy East and West* 45 (January 1995): 97–104.

26. See R. J. Zwi Werblowsky, "Some Observations on Recent Studies of Zen," in E. E. Urbach et al., eds., *Studies in Mysticism and Religion Presented to Gershom G. Scholem* (Jerusalem: Magnes Press, 1967), 317–35 and the review of Benz's book *Zen in Westlicher Sight* in *The Eastern Buddhist* N.S., 1 (September 1965): 126.

27. See chap. 2, "The Rise of Zen Orientalism," in Bernard Faure, *Chan Insights and Oversights*, especially pp. 52–74. Quotes on pp. 53 and 63.

28. Sharf, "The Zen of Japanese Nationalism," 1–43. Quote on p. 40. The article was reprinted in revised form in Donald S. Lopez's excellent collection, *Curators of the Buddha: The Study of Buddhism under Colonialism* (Chicago: University of Chicago Press, 1995). Also see Sharf's follow-up piece, "Whose Zen? Zen Nationalism Revisited," in Heisig and Maraldo, *Rude Awakenings*, 40–51.

3

My Lunch with Mihoko

Ellen Pearlman

Allen Ginsberg lay in a coma, dying. An oxygen tube laced across his nose as he tossed and turned against his portable hospital bed. Sitting beside him that early April night, I held his cool, surprisingly delicate hand and meditated with him despite his coma. I breathed in, and he breathed in, then breathed out. Both of us became one breath of bare attention. Suddenly, as if distracted by a thought, he tossed and turned, like a balloon trying to break its tether. His bed in his East Village apartment was placed to face the traffic below. Buses swooshed by, horns blasted, and the soft *tching tching* of delivery boys' bicycle bells clanged as they wove their way through traffic. Friends, relatives, and former lovers—some famous, some not—came and went. Off to one side of the room sat Gelek Rinpoche, a Tibetan lama, with three other monks performing *pujas* and prayers. I served them tea, then sat down among them to practice.

Two hours later Allen was dead of a massive heart attack.

It seemed as if a linchpin of the universe had been removed, and the firmament shifted. An ancestor, a keeper of the flame of knowledge—at least for me and others of my generation—was extinguished, but it wasn't only Allen who had died. It was also the first wave of those who had discovered and engraved Buddhism into the New York avant-garde. John Cage had died a few years previously; William Burroughs, Gregory Corso, Jackson Mac Low, Nam June Paik, and others would soon follow.

As I grieved, I thought about how Allen and I, both agnostic Jews from Eastern Europe, became Buddhists. What forces had shaped our commitment? In my twenties I was part of, depending how you looked at it, a second wave of Buddhist transmission to America: Allen had been one of the first who went to the East to study with revered Buddhist masters. In New York, I knew increasing numbers of artists developing Buddhist inclinations. In Boston, I had walked into Memorial Church at Harvard University and was engulfed by a Phillip Glass's opera, *Einstein on the Beach*. The music's repetitive, pounding, varied tempo was a representation of exactly what I had experienced during meditation retreats. I found this same sensibility in the work of other artists, in readings by the poets Ann Waldman and Patti Smith, and at John Cage concerts at the Museum of Modern Art. But to most people in the art world, Buddhism was just a buzz word. I interviewed many people in the New York creative world, and practically all roads, without exception, led back to the Japanese scholar Dr. D. T. Suzuki. Everyone, it seemed, had read him, especially in the 1940s and 1950s, before ordained Buddhist teachers were readily available in the West.

Zen Buddhism, admittedly, is not my specialty, for my real training is in South East Asian Vipassana and Tibetan tantric meditation, which I have pursued for the past thirty-five years. During my research, the more I read Dr. Suzuki's work, the more I wanted to know about Suzuki the man. Who was this unassuming person who had, as far as I could tell, helped change the direction of American culture? I found myself especially surprised by the controversy over Suzuki's activities in Japan during World War II. Seeking to discredit him, some critics accused him of imperialistic, militaristic sympathies. Why was this man, who had opened the door for so many others, having the door shut on him? I wasn't a Suzuki scholar, nor do I speak Japanese; yet I wanted to investigate the claims against Suzuki. It was true Suzuki's teacher, Shaku Soen, had a militarist, nationalistic perspective, consistent with what critics refer to as "Nihonist." But Soen lived on the cusp of the twentieth century, the early stage of relations between America and Japan. What else could he have done? America thought it was superior to Japan, but Japanese thought they were better than Americans. The Japanese thought Westerners smelled bad because they didn't bathe, while Westerners thought the Japanese had bizarre customs and rituals. Did that make either Japanese Nihonists or Americans chauvinists?

To help answer my questions, I located Dr. Taira Kemmyo Sato of the Three Wheels Organization in the United Kingdom, who studied with Dr. Suzuki until the day he collapsed and died of an intestinal obstruction at age ninety-six in Japan. He suggested I get in touch with Mihoko Okamura, Dr. Suzuki's secretary for the last fifteen years of his life, now living in Kyoto, Japan. He would make the necessary introductions. I was thrilled but scared. First I wrote her, then I called. She picked up the phone, answering in clear, precise English, since she had been raised in California and New York. After I hung up the phone I was profoundly affected by the story she had told me of how she had been in her pajamas, sick with a cold, listening through the wall next door when Allen, Jack Kerouac, and Peter Orlovsky first met Dr. Suzuki in the early fall of 1957, on the eve of Jack's publication of *On the Road*. I had already read two accounts of that meeting, one from Suzuki and one from Kerouac. Suzuki had noted, "The 'Beat generation' is not a mere passing phenomenon to be lightly put aside as insignificant. I am inclined to think it is somehow prognostic of something coming, at least, to American life."[1] I now felt speaking to her was like receiving a baton of live human contact, passing from generation to generation. What else could lineage possibly be?

I flew to Kyoto to visit her, feeling I was reaching back to the time in New York when Suzuki taught at Columbia University. I stayed in a small guest house right next to Daitokuji Temple, an important Rinzai temple in Japan. Waking up on my futon in a three-tatami-mat sized room, I went downstairs and made arrangements to meet Mihoko the next day, then took a bus downtown to see the sights. Especially memorable was a small, local temple. It was about noon, and I wandered among the beautifully pruned gardens, trees, chirping birds, and stone walkways. I entered a peaceful, well-tended graveyard. Rows of neat, narrow stone columns were flanked by thin wooden strips of calligraphic inscriptions that made softly clacking sounds, shimmying with the breeze. Some, weathered with age, had turned from bamboo tan to soft slate grey. Ancestors, I thought; I have stumbled onto a site of ancestors. An official plaque stated that the temple was Choko-do, an Amitabha Buddha temple dating from the twelfth century. Many of the 1,800 temples in Kyoto had placed small English-language plaques on their outside walls, explaining a particular site's historical importance.

Next, I saw priests wearing long, fluttering, translucent white robes draped over aqua and turquoise under-robes standing on either side of the gates. Atop their heads were tall, peaked, intricately woven black rattan hats. Holding fans, they smiled, nodded, and indicated I should enter. They walked with me over to a spigot. One priest dunked a small bamboo ladle into the water to rinse my mouth with and pointed at the receptacle where I should spit it out. Strange, discordant music sounded. The priests bowed to one another, and gestured for me to follow, and we entered an open room hung with white and red brocades. Two flute players and two drummers were playing high-pitched music, as the elder priest unfolded a calligraphic scroll chanting in a clipped, singsong way. There was only one other person present, an old man who appeared to be the sponsor of the ceremony. The younger priest leaned over a pewter urn incised with calligraphic inscriptions, while the older priest held a staff of long, squiggly strips of white paper, waving it around. Everyone bowed. The music continued and the younger priest walked into an intricately arranged inner chamber, his head but not his torso hidden from view. Platters of perfectly arranged food were carried into the inner chamber by the older priest and the sponsor. A fresh green sprig with white paper woven into a zig-zag pattern was waved around as both priests clapped and bowed. The pewter bowl was uncovered, a miniature ladle dipped in, and its contents poured into small, white, ceramic saucers from which everyone drank. The monks motioned that I, too, should drink the water. The food was carefully carried from inside the inner chamber to an outside shrine, and the ceremony was over, the monks lining up and bowing to me as I left. We had not spoken one word to each other during the entire event. Stepping outside, I read the temple's plaque: It was the Ichihime Jinja Shinto Shrine of the Five Goddesses. The shrine's water was traditionally used in the first bathing ceremony for the imperial newborn infant. The last line stated: "Its miraculous virtue is especially renowned for protecting women from evil." In less than twenty-four hours in Japan, I had made contact with ancestral spirits, been ritually cleansed in a Shinto ceremony, and protected from evil. I was now prepared to meet Mihoko, a living representative to me of Dr. Suzuki.

She had luminous, dark, indigo blue hair, as some older people in Japan do dye their hair fuchsia pink or lime green, a flip on Western ideas of punk. Now in her seventies, forceful and forthright, she shook my hand as we stood on the wooden steps by the carp pond in front of my tiny guesthouse, saying "hello" in her elegant, clearly enunciated English. "My husband is waiting in his car; I am taking you around today," she announced, and we drove to Ryoanji Temple. Using a professional video camera, I put my headphones on and started shooting the moment we stepped into the compound of the famously enigmatic Ryoanji Garden. She mentioned she was working on a photo book of remembrances of Dr. Suzuki and had recently opened the contents of cartons of boxes she had been saving for forty years.

As she briskly walked down the path in Ryoanji Garden, she said, "The worst and the best thing about the human being is they have intellect. And the intellect divides the subject from the object. What Buddhism is insistent about is that reality can take place *only* when the subject and object are whole." We walked into the famed raked-stone "dry" garden, along with a cluster of Japanese school children furiously snapping pictures of each other. Everyone, she informed me, had their own interpretation of the garden's fifteen rocks in the Ryoanji Garden. She said each piece was individual, but also held the universal. I asked about her personal history and she said grew up California, but during World War II, when she was nine years old, her family was sent to the Japanese interment camps in the desert. She did not linger on that memory but asked me, "What is it *now* for the person? *Now* is the most important moment, because it is *now* from where you measure your past and future. When you have that *now*, even in death it is not a problem." Mihoko turned to me as I gazed at those immortal fifteen rocks. "The purpose is to answer the question of who you are. Those stones and the sand and the way it has been composed, it is both the question and the answer."

We continued walking around the garden. Her father, Frank Okamura, had been a gardener at the Brooklyn Botanic Garden as well as a bonsai master, so she was well qualified to discuss the moss on the rocks and the exceptionally well-pruned trees. As the bamboo leaves rustled in the summer breeze, she pointed out the renowned square water basin with the inscription "I learn only to be contented." I then asked her about the recent attacks on Dr. Suzuki. She drew her shoulders together, shrugged, and replied, "Young academics, the new generation, they always have an axe to grind. They will pick up anything that will support that axe. They are not looking at what went before or what went after the statements, because statements are their commodity. They see a string of words which will support their viewpoint and they pick it up without any strings attached, and I think that is a crime, really."

I replied, "I read somewhere that if you did not support the wartime effort in Japan you were either surveilled or jailed."

"Look," she said, "there are all kinds of Japanese, and there are all kinds of Germans, and you can't really package them together. It so happens that Suzuki was an antimilitarist, period. And people are not going to see that about him if they see that a few Zen priests were pro-militarist. They don't realize his wife was American, and forget his long history of being in America. They don't realize he kept saying, with the risk of being arrested, that Japan should not have gone to war with America. War is a materialistic thing and you cannot beat American materialism." We left the rock garden and wandered among the blooming lotus flower ponds. A caretaker gently raked the surrounding grass with a plain bamboo rake, a timeless and simple gesture. Mihoko said in her no-nonsense way, "There were pro-militarists among the Buddhists, no doubt about that. It was in the air. If you find an impure air, you have to breathe it sometimes, you see? But that does not mean that everything is contaminated."

"Maybe it was the fear of imprisonment?" I asked.

"If you are brainwashed, and that is what they do in such times, you are brainwashed by the entire society. I am sure a lot of Germans were brainwashed. What do you do under such circumstances? Dr. Suzuki was not brainwashed. It's quite simple. The militarists came in and told all the university students, 'You must go to war and die for your country.' Dr. Suzuki got up and said, 'No, you come back alive, because without you Japan will not have a future.' He was able to say that with the militarists right there, and if they dared to arrest him they could have done that. His position was such that they did not arrest him. That doesn't mean he was pro-militarist. And I know from my own experience of having been with him for fifteen years that he never had any thoughts in that direction."

I countered, "But some people also felt that he thought his country's culture was superior to others."

She stared directly at the camera, as if she was trying to tell the world something through its lens. "He never forced anyone to think in his way. He was not a proselytizer in any sense of the word, and in fact he criticized proselytizers of other cultures. He just said what he thought. Words are words and they can be twisted in any which way."

Back at the car her patient and attentive husband of many years was waiting. We were, I was informed, going to a small restaurant on the grounds of Daitokuji for lunch. She casually mentioned she had tutored the head Roshi in English, and I understood what a profound honor that was, and realized just how gracious she was to take me to lunch in this refined and hidden spot. We walked into a small, traditional-style restaurant with low black tables on tatami mats rimmed by shoji screens and painted panels. I set my camera up on a tripod directly across from her. The kimonoed waitresses tiptoed behind the screens and brought us scores of small lacquered bowls, each with one or two morsels of food. Mihoko instructed me on how to drink my tea. She said I should hold it once, and then turn it two times so the correct side of the cup faced the person sitting opposite me.

"So that is the way a proper person has their tea," I stated.

"Well, ceremonial tea," she answered. "Wipe the place where you soiled the cup with your mouth, and then turn the cup the other way. Now you are finished."

As we toasted one another with little crystal glasses of fragrant plum wine, I said, "All the descriptions I read describe you as being in your late teens or early twenties and being confused and despondent until you met Dr. Suzuki."

"I was despondent," she agreed, nodding her head, "in the sense I didn't find the world important enough to live in. A lot of teenagers have the same feeling. I think that is how we grow up. But I was insistent on having an answer to all of this, and I found somebody who could do that for me. He said, you are here Mihoko-san, you are fifteen now and you are just knowing what it means to learn. In other words—asking questions is the first step you take, asking good questions so that you will know when the answer is there. Without asking questions there is no answer. So in Zen that is the most important. The first step in Zen is to doubt. Have a good doubt."

"So you had an existential crisis?"

"Exactly. What am I doing here? What is it all about? Who are you? That kind of thing."

The waitress brought out more bowls of delicately sliced, artfully arranged dishes. I tried something she said was the outer skin of tofu, soaked in marinade. "It was an extraordinary experience," I said, opening the skin, "that Buddhism came to the West during the twentieth century. It will never happen again, it cannot be repeated."

"Not exactly the same, but the same quality, because enlightenment is enlightenment," she responded. "The form may change, but the inner quality doesn't have to change."

"Because the nature of mind is changeless," I countered.

"That's right," she said, eating the rice with her chopsticks, holding the black lacquered bowl close to her mouth.

"Someone who practices tea ceremony, flower arrangement, archery or kendo or judo or any Noh play or Japanese dancing, any of those things which are considered Japanese culture, these are exercises in emptying your mind of the ego. It is central that you learn to encounter your ego through practice," she explained. "That is what you do when you practice calligraphy. You can see your ego moving at the tip of the brush, but how to get beyond the ego through practice is the issue. It is like chanting a mantra a thousand times a day, but the first time you chant the mantra and the thousandth time you chant the mantra, there is a different quality because you go through a certain stage of your own consciousness or awareness. The fact that you repeat, repeat, repeat—this is, in Japanese culture, an important thing. It is true, for instance, even in sword play. The first strike you make is not the best strike, so you have to practice striking and non-striking so they are the same dimension. The Buddhist monks brought the discipline that is required of monks to the social level of everyday life for children, housewives, craftsmen, swordsmen, even the Daimyos."

"But when these ideas were introduced by Dr. Suzuki to America in the 1950s," I responded, "it was very rare. Almost no one had heard about them."

"If what you just said is true, Suzuki should not be accused of being an imperialist because he is not saying something very original for the Eastern mind. For the Western mind it is something very original, isn't it? You just said that. It has nothing to do with nations or particular groups of people. That is why he was not an imperialist. It belongs to human nature, and it was this human nature that is required to be saved. That is all he was saying. And it has nothing to do with imperialism. Why is he being called an imperialist? I don't know; it's stupid."

"I meant nationalist, Nihonist," I said as the waitress brought us shaved slices of a sweet, gelatinous dessert.

"Oh, for God's sake!" she exclaimed. "I must say, there is no culture like the Japanese culture, from what we were discussing. Because if you pick up a flower or try to put it in a vase in a non-effort way, that is Zen or Buddhist, and has nothing to do with nationalism, not at all. The flower speaks, not the nation, not the culture, not the person who put it in there, it is the universe, right there."

"Why didn't Dr. Suzuki actively reach out more to the Beat generation?" I asked.

"Oh, he did, but he didn't go and sit with them, that's all. He tried to veer people to do meditation, to be quiet within themselves. That is more proof he wasn't a nationalist. In human history, in Christian history, for instance, you can be quiet without sitting down in a particular posture, though he did say *that* is the best posture for being quiet. He felt that the Indians had done quite well in showing that folding your legs up and putting your body in one place and keeping your spinal cord straight was probably the best way for a human being to reach serenity. Yet he did not think that was the only way to arrive at it. It does not matter what language you do it in. He found Traherne, the mystic in England, interesting, and William Blake. He loved Meister Eckhart very much. 'I wish Eckhart was here, I would like to talk to him,' he would say sometimes. Being quiet and being able to face everything that goes on inside of you, good, bad, and evil, and then coming to the realization, ahh, this is what it is all about. And maybe sitting is not the way for Western people to arrive at that."

"I have read," I told her, "that later in his life, Dr. Suzuki felt very close to Pure Land practice."

"His mother was a Pure Land person, and when he came back from the United States he did a few requested translations of important Pure Land texts. Then he went to teach at a Pure Land University which is where I am teaching now, Otani University.[2] So people think he became involved toward the end of his life, but it is not that at all. The practice tells you to repeat the mantra, and I have a theory about that. It was mainly meant for the average person who was a laborer and had to work with their hands all day long. They could not sit down in an aristocratic way in a Zen temple and do zazen. They had to make a living from morning until night. The way for such people to meditate is to recite a mantra. That is another way of going through the day with what Dr. Suzuki used to call 'uniformity of mind,' without the mind getting excited or angry or upset about something. It brings you sanity."

And with that our meal ended. Mihoko's husband had gone back to work, so she called a cab, which quickly arrived. She dropped me off on the pebbly little side road by my guest house, and got out of the car to say goodbye. Standing there, she glanced up at a black and white Japanese crest adorning one of the neat white neighborhood stucco houses. "Amazing," she said. "That crest up there is my family symbol. I never knew it was here before."

I turned and focused on the black and white circular design, and saw it was a delicate butterfly. I remembered my dreams after we spoke on the phone in the spring, dreams of butterflies and chrysalises. Now I realized why I had them and what they meant. Ours was not an ordinary meeting, at least not for me; it was a kind of transmission.

I told Mihoko I had dreamt of her family crest before I knew she ever had a family crest and had made drawings of it. I know this touched her. Before I left she gave me her personal fan as a gift. It had calligraphies of humorous animal characters that she said were the first Japanese cartoons. When I arrived back in New York, I placed it on my shrine. And that is when I knew, without a doubt, lineage had come full circle.

Notes

1. D. T. Suzuki, "Zen in the Modern World," *The Japan Quarterly* 5:4 (October–December 1958): 453.
2. Mihoko has since retired from this position.

Part II

Dharma: Doctrine, Belief, and Practice in America

4

What Can Buddhist No-Self Contribute to North American Bioethics?

Michael C. Brannigan

How can the Buddhist teaching of no-self contribute to a field that presumes the existence of an independent, unique, and private individual? North American bioethics and its manifestations, particularly in the United States, assume without question that each one of us is a self, a unique person, a moral agent. This individual moral agency is the fundamental starting point for self-determination, autonomy. Indeed, the key principles in North American bioethics of autonomy, beneficence, nonmaleficence, and justice support the centrality of the individual self. Beneficence protects the best interests of each individual patient; nonmaleficence safeguards each individual patient from undue harm; justice balances individual interests with those of the group. Suggesting that the radical notion of no-self can offer anything constructive seems to make little sense. This does not discount the worth of other Buddhist teachings such as Buddhist virtues, particularly that of compassion (*karuna*) in a world of suffering. Yet is there any value in Buddhism's leading idea of no-self, *anatman*? I submit that *anatman*, immensely puzzling for those of us conditioned to assume a separate self, has rich significance for North American bioethics.

No-Self and Medical Futility

Buddhists would be among the first to confess that we have a deep-seated need to posit a private identity. We naturally intuit a personal, independent self. Suspected by his fellow monks that he must be enlightened since he does not assume a separate self, the ailing monk Khemaka admits that he still feels pain and discomfort and reassures them that he is not enlightened, not an *arhant*. He goes on to point out that the feeling of " 'I am' has not been overcome, although I don't assume that 'I am this.' "[1]

Despite this strong intuitive pull, however, Buddhist analysis reduces experience to five sheaths, or aggregates (*skandhas*). These five aggregates (called "clinging aggregates" in the *Khemaka Sutta*) consist of form (*rupa*, referring to matter), sensation (*vedana*, these being pleasant, unpleasant, or neutral), perception (*samjna*, producing mental images), mental formations (*samskara*, especially volition), and consciousness (*vijnana*, encompassing recognition). These sheaths undergo constant change as do all things. Such is the Buddhist truth of *annica*—all things are impermanent. Therefore, there is no enduring identity, no individual self, for such a self suggests an entity that is separate and permanent. This fundamental truth of no-self, *anatman* (Pali, *anatta*), categorically differs from our customary way of thinking and constitutes the radical core of Buddhist teaching, a core that is maintained in both Theravada and Mahayana traditions.

Nevertheless, as with Khemaka, we undergo profound difficulty acknowledging this truth of no-self. We need to be secure in a sea of impermanence. "O bhikkus, this idea that I may not be, I may not have, is frightening to the uninstructed worldling."[2] We "uninstructed wordlings" have an inescapable need for a permanent "I," and this leads to harmful attachment, egoism, and conceit. As the celebrated *Dhammapada* reminds us, clinging to the illusion of a permanent and independent self generates suffering:

> "All conditioned things are impermanent," when one sees this in wisdom, then one becomes dispassionate towards the painful. This is the Path to Purity.
> "All conditioned things are *dukkha*," when one sees this in wisdom, then he becomes dispassionate towards the painful. This is the Path to Purity.
> "All states (*dhamma*) are without self," when one sees this in wisdom, then he becomes dispassionate towards the painful. This is the path to Purity.[3]

This essay explores the value of Buddhist no-self within the context of the controversy in North American bioethics regarding so-called medical futility, an issue with profoundly far-reaching implications and one that some may claim to be ultimately irresolvable. First, by way of introduction, here are some general remarks about bioethics. Since its inception in the early 1970s bioethics has developed into a rich field incorporating not only the perspectives of its foundational disciplines of philosophy and theology, but also those from medicine, nursing, biology, ecology, sociology, anthropology, literature, and law.[4] It continues to influence public policy with respect to issues in health care such as advance directives and brain death legislation and the life sciences including stem cell research.

Bioethics has grown beyond its North American origins, and with an increasing interest in intercultural bioethics, the pressing question is whether or not there are valid grounds for a global bioethics. This latter concern is no doubt poignant since various philosophical, religious, and cultural worldviews appear to have irreconcilable premises. Incongruities among these worldviews surface in dramatic tensions such as female genital circumcision, patterns of spousal abuse, requirement of a husband's permission for consent, international human subject research, and global health disparities. It is precisely this dynamic nature of bioethics and its burgeoning across cultures that compels us further to consider Buddhist teachings, in this case the idea of no-self, and potential applicability to a field that resonates with voices from various disciplines, and now voices from many cultures.

Given this, what is the problem regarding medical futility? The bare bones of the controversy refer to the use of medical treatment that, in the professional judgment of clinical providers, is not medically effective and offers little in the way of medical benefit. In itself, this presents no problem if there is agreement between providers and patients, their surrogates, and their families that intervention ought to be discontinued. However, problems surface in the absence of such agreement, when, for instance, family members insist upon providing this treatment at all costs. Bear in mind that in most cases, this problem arises in cases where patients cannot decide for themselves. It often comes down to an outright conflict between what patients' surrogates and/or their families want versus what health professionals consider to be medically indicated. In order to understand why the matter of medical futility has erupted as a particular issue in American health care, let us review its clinical and sociocultural contexts in the United States. This enables us to further understand the complexity of the issue of medical futility. It also prefaces our later discussion of how the Buddhist teaching of no-self can be especially relevant vis-à-vis certain sociocultural components.

Clinical Context of Expectations

In the United States, public expectations of specific interventions, particularly those that keep patients alive (ventilators, dialysis, antibiotics, medical feeding, and so forth) are often unrealistic. Patients themselves may believe that certain interventions will restore them to some level of normalcy when in fact these may only function to keep them alive. Some interventions may incur more harm than benefit. Unrealistic expectations lay the groundwork for potential conflict. Media portrayals of medical science and technologies no doubt factor into this. I know of patients who, after meeting with scores of specialists and still not hearing what they want to hear, seek their "miracles" at places like the Cleveland Clinic or the Mayo Clinic. At the same time, clinicians feel pressured to apply nearly every relevant test, driven also by the fear of medical litigation, further fueling a good deal of the ongoing antagonism between physicians and lawyers.

Clinical Context of Definitions

There is no consensus on the definition of medical futility. Suppose we rely upon a strict quantitative measure, for example, reviewing whether or not this treatment had been successful in at least one of the last one hundred similar cases.[5] But cases are not identical. Moreover, who makes the determination? Even with strict empirical criteria, values are naturally imbedded in the assessment. Should the determination of futility be based upon quality of life criteria? Again, who makes the call? In many if not most cases of medical futility, the patient is not able to decide for herself or himself, and the surrogate or a family member is the one who insists upon continued treatment. Setting forth qualitative criteria requires having to weigh whose values count more so than another's.

Clinical Context of Resources

Intervention that is marginally beneficial could be used for another patient who may stand to gain from that same intervention. Medical resources are in high demand, but the supply is thin. Should cost containment and resource allocation figure into the determination of medical futility? Clearly, the danger here lies in making cost-cutting decisions at the bedside, where the physician's principal duty should center on the patient. Let us now situate medical futility within America's sociocultural context, where the value of the Buddhist notion of no-self becomes more evident.

Sociocultural Context of Technological Imperative

First, consider the near obsession that our culture has with technologies. Given our strong pragmatic bent—we essentially value things in terms of their "usefulness"—we are driven by what has been called the "technological imperative."[6] Since we have the technologies, we feel compelled to use them. This imperative is strikingly apparent in the medical setting. Because we have the MRIs, the renal dialysis machines, and so forth, then we must use them. This makes sense if the application is effective. Yet maximal use in no way equates with optimal use. This gets to the core of some of the most plaguing issues in the use of scarce medical resources. From neonatal intensive care to adult patients who are nearly brain dead, medical technologies pervade medical practice. This naturalist fallacy—because these technologies *do* exist, they *ought* to be used—reflects a fundamental disposition in our culture. The standard-bearer of meaning rests upon *application*, so that applying these technologies becomes an end-in-itself rather than a means to an end.

Patients' Moral Rights

The previous discussion provides a backdrop to two other sociocultural features: emphases on patients' rights and views of life, aging, and death. Here, the Buddhist idea of no-self can help to broaden and enlighten our perspective as well as possibly contribute toward some resolution.

For well over three decades, North American bioethics has touted the importance of patients' rights. When the eminent theologian Paul Ramsey published his *The Patient as Person* in 1970 and made the remarkable claim at that time that patients are in essence "persons," that is, moral agents, this started a tidal wave of advocacy upholding patients' fundamental moral right to be self-determining, to make decisions for themselves, to be autonomous. Espousing patient autonomy recognizes that our dignity lies in our moral right to exercise our individual freedoms, most importantly, the freedom to make our own individual decisions with respect to our health care and well-being. Autonomy has become the cornerstone principle in North American bioethics. For this reason, quite a few ethical conflicts arise when this principle clashes with other key principles, especially the principle of beneficence, acting in ways that will bring about the best interests of the patient.

This is particularly evident in end-of-life decision-making. Prior to the patients' rights movement in America, it was considered to be a professional and moral imperative to keep a patient alive on ventilator support if this sustained the life of that patient. Attention then turned to considerations of what the patient would want. Eventually, the exercise of patient autonomy as a genuine expression of the patient's competent, clear, voluntary, and informed decision in many cases trumped the principle of beneficence, even if this resulted in the patient's death. Doing so meant honoring that patient as a person, as a moral agent.

Note here that the philosophical underpinnings of autonomy presume autonomy to be a manifestation of an individualized moral right, so that self-determination rests upon a notion of self that is individual, personal, and private. Self-determination in the North American context assumes a privileged center of meaning referred to as a self. Buddhism rejects this. Nonetheless, in my opinion, this fundamental ontological difference does not diminish the need for nor preclude the possibility of reassessing our Western view of autonomy from a Buddhist perspective. Indeed, doing so only helps to enrich our metaphysics of personal identity. At this point, therefore, let us step back and reconsider the Buddhist view of no-self and examine it from another angle.

No-Self as Pratityasamutpada

No-self can be viewed on two basic levels. On the most direct level, as described here and as noted in the classic texts, no-self means precisely that—the absence of an independent, permanent substance or entity called "I." This level clearly stipulates that there are no grounds to suppose the existence of a unique, individual, or permanent self. The belief in an independent self is the principal illusion from which Buddhist teachings seek to release us, since clinging to this illusion lies at the root of our suffering.

On a second, inferential level, no-self is more positively described in terms of the Buddhist teaching of *pratityasamutpada* (Pali, *paticca-samupadda*), dependent origination. The pairing of the terms, *pratitya* meaning "mutually dependent" and *samutpada* referring to "origination," nicely spells out the idea of simultaneous cause and effect, that is, that we are not only dependent upon but also conditioned by all else.[7] *Pratityasamutpada* also translates as "conditioned genesis." Yet bear in mind that both "genesis" and "origination" can mislead us into assuming some particular starting point. The real meaning behind the idea is that there is no such point, and that all things remain relative, conditioned, and interdependent. The *Majjima-nikaya* cites the ceaseless and symbiotic relationship between "this" and "that":

> When this is, that is;
> This arising, that arises;
> When this is not, that is not;
> This ceasing, that ceases.[8]

Pratityasamutpada is also described in more complex fashion via the intricate chain of causation among the twelve links: ignorance (*avidya*), mental formations (*samskara*), consciousness (*vijnana*), the psychophysical state (*namarupa*), six "gateways" of sense perceptions (*sadayatana*), contact with senses (*sparsa*), feelings (*vedana*), craving (*trsna*), grasping (*upadana*), coming into existence (*bhava*), birth (*jati*), old age and death (*jaramarana*).[9] Each link not only conditions but is conditioned. Each is interdependent and relative to each other.

Though this seems complex, it essentially means that all existing things, or *dharmas*, come into being and pass from being through a fundamental ontological interdependency. "Those who see Dependent Origination, see the Dharma. Those who see the Dharma, see Dependent Origination."[10] *Dharma*s therefore reveal the truth of *annica*, impermanence. At the same time, this entire scheme reflects an ontological interdependence that is both spatial and temporal. Spatially this occurs through interrelationships, temporally through continuities. This ontological interdependence conveys the fluid nature of existents and the perennial act of becoming that occurs through space over time. Nevertheless, we worldlings, enmeshed in ignorance (*avidya*), do not recognize existents as ultimately impermanent and changing. We attach ourselves to the illusion of permanence and pay a dear price. Clinging to a permanent self spawns all sorts of anxieties and suffering. Suffering ultimately comes about due to this epistemological confusion.

Again, this Buddhist teaching of *pratityasamutpada*, the notion that all of existence is so intertwined that no one thing, person, or event is independent, separate, solitary, and void of any impact or effect, is another way of understanding no-self. Nothing occurs in isolation. My every act has an impact upon some thing, some other. We all live and act together in a vibrant web of interdependency and interconnection so that relationality in essence defines our being. We are being-with-all-else-that-is. Now let us apply this to the issue of medical futility.

Pratityasamutpada as Spatial Interrelation

In the clinical setting, a proximate, visible relationality is evident in that decisions at the bedside affect not only the individual patient, but other parties such as family, loved ones, friends, and so forth. What is less evident is that, according to *pratityasamutpada*, the relationality extends throughout the living sphere to strangers, persons at the other end of the world, all within the community of living beings, animals, insects—all of sentient being is somehow touched by the decision made by an individual patient. An individual, "autonomous" choice thereby operates on two levels: the familiar level of an individual decision affecting loved ones and the ontological level of the decision affecting all of being.

At the first level, non-Buddhists may assert that the individual patient whose choice naturally impacts upon family and friends is still an independent, separate, and private self. They may claim that the individual patient remains his or her own self, and that any deed remains his or her own and does not in essence affect the essence of the others, that there is no ontological relationality. Buddhist no-self reaches deeper and further. As we see in *pratityasamutpada*, the heart of the matter lies precisely in the relationality among all living beings. It is precisely our shared essence that is radically distinct from our conventional understanding of how the individual views his or her identity as well as the exercise of his or her rights.

Buddhist no-self in terms of an ontological relationality contributes significantly to the controversy over medical futility by reminding us that the individual or collective demand for treatment, whether futile or not, affects all parties. We allocate treatments in ways that affect costs of treatments, thereby affecting the institutional use of such treatments. Also, allocating treatment to this particular patient takes away that treatment from another patient who may stand to gain, and this affects not only other potential candidates but also ever-widening circles of others. *Pratityasamutpada* reminds us that a single decision by an individual to maintain medically futile treatment, as with any decision, any act, produces immediate and long-range ripple effects.

No-self as *pratityasamutpada* awakens us to the scope of impact that is less visible though far-reaching. Visibility is a superficial measure in that we tend to not weigh in factors we do not see. Because our disposition is thus parochial in that our ultimate concerns rest within our proximate circles of who and what matters, those outside of our circle of meaning are considered less important. After all, it seems morally counterintuitive to assign equal meaning and value to perfect strangers. To illustrate, an earthquake in Pakistan is indescribably devastating in its scope of human fatality, suffering, and misery. Yet it is still "over there"; though our hearts go out to the Pakistanis, it still does not *ultimately concern us*. In the same way, the scope of moral concern in a situation regarding medical futility is restricted within a proximate circle of visibility.

No-self and its manifestation as *pratityasamutpada* beckons us to consider the nonvisible implications of our visible act. It releases us from a self-imposed prison built on the false premise, the illusion, that only the local and the visible is what is real. Buddhist no-self can release us from this prison. Its emphasis upon an ontological relationality among all living beings forces us to imagine and consider the scope and profoundly far-reaching impact of our actions.

Views of Life, Aging, and Death

Another crucial sociocultural component in the United States concerns our views regarding the spectrum of life, aging, and death. Let us first consider views toward death. The fact that our culture has a genuine problem dealing with death is not news. Media portrayals of death and dying continue to be skewed and unrealistic and reflect our fundamental unease with mortality. In reality, death as it is played out in hospitals and in nursing homes (most Americans die in institutions and not in their homes) often occurs in a slow, extended process. This real face of death is not photogenic; it is one that we Americans prefer to ignore.

This is particularly so in the American medical setting, where we deconstruct mortality by attempting to medically manage the process of dying through various life-sustaining technologies. This management of mortality not only consumes much of our health care energies, but also our health care resources and dollars. It also reinforces unrealistic expectations regarding medical treatment so that medically managing death and dying and our cultural rejection of death sustain each other in a vicious circle. Indeed, our health care system is dominated by a biomedical model that, despite emphases on patients' rights, hospice work, and advance directives, still sees death as the ultimate enemy and works to its fullest extent to stave off death by any means, even to the point of keeping patients marginally alive, so long as they are alive.

This problematic affects how we view life. In the United States there is now a wave of growing interest in protecting life at all costs, particularly saving the life of the "innocent" such as the "unborn," marginal groups including minorities, elderly, and disabled, even the cluster of human cells known as the pre-embryo. Though reasons for this momentum are numerous, it reflects a long-standing cultural ethos regarding views of death and how this impacts upon our views regarding the continuum of life, aging, and death.

This cultural vitalism and problem with death in turn impact upon our views toward aging. For many of us, aging, especially old aging, represents a dying. Old age and death are feared allies. In contrast, old age and death (*jaramarana*) constitute the twelfth link of dependent origination. Birth necessarily leads to it. There is no birth without it. It necessarily leads to rebirth. Nevertheless, as a culture, we dread old age because we find no value in it and it embodies the inevitability of death. Consider the extremes we go to in order to avoid the façade of aging. The cosmetic industry and the popularity of extreme makeovers are testaments to our cultural obsession with not looking old.

Much of this rests upon our fundamental views of time. Our U.S. culture tends to focus more on the present and the future. In view of America's history in struggling to shape new opportunities, and the fact that our nation is still young, we place a high premium on promise, potential, and hope. Future-oriented and pragmatic, we cherish youth and young adulthood, phases that embody promise. Deaths of infants and children signify the death of promise and represent the ultimate tragedy. After a certain time in our lives, however, we diminish or abandon ideas of usefulness. When we combine a culture whose time-consciousness is essentially future, that values usefulness and productivity, and that militates against the fact of death, the consequence is an America where aging represents an overriding crisis.

The crux of the matter is that we as a culture lack a fundamentally coherent and consistent philosophy of life stages. We assign an intrinsic value to youthfulness and young adulthood in that these stages embody promise and potential. At some point along the spectrum of life, we cease to assign value and thereby do not assign an intrinsic value to aging as a good in-and-of-itself. When the elderly assimilate this view—how could they not since it pervades our daily lives so that reaching middle age can be filled with apprehension, fearing one is about to "cross the line"—they can easily feel disenfranchised, disconnected in a world that chooses to minimize their worth or else ignore them altogether. A coherent philosophy of life's stages has a seamless continuity so that a constant meaning is sustained through and permeates each stage, so that each stage naturally interacts with all others. It means that there is an inherent meaning within each stage, so that meaning is not derived from nor dependent upon another stage.

Some critics may argue that we do assign meaning to life's stages. Look at birth, intrinsically meaning new life, possibility. Consider childhood, intrinsically reflecting wide-open joy and discovery. Look at adolescence, meaning learning and youthfulness, and preparing for one's social spot in life. Consider adulthood, representing responsibility, societal contribution, productivity. But when we look at older adults, or those retired, or the elderly, *as a culture* we stop there. Do we *as a culture* assign any intrinsic value to aging?

Critics again may respond, "It depends. An old person can still be youthful. Can still be full of vigor and exercise body and mind. An old person can even be productive. Can volunteer in hospitals, food kitchens." But what is happening here? We assign value to an old person because of that old person's youthfulness, or because of that old person's productivity (and social worth). But do we assign value to the old person *because* he or she is *old*? In attributing intrinsic worth to growing old, we do so precisely because the person is growing old. By admiring an old person's youthfulness and/or productivity, we assign *value* to youthfulness and productivity, values that we have assigned to earlier stages in life.

I well remember Elsa Gidlow, a beautiful, eighty-year-old poet who lived in Mill Valley just beyond Sausalito. Nearly totally self-sufficient, she grew her own herb garden, cut her own wood, walked with a brisk step, stayed mentally sharp, and wrote sparkling poetry. I admired her greatly—for her youthfulness. I did not admire her for *being old*, but for acting young, and in so doing I unwittingly gave in to the cultural ethos.

Pratityasamutpada as Temporal Interrelation

Pratityasamutpada in terms of temporal relationality helps to address this profoundly difficult and far-reaching problem. It offers a unique parameter for constructing a coherent life stage philosophy. It asserts an interconnectedness among the three time modes of past, present, and future. Each mode interpenetrates with the other. Thus, the past is not past in terms of no-longer-being; the past is not static, reified,

and thereby over with. Within a framework of ontological relationality, time's dynamic is such that past enters into the present and
flows into the future. Just as there is no permanent or independent
entity, there is no separate, compartmentalized moment in time. In the
Sabbasava Sutra, we read the Buddha's warning to his fellow monks
(*bhikkus*) to not engage in unwise reflections such as:

> Did I exist in the past?
> Did I not exist in the past?
> What was I in the past?
> How was I in the past?
> Having been what, did I become what in the past?
> Shall I exist in future?
> Shall I not exist in future?
> What shall I be in future?
> How shall I be in future?
> Having been what, shall I become what in future?[11]

In the same way, we can fragment the cycle of being and becoming so
that we ignore time as being/becoming in its totality. In reality, each
moment is a rising and a falling, a birth and a death. Herein lies the
truth of *annica* or impermanence. In this fashion, each moment is all
there is. Since each moment is carried into the present from the past
and flows into the future, being is becoming. There is a perfection in
each moment. No one time modality is superior to any other.

A coherent philosophy of life stages is possible if we are willing
to reconsider our view of time in light of a radically new vision of
time/being/becoming that we find in the Buddhist teaching of interconnectedness. A coherent and consistent philosophy of life stages
assigns intrinsic value to each stage, each moment in life. It assigns
an intrinsic value to each moment since each moment incorporates
all the others. Aging therefore possesses an intrinsic value because it
incorporates all moments leading up to that phase and all moments
that follow.

Pratityasamutpada as temporal interconnectedness enables a
coherent approach to life stages whereby each moment carries its own
intrinsic worth. Our cultural angst regarding death and aging is both
derived from and sustains this lack of a philosophy of life stages.
As long as we continue to have a fragmented outlook toward the
spectrum of life and death, conflicts such as those regarding medical
futility will continue to surface.

Conclusion

The Buddhist view of no-self is rich in application, and this is illustrated with respect to the painful debate over medical futility—whether or not to maintain treatment considered medically futile in the face of demands that such treatment continue. Despite no-self's conceptual gravitas, it makes sense to think of it in terms of *pratityasamutpada*. And though the formulation of dependent origination is rather complex, in its essence it is deceptively simple yet profound. It refers to our fundamental ontological interdependency in that no one thing, living being, or event is separate from the fabric of being.

This ontological interconnectedness reveals itself spatially and temporally. Spatial interconnectedness sheds light on the meaning of the individual person. Surely, each one of us is unique and individual on a conventional level. Yet on the deeper level, we are in essence intertwined. Thus, individual decisions we make for ourselves as patients affect not only family and friends, but all living beings. This relational view of self and self-determination widens the scope of concern and in so doing extends the moral community to all living beings. *Pratityasamutpada*, the expression of no-self in terms of spatial interdependency, reminds us of our shared humanity and essence. It guards us against misplaced assumptions of autonomy as merely a private affair.

Temporal interconnectedness lays the groundwork for a coherent philosophy of life stages. In this way, the later stages in the rhythm of being/becoming possess intrinsic value as do all prior stages. In this dance, each moment rises and falls, each moment is the beginning and the end. Each moment is connected with and flows into and from all others. Each moment embodies the past, present, and future. Growing old is not divorced from the rhythm of life, but in fact plays a key role. Growing old is intrinsically meaningful and valuable. In this temporal interconnectedness, life's youth, growing, aging, and ending comprise life's truth and beauty. This would no doubt impact upon how we view old age and death (*jaramana*), enabling us to naturally think of them as inherently valuable, final steps in the dance.

Notes

1. From *Khemaka Sutta* in *Samyutta Nikaya* XXII.89, trans. Thanissaro Bhikkhu (accessed Insight edition 2005), at http://www.accesstoinsight.org/index-sutta.html.

2. From *Majjhima-nikayatthakatha, Papancasudani*, II, 112, cited in Walpola Rahula, *What the Buddha Taught*, rev. ed. (New York: Grove Press, 1959), 56.

3. *Dhammpada*, 277, 278, 279, cited in Rahula, *What the Buddha Taught*, 134.

4. The term "bioethics" was first coined in 1971 by University of Wisconsin biochemist Van Rensselaer Potter (1911–2001).

5. See L. J. Schneiderman, N. S. Jecker, and A. R. Jonsen, "Medical Futility: Its Meaning and Ethical Implications," *Annals of Internal Medicine* 112 (1990): 949–54.

6. See David Rothman, *Beginnings Count: The Technological Imperative in American Health Care* (New York: Oxford University Press, 1997); Arnold Pacey, *The Culture of Technology* (Oxford: Basil Blackwell, 1983); Jacques Ellul, *The Technological Society* (New York: Vintage, 1964).

7. See Akira Hirakawa, trans. and ed. Paul Groner, *A History of Indian Buddhism: From Sakyamuni to Early Mahayana*, Asian Studies at Hawai'i, No. 36 (Honolulu: University of Hawai'i Press, 1990), 48.

8. *Majjima-nikaya*, cited in Rahula, What the Buddha Taught, 53.

9. David J. Kalupahana, *Buddhist Philosophy: A Historical Analysis* (Honolulu: University of Hawai'i Press, 1976), 31–33.

10. *Majjhima Nikaya*, Vol. 1, trans. I. B. Horner, Pali Text Society Translation Series (London: Luzac, 1954–1959), 119, cited in Hirakawa, *A History of Indian Buddhism*, 49.

11. Cited in Rahula, *What the Buddha Taught*, 101.

5

A Contemporary North American Buddhist Discussion of Abortion

Rita M. Gross

In current North American discourse, abortion certainly is a contentious topic. Elections are decided by candidates' stands on abortion, and one of the most feared developments in United States' law is overturning the Supreme Court decision that legitimatized abortion, which many fear could happen with new Supreme Court justices. Despite the importance of this issue, it is only rarely discussed in North American Buddhist contexts. It is widely assumed that Buddhists would be unequivocally anti-choice because of the strong position against killing encapsulated in a common version of its first precept, binding on both lay and monastic practitioners: "do not take life."

However, I will claim that such a knee-jerk reaction is based on superficial understandings of Buddhist ethics and lack of deep contemplations of the harm wrought to both women and the ecosystem when women are forced to complete unwanted pregnancies. To me, as a long-term (thirty years) practitioner of Tibetan Vajrayana Buddhism and a lifelong feminist, the argument that Buddhists must be anti-choice does not seem so simple and obvious. Of course, Buddhists would never prefer abortion to other options such as reliable birth control. Through no failure of their own, those other choices are not always available to people, which complicates ethical choices considerably. While traditional Buddhists would agree with anti-choice advocates that abortion ends "a life" (but not "life," which is beginningless and endless), a nuanced understanding of Buddhism's first precept argues that Buddhists have an ethical obligation to minimize as much as possible the amount of harm their lives cause to the inter-dependent matrix of relative existence. This understanding is quite different from absolutist claims that abortion is always wrong, though abortion is always to be avoided, if possible. The most effective way to avoid abortion is to avoid unwanted pregnancies, but once an unwanted pregnancy is in place, the ethical situation changes.

In this essay, I will reflect as a Buddhist critical and constructive thinker, first on discourses on abortion prevalent in North American politics, and then offer Buddhist interpretations of these arguments. My arguments also depend on my lifelong commitment to feminism, which I define as commitment to women's status as complete human beings, rather than adjuncts to humanity whose purpose is to take care of men and children, while ignoring their own visions and longings. I have brought these two stances, Buddhism and feminism, together in many other contexts and will not review those arguments here.[1]

Common North American Positions on Abortion

North American rhetoric on abortion, like most North American poli-tics, reflects entrenched dualistic positions, with little sympathy for and understanding of why others would take different positions. Will-ingness of many to impose their version of right behavior on others who would do things differently is also characteristic.

The most unfortunate and inaccurate aspect of North American debates on abortion is, in my view, naming one of the two usual posi-tions "pro-choice" or "pro-abortion," while the alternate position is almost always named "pro-life." This naming is completely inaccurate because no one is "pro-abortion." I have never understood why pro-choice advocates have let this linguistic convention go by relatively unchallenged. Buddhists appreciate greatly the power of language and have long insisted that precise and accurate language does make a real difference in how one deals with practical life-and-death issues. With so much at stake for women's well-being in this case, the impor-tance of accurate language cannot be overemphasized.

If we are to use the usual terminology, I do not believe anyone is pro-abortion and that everyone is pro-life. No one would say that somehow life is incomplete without experiencing an abortion or that it is in any way, shape, or form a desirable experience. It is simply less odious than the alternatives. Therefore, those who favor the avail-ability of abortion are pro-choice, while those who would deny that availability are anti-choice. I think the emotional heat surrounding this issue could be lessened if all sides understood that people can be pro-choice or anti-choice, but no one is pro-abortion. Most pro-choice people are also pro-life, in that they cherish and nurture life in general. Furthermore, the position of being both anti-abortion and pro-choice is utterly consistent; one can prefer both to avoid abortion and reluctantly choose it as the lesser of two evils in some cases. It is a conceptual mistake to cast the debate in terms of pro-abortion versus pro-life. Either one is anti-choice or one is pro-choice. Those are the alternatives.

We should be clear that all Buddhists would prefer conditions in which women would never need abortions, but currently, those conditions do not prevail, due to inadequate birth control mechanisms, their lack of universal availability, and insufficient education and socialization to inculcate the virtue of always using birth control except when pregnancy is the desired outcome of sexual activity.

Perhaps this linguistic inaccuracy in framing the debate has slipped by because pro-choice advocates in North America have been relatively insensitive to the moral ambiguity of abortion. They have been so focused on the needs of women for reproductive freedom and control that they have usually overlooked the fact that abortion is undesirable, and as a result have not shunned the label "pro-abortion." They have been comfortable declaring that the fetus is a mere "blob of tissue." Because they are so focused on the rights of women, the status of the fetus as a developing human being has not registered. Nor have they always acknowledged the grief and discomfort that having an abortion can bring to women who make that choice, though recently some pro-choice advocates have begun to write of this dimension of the abortion issue.[2]

As with all North American political issues, pro-choice advocates have been quite strident in advancing these positions. I believe that such stridency and insensitivity to the moral ambiguity of the situation have actually polarized the debate more than necessary and may have diminished support for the "pro-choice" position.

The North American debate has also focused mainly on rights, especially a "right to privacy" as opposed to a "right to life." By contrast, Buddhist thought usually emphasizes mutual obligations and interdependence over individual rights because the whole category of the "individual" as metaphysically real is highly suspect in Buddhist analysis (though individuals are real enough in analyses of the relative world). Buddhist debate on the topic of abortion would not be framed in terms of individual rights. It would be famed in terms of compassion and alleviating suffering. The North American debate may necessarily be focused on the issue of "rights" because of the con-straints of constitutional law in the United States and the individual-ism of the Western religious and philosophical heritage. But framing the arguments largely in terms of rights rather than care and concern for others also lends a harsh, divisive tone to the debate that polar-izes people into extreme positions with little empathy for the concerns that drive those on the other side. While I agree with the conclusions reached by those who frame their pro-choice arguments in terms of rights, as a Buddhist, I get there using different arguments.

The North American debate also focuses, though to a lesser extent, on certain slippery slope arguments: if we allow abortion, what will be next? Currently, one of the most contentious slippery slope arguments concerns late-term abortions. It is hard for me to imagine that most women would prefer a later-term abortion to a timely abortion. From a Buddhist point of view, as I will discuss later, mindfulness is a cardinal virtue and practice: one should be aware that one is pregnant and that one cannot have a child well before a late-term abortion would come to pass. I do not think there would be much sympathy for late-term abortions among Buddhists, except to save the life or fundamental health of the mother, or possibly in the case of a severely deformed or deficient fetus.

Another version this slippery slope argument goes something like this: if we allow abortion, why not infanticide or child sacrifice? After all, if the pregnancy is not interrupted, there will be a child eventually. The best answer to this slippery slope argument is that denial of abortion *does*, in fact, lead to infanticide. I am not thinking only of the desperate cases of confused teen mothers who give birth secretly and dispose of their babies; I am thinking of widespread cul-tural practices of exposing infants who overtax the carrying capacity of their societies. I am also thinking of more subtle forms of infanti-cide, of the neglect often suffered by children already born to parents who are unprepared to care for them properly.

Slippery slope arguments also go the other way. Some would outlaw relatively safe and reliable methods of birth control, such as the pill and IUD, on the grounds that they actually prevent a fertilized egg from implanting in the uterine wall rather than preventing the union of egg and sperm. Thus, it is argued, these methods of birth control actually cause very early term abortions. But is it reasonable to use the loaded term "abortion" for a situation in which the woman's menstrual cycle is not disrupted and the presence or absence of a sup-posed fetus would be difficult if not impossible to detect? Besides, if these methods are not available, all that remains are inconvenient and relatively unreliable barrier methods of contraception. And then, next, some will complain that "abortion" is practiced if the egg and sperm, who could have united, are separated by a barrier, which seems to be a less pious way of restating the Roman Catholic position that every sexual act must be open to the potential transmission of life.

I have heard of instances in which the slippery slope has also gone even further in the other direction, going so far as making the claim than menstruation is equivalent to abortion. Menstruation is evidence that a woman who could been have pregnant is not, which constitutes a kind of abortion. Women should always be pregnant or nursing, it seems, which would be extremely oppressive to women. Strange though this logic may sound to many contemporary readers, it has been used in some Hindu contexts as an argument for having girls marry before puberty; every time an unmarried girl menstruates, her father, who has not gotten her married off quickly enough, has committed an abortion.

The strangeness of this argument indicates the tenuous nature of slippery slope arguments against abortion altogether. There is always a slippery slope in any moral dilemma. Things are not discrete and separate but in process, in interdependent continuity. There is no magic, definitive, black-and-white point that clearly separates one part of a process from another, a point that is basic in the Buddhist views of how things work. Therefore, moral situations are complex and ambiguous, not simple, black-and-white dichotomies. Yet choice and action are required. Common sense should indicate early abortions are preferable to late-term abortions or the many forms of infanticide, and that menstruation, rather than indicating an abortion has been committed, indicates that one is not necessary. Slippery slope arguments are meaningless and have no place in reasoned, caring discussion and decision-making.

In North American debate, one of the great perversions of abortion, its use for purposes of sex selection, is rarely discussed because it does not seem to be a motivation for abortion in North America. Abortion is widely used for this purpose in some parts of Asia, however. Because gender discrimination is unacceptable from a normative point of view in Buddhism, this use of abortion could never be acceptable to Buddhists. It is doubly negative, in that it compounds something Buddhists would rather not have to do—commit an abortion—with another practice that is fundamentally un-Buddhist—gender discrimination—even if it has been widely practiced in Asian Buddhism.

Compassion as the Basis for a Pro-Choice Position

To me, it has always been utterly clear that abortions must be safe and legal so long as birth control is not 100 percent reliable. Even with today's birth control, which is not completely reliable, abortions could be quite rare, needed only in cases of rape or birth control failure, if education and awareness surrounding sexual activity were dealt with much more skillfully. But abortions must be safe, legal, and as rare as possible because the costs of the other option are simply unbearable to women and to the ecological matrix supporting the lives of us all. The human costs to women are staggering when they are forced to complete unwanted pregnancies. I can imagine few things crueler to a woman than to force her to bear a child she does not want to have. It is very hard for me to understand the mind-set of those who would force her to do so by outlawing abortion altogether if they could and by creating restrictions that make it extremely difficult to obtain abortions even though they are legal. It is impossible to imagine that they have even an ounce of empathy for a woman pregnant against her will, who may well have been using birth control that failed, or who may have been poorly educated about her own sexual safety, or who may have been seduced in some way. Why punish the woman with such a horrible burden? What would compassionate feelings for the suffering woman dictate? That she be forced to go through an unwanted pregnancy, with all the social, emotional, and career losses that can be entailed by such a fate, or that she be allowed to end the pregnancy with both regret and relief? Needing an abortion is never a woman's first choice. Why make her suffer so much more by denying something so simple? Worse yet, why make her risk her life by forcing her into unsafe and illegal options?

In all the North American debates about abortion, this one factor, the suffering state of mind of a woman pregnant against her will, which should be the number one priority framing the discussion, is utterly forgotten. The anti-choice advocates have lots of sympathy for the fetus (though little sympathy for the child once it is born) but don't care at all about the suffering they would cause women. The pro-choice advocates are so caught up in often aggressive arguments about rights that they also seem to gloss over the suffering woman who simply cannot have a child or another child in her current circumstances. Whatever a Buddhist might conclude about abortion (and many Buddhists would not agree with me that abortion is sometimes that least harmful solution to a difficult situation), any Buddhist who is careful to bring Buddhist values into the discussion would remember the suffering woman first and would seek compassionate solutions for her.

What Is the Real Agenda Driving the Anti-Choice Position?

It is clear to me that a woman could hold ethical, philosophical, and religious views that would make it impossible for her to end an unwanted pregnancy medically, even though she might pray that divine intervention would solve her problems. When I comment on the anti-choice position and its rhetoric, I am not directing my comments to such individuals. I am talking about a well-organized movement that seeks to dictate its ethics to all people, whether or not they share that ethic.

I do not find the claims of the anti-choice movement—that it is really pro-life, that its main concern is saving lives—at all credible. The same people who are so opposed to abortion usually also support wars and American military intervention all over the planet. They usually support the death penalty. Often they support and advocate technologies that are destroying the environment, which is the life support system of us all. Often they hunt and fish. They usually eat meat and are rarely concerned about animals' safety and well-being. Furthermore, anti-choice concern for the fetus often ends as soon as it is born. The same people who so adamantly deny women abortions also often oppose spending for social programs that would better the lives of these women and the children they force them to bear. If one is pro-life, then one needs to be consistently pro-life. If one is not consistently pro-life in a thoroughgoing manner, perhaps some other agenda is actually the main, though unstated, agenda.

What of a hypothetical, imagined society that was genuinely pro-life in all its laws and practices? Presumably, there would be many fewer occasions in which an abortion might be necessary in such a society. Finding truly effective and safe birth control would be a much higher research priority than it is in our society at present. Sex education would be realistic, birth control available to all and its use considered a moral imperative except on the rare occasions when people wished to conceive a child. All children who were born would be adequately cared for, and women would not be stigmatized in any way, no matter the circumstances under which they bore children. But might rape or failure of birth control still occur? Yes, and on those rare occasions, it would still seem cruel and uncompassionate to force a woman to carry through an unwanted pregnancy. However, unless many policies and practices change radically, the question about abortion in a truly pro-life society remains completely hypothetical. We do not live in a society that practices pro-life ways of living in any arena other than involuntarily pregnant women.

The claims of the anti-choice movement to be pro-life become even less credible when we realize that their positions on related issues actually make unwanted pregnancies, and therefore some abortions, *more*, rather than *less* likely. The same people who fight to make abortions illegal or difficult to obtain also often want to restrict access to birth control, to make it difficult or impossible to obtain the morning-after pill, and to teach "abstinence only" sex education programs to children and teens. It is extremely difficult to understand, for example, how the Roman Catholic Church can justify forbidding birth control, given its unequivocal anti-abortion stance. That its spokesmen then go on to claim that they are actually pro-woman, and respect and revere women, is even more mysterious. One would think that if the goal is to stop abortions, then every possible means of preventing unwanted pregnancies would be very high on the list of priorities of such groups. But no! Also high on their list of priorities is prohibiting the very things that reduce or eliminate unwanted pregnancies—reliable birth control and realistic sex education that is mindful of the sexual urges of adolescents and the likely outcome of those urges. I could take the pro-life movement much more seriously if its advocates worked as hard to prevent conception, to prevent unwanted pregnancies, as they work to prevent abortions. Because their policies actually encourage unwanted pregnancies, it is hard to take their claims to be pro-life at face value.

So what is going on? What is the real agenda? At its most innocent level, I have always thought that abortion has been deemed so awful by so many religious thinkers because men can much more easily identify with a fetus about to be aborted than with a woman who simply cannot have a baby. These men have never been and will never be in the position of such a woman. And all the laws and most of the religious texts about abortion have been written by such men. The dominance of such men's voices in the abortion debate (despite the fact that many women are actively anti-choice) probably explains why we so seldom hear the anguished first person voice of a woman suffering under the load of an unwanted pregnancy in the debate. We need the voices of highly educated, articulate, and deeply spiritual women to be much more public in explaining why abortions must be safe, legal, and rare.

At a more hidden level, it is difficult to avoid the suspicion that many in the anti-choice movement regard unwanted pregnancies as an appropriate punishment for having sex they deem as illicit. One often hears that sex education should not include how to use birth control because such knowledge encourages teenagers to have sex. Conversely, one hears that fear of pregnancy is the only way to stop people who "shouldn't be having sex" from having sex, which justifies keeping birth control out of their hands. When young women have sex anyway and become pregnant as a result, the pregnancy is regarded as punishment for breaking the rules. There is no question that such attitudes toward young women and poor women are common (rich women can usually find ways to have an abortion even when it is illegal). Furthermore, the men who cause the pregnancies do not suffer the same stigmatization or have their lives totally disrupted by an unwanted pregnancy. I suspect that if unwanted pregnancies caused as much disruption, anguish, and suffering to men as they do to women, there would be much less opposition to the pro-choice position.

The most secret agenda, often not so well hidden, is to keep women tied to their traditional and subservient positions and roles. If women can be subjected to random pregnancies they do not want, then independence, dignity, and freedom for women do not truly exist. A woman's dreams for her life can be ruined by an ill-timed, unwanted pregnancy, and it is possible for her to suffer such a fate even if she is always diligent about using birth control. All contraceptive devices fail on occasion. If abortion were not available in such circumstances, a woman would be reduced to the status of a virtual slave, subject to the will of others who control her body. And there do seem to be some people who are just plain mean, who don't want women to be regarded as fundamentally free and independent human beings in the same way that men are. They want to be able, always, to hold the possibility of unwanted, forced pregnancy over women as a means of control and as denial of their humanity, freedom, and dignity.

Buddhist Arguments toward a Pro-Choice Position

I would argue that the abortion issue is best placed in the context of discussions about human sexuality altogether and discussions about the desirability of controlling fertility. Is sex part of the communication that occurs between committed adults, or is sex primarily for the purpose of procreation? Should people be allowed, or even required, to control their fertility for the sake of the overall well-being of the planet and their own children? Buddhism has never regarded sex as something laypeople need to avoid except to procreate, and Buddhism has never promoted unlimited fertility or lauded large families, or even required its adherents to reproduce as part of their religious duty.[3] Before articulating a Buddhist pro-choice position, I think it is essential to understand more fully Buddhist views on sexuality and birth control.

As an overview, it seems that there would be little, if any, opposition to the use of birth control from a Buddhist point of view, but that abortion would be a different matter. There is no question that Buddhists would want to avoid abortion, and the most effective method of avoiding abortion is avoiding conception. But it is also case that in one Buddhist context, that of contemporary Japan, one of the main functions of Buddhist temples is offering services that comfort those who have found it necessary to have abortions and help the aborted fetus continue on its journey.[4] To understand this seeming contradiction, we have to start with traditional Buddhist attitudes toward sexuality, and with traditional Buddhist understandings of birth and rebirth.

The first step in developing a thoroughgoing pro-choice position is recognizing the moral legitimacy of not reproducing. The first choice that needs to be in place is the ability to choose not to be a parent, whether one is married or single. Many religions do not even allow their followers, especially women, to make that choice, but Buddhism has always been different. It has always celebrated nonreproductive lifestyles for both women and men. Most religions regard reproduction as a religious duty and command their followers to reproduce, but Buddhism has never been driven by the command to "increase and multiply" and has always recognized that human fertility can be a problem, that having children is not always so desirable. Human fertility can be a great problem, both for individuals and for societies, as well as the earth. I would argue that recognizing how much harm is done by too much human fertility, or human fertility in the wrong times and places, is an important step in building a pro-choice position. I would also argue that this issue is largely unrecognized by masses of people who think that pregnancy and childbirth should always be celebrated.

If one makes the choice to remain childless, three methods are available for carrying it out: celibacy, birth control, or abortion. For much of human history, birth control was relatively unavailable, which is why people have always practiced abortion, or, in more dire cases, infanticide. It is often difficult for people living in our era to imagine what life was like before the advent of relatively reliable birth control, and I think that lack of imagination makes it difficult to understand some aspects of traditional religions. Without relatively reliable birth control, celibacy was the only way to avoid conception, and that option was widely used and celebrated in Buddhism. Much of the time, Buddhist literature focuses on why men would want to be monks and avoid parenthood, but there was also some recognition of the difficulties motherhood presented for women. In fact, in a statement that has offended many Western Buddhists, it was argued that a female rebirth was less desirable than a male rebirth, precisely because of the pain, limitations, and liability imposed by pregnancy and childbirth, among other aspects of female biology. In any case, being able to avoid pregnancy and childbirth is essential to a pro-choice position, and Buddhism provided this to women by including a nuns' order from the beginnings of Buddhism to the present day.

This is not the place to discuss the issue of whether or not the Buddha wanted to found a nuns' order. Nor is it the place to discuss relative lack of support and enthusiasm for the nuns' order historically or the lower standards of education that generally prevailed for nuns.[5] The point is that the nuns' order provides an alternative to reproductive roles for women, and being able to choose not to reproduce is essential for women (and men). I would also argue that in situations in which women (or men) cannot survive outside an extended family or some other social institution that replaces the extended family, and in which reliable and effective birth control is not available, monastic institutions provide the only method for women to be able to survive in nonreproductive roles. These describe the conditions of most humans for most human history. These days, it is difficult to argue for the benefits of nunship because it is widely misunderstood as simply a denial of sex, which seems unattractive to most contemporary Westerners. However, I would argue that women generally fare better in situations in which the alternative of nunhood is available, simply because it is an *alternative* to wifehood and motherhood in situations in which being a self-supporting career woman with or without children is not possible.[6] I would also point out that a significant revival of nunship is occurring in Asian Buddhism. Ordination is now more widely available and the standards of education are improving in all versions of Asian Buddhism. Many women gladly choose this option instead of male-dominated marriages. Based on my friendships with Asian and Western Buddhist nuns, I would also say that they appreciate their community life and have no desire to strike out as independent career women instead. The many positive dimensions of this institution should not be overlooked in building a thoroughgoing Buddhist pro-choice position. Though imperfectly available and supported throughout history, I would argue that initiating and maintaining a nuns' order constitutes some traditional recognition of women's ability to choose not to reproduce.

When we discuss Buddhist reasons for choosing celibacy over the householder's life and Buddhist views of sexuality, we gain further insight into how Buddhists might think about women's right to choice. I cannot stress enough when discussing these issues that Buddhist views of sexuality and celibacy have nothing to do with concepts such as purity and impurity, sin, or the evils of sexual pleasure. The reasons given for celibacy have always been basically the same: Life is short and there isn't time for everything. Some choices must be made, and those who engage in sexuality usually also have children. Therefore, they need to pursue economic activity in addition. The results are two—attachment or clinging, and insufficient time for study, contemplation, and meditation. Both militate against deep insight, freedom, and peace. The freedom of monastic life is frequently compared to the cramped, claustrophobic, hurried life of a householder, and the celibate monastic lifestyle sounds much better. This is not the place to debate this assessment of the virtues of monasticism versus the householder lifestyle, though I find these Buddhist arguments cogent, especially if one cannot easily be both sexually active and childless. The point is that, given this evaluation of the virtues of monasticism, if women did not have the ability to pursue this lifestyle, the situation would be extreme for women. It is one thing to be forced to be a wife and mother in a cultural situation in which those are the valued only options for women; it would be entirely different if the disvalued householder life were the only option for women.[7]

The strict monastic codes against sexual activity of any sort have little spillover into the sexual lives of laypeople. The Buddhist attitude is not that sex is *tainted*, but that it leads to problematic results if, and only if, one is seeking freedom from conventional life and concerns. Buddhists, with their assumption of rebirth, have also always stated that monasticism is not for everyone, at least not in this life. For laypeople, sex is not a guilty pleasure that should be indulged in only because reproduction is its outcome. Laypeople are bound only by the Fourth Precept, not to misuse sexuality or to engage in improper sexuality. There are no detailed, extensive law codes defining laypeople's behavior; those are reserved for the behavior of monastics (and they are detailed!). It is commonly claimed that sexual morality for Buddhist laypeople generally follows the norms of the surrounding culture, and I think this is an accurate generalization. This means that there is latitude for contemporary developments, and most North American Buddhists who comment on sexual ethics claim that the meaning of not misusing sexuality is not harming sexual partners in any way, *including* the psychological harm of misleading one's partner about one's commitment to the relationship, indiscriminately seducing people, or any other imaginable way of using sexuality to harm another being.

I know of no instance in which using birth control is considered to be misusing sexuality. I have only seen the issue discussed in a few contexts. In one case, a student asked a traditional Tibetan teacher who is a monk if family planning is permissible. The teacher replied that he had no "fixed opinion" on the matter, but added that he could see "no great fault in preventing conception." The student pressed him, suggesting that to use birth control might "prevent a mind from taking rebirth." The teacher's response is interesting, especially in light of the arguments I have been making about the importance of the nuns' option. He replied, "Is it then non-virtuous to be a nun? For instance, a woman who could have had five children, by becoming a nun before she had any children, would have prevented five beings from taking rebirth. Would that be a non-virtuous action?"[8] He seems to be saying that if it is permissible to prevent conception by being celibate, it is also permissible to prevent conception by blocking the union of egg and sperm. Only if conception has already taken place might he see a problem. In general, Buddhists seem to see a major difference between *preventing* conception and *stopping* the process once conception has occurred.

In fact, all Buddhist logic would argue that birth control is absolutely essential to proper engagement in sexuality. The fact that abortion is always considered problematic and something to be avoided is itself the strongest argument in favor of birth control. The only other option is to refrain from sexuality except when pregnancy is the desired outcome, and Buddhists have always considered that advice to be unrealistic for laypeople. If people had so little desire for sexual activity, they would probably be monks and nuns! Of course, this logic requires the availability of birth control without moral or economic discouragement from using it. If birth control is available, however, there would be less sympathy for "accidents" occurring because people fail to use it. Mindfulness and awareness are key principles

that should accompany all Buddhist activities. Being swept away in
the passion of the moment and failing to use available birth control
or simply failing to use it routinely could probably be considered
improper and harmful uses of sexuality.

To understand the need both to limit conception and to avoid
abortion, it is necessary to understand how Buddhists have traditionally thought of human birth. This is almost impossible to understand
if one does not remember the Buddhist assumption of rebirth, so
culturally foreign to so many Westerners. Any birth is, by definition, a *rebirth*. For conception to take place, *three* things, not just two,
must coincide. There must be sperm, a fertile egg, and a being seeking rebirth. If the third component is not there, pregnancy will not
occur, no matter how many sperm and fertile eggs are present. Thus,
one is conceiving or aborting an ongoing lifestream. (This does not
contradict Buddhism's assertion of fundamental lack of a permanent
abiding self, but the explanation is too lengthy and complex for this
context.) Traditionally, many Buddhists have regarded the moment of
sexual intercourse itself as the moment at which rebirth occurs, if it
is going to happen. Some texts say that the being in the intermediate
state sees its future parents copulating and rushes in to find a new
body. They also say that if the being is attracted to the father, it will be
reborn as a female, and vice versa. So, clearly, a traditional Buddhist
position on a life beginning at conception would be as conservative
as that of Roman Catholicism. How is it, then, that Buddhist temples
in Japan also perform services on behalf of women and couples who
have had abortions?

Again, the Buddhist understanding of the life process probably
makes some difference. Buddhists would say that *a* life begins at conception, but they would never say that *life* begins at conception. Lives
are not discrete, independent entities in Buddhist thought; they are
all parts of an interdependent, ever-changing matrix. A life will be
relatively stable for a short period of time, but it has no independent
existence by itself. It is completely and totally interdependent with its
matrix. *Life*, rather than individual lives, is beginningless and endless.
It is a process, the matrix in which individual lives come and go. It is
utter nonsense to claim that *life* begins at conception. All that begins
at conception is a specific, concrete lifestream that has gone through
many births and deaths, and probably will go through many more.
The beginning of *a* life is awesome, but it is not quite on the level of
the beginning of *life*. I believe that confusing *a* life with *life* is a huge
conceptual mistake, and that this conceptual mistake drives much of
the contentious North American debate on abortion.

To return to issues surrounding birth control and rebirth, one might think that because one would be conceiving—giving a body—to an ongoing lifestream, there would be some premium on getting as many bodies as possible into circulation. One could think that this would be the case, especially for human beings, given that human rebirth is considered to have more opportunities for positive developments than any other rebirth. However, this logic is nonexistent or rare in Buddhism because rebirth itself is guaranteed for any being still in *samsara* and only a *fortunate* rebirth has much potential. A human rebirth, in and of itself, is relatively fortunate, but only a rebirth in which one has the potential to practice deeply and develop insight into profound reality is considered to be a *precious* human birth, as opposed to merely a human birth. To be so fortunate, a human being needs sufficient material, emotional, and spiritual resources, and the birth would be less than fortunate if its family, community, or planet could not or will not provide such resources. Thus, limiting rebirths to those that can be properly nurtured will require some use of birth control in most or all cases. This argument is very strong in Buddhism, and is the basis on which one could argue that birth control is *required*, not optional, because one is causing great harm to many beings by indulging in uncontrolled and unlimited fertility.[9]

Traditionally, however, it is said that the situation changes drastically once conception has occurred. The lifestream that was in the intermediate state between death and rebirth (*bardo*) changes into a sentient being who is now between birth and death. To stop the life process of a being between birth and death is killing, something that should be avoided. On the other hand, concerning the being in the intermediate state between death and rebirth, it would probably be said that this being simply was not karmically situated to be able to connect with the egg and the sperm that do not come together because of the presence of birth control. There is no question that the usual traditional Buddhist position on abortion regards it as extremely unfortunate. Yet in some Buddhist countries, abortion is widespread and one finds very little of the dogmatic, contentious rhetoric that surrounds most North American discussions of abortion in Buddhist contexts.

Why? At base, probably because Buddhists recognize the impossibility of truly keeping the precepts, regard fixed mind and dogmatism as problems rather than virtues, and do not regard expressions of anger, aggression, and confrontation as helpful in any way, especially in a situation that is already broken and wounded. Of course, no one would deliberately set out to have an abortion. But what does one do when a pregnancy is impossible and destructive? The First Precept asks us to do no harm and to avoid taking life. The fact of the matter is that it is impossible to keep that precept perfectly in the interdependent web of life and death, the web in which life feeds on life. Buddhists have always known and conceded that. To be alive is to take life. Even being a vegetarian does not solve the problem of taking life to stay alive; many insects and small animals lose their lives as a result of agricultural processes.

A more precise application of the precept would be to try to choose the least harmful alternative and to regret what harm is inevitable. Another Tibetan teacher comments that Buddhist farmers would kill insects with regret and with a sense of feeling for the insects, rather than just regarding them as pests. He goes on to make the case that Buddhists should not engage in moral absolutism because we always have to take "the situation and a variety of factors into account." To make the point as strongly as possible, he then states: "For example, abortion may not be a good thing, but in certain circumstances it may be more beneficial to have an abortion than not to have one."[10] When complete nonharming is impossible, the only alternative is to take the less harmful course of actions. Anyone who cannot imagine circumstances in which abortion is the least harmful alternative is either inexperienced or lacking in imagination.

The difficulty and uniqueness of a situation in which abortion may be necessary is that it is impossible to avoid harm, no matter what course of action is taken. When an unwelcome pregnancy has occurred, harm will be done, no matter what course of action is taken. The very word "unwelcome" makes this clear; the time and circumstances are not appropriate for childbearing. Either the fetus will harm its mother, family, community, and environment in ways too numerous to count, or this particular lifestream of the fetus will be ended and it will be asked to move on to another existence. Women have dreams and visions for their vocation, including a spiritual vocation, and those dreams and visions of the purpose of her life are greatly harmed when a woman who does not want to bear a child is forced to remain pregnant. Biographies of Buddhist women saints often contain stories of how harmful forced marriage and maternity can be to women. The fetus will suffer whether or not abortion is the option chosen; being an unwanted child is not a good fate. In addition, societies and the environment are greatly harmed when asked to support populations far beyond their carrying capacity. The question is, then, in each situation, what choice results in the least harm?

As mentioned several times already, Japan is a nation with a large Buddhist population, and at a certain formal level, Buddhism is as anti-abortion as Roman Catholicism. Yet the rate of abortion in Japan is quite high, much higher than in the United States, partly because birth control is relatively unavailable. What is the practical response of Japanese Buddhists to such difficulty? All forms of Japanese Buddhism provide a ritual of grieving and forgiveness for those who suffered an abortion—both parents and fetuses. This ritual is commonly and publicly performed; mementos of the ritual are quite obvious in many Japanese Buddhist temples. One scholar who has studied this ritual in depth remarks that this way of dealing with the ambiguity of abortion means that Japanese society is not torn apart by the issue.[11] In a few North American Buddhist contexts, such ceremonies are also being adopted, and I would argue that offering compassion and comfort to all who suffer through an unwanted pregnancy and an abortion is far preferable to condemnation, guilt-tripping, and legal punishments.

Conclusion

I would like to make a few comments in conclusion. First, I think that North Americans in general could learn a great deal from Buddhists about how to live with the fact that abortions will occur. We could learn that the contentious, bitter, mean struggle that goes on over abortion is completely counterproductive, and we could learn that rituals of healing and compassion for those who have found abortions necessary are more recommended than ignoring or condemning such people.

Second, we could reflect that those who don't believe in abortions shouldn't have them, but that this is not a matter to be imposed on others. I can well imagine people who would not consider abortion for themselves under any circumstances and I do not seek to end their pregnancies even if I think they are inappropriate, even harmful to general well-being and planetary sustainability. Why do so many people feel so self-righteous about making the reverse decision for me? Perhaps the greatest ethical superiority of the pro-choice position over the anti-choice is the fact that it can accommodate those who would make other ethical choices, rather than forcing its own ethics onto them. In any sane and free society, it is always more desirable to find ways for people with differing values to coexist than to promote continual strife between them. The pro-choice position can do this, whereas the anti-choice position does not.

Third, we could learn that abortion always results from some failure of birth control and unite our efforts in eliminating that failure in as many ways as possible. If only all the anti-choice forces in North American, including many religious organizations, also became adamantly pro birth control and pro realistic sex education, imagine how many fewer abortions would happen.

Notes

1. Rita M. Gross, *Buddhism After Patriarchy: A Feminist History, Analysis, and Reconstruction of Buddhism* (Albany: State University of New York Press, 1993).

2. Frances Kissling, "Is There Life after *Roe?" Conscience: The News-journal of Catholic Opinion* 25:3 (Winter 2004–2005): 11–18.

3. I have discussed these issues in much more detail in two essays. See Rita M. Gross, *Soaring and Settling: Buddhist Perspectives on Contemporary Social and Religious Issues* (New York: Continuum, 2000), 75–124.

4. William LaFleur, *Liquid Life: Abortion and Buddhism in Japan* (Princeton: Princeton University Press, 1992).

5. The arguments are discussed in Gross, *Buddhism After Patriarchy*, 32–40.

6. For a more extended discussion of this argument, see Rita M. Gross, "Buddhism," in *Her Voice, Her Faith: Women Speak on World Religions*, eds. Arvind Sharma and Katherine K. Young (Boulder, CO: Westview Press, 2003), 91–95.

7. The nuns' order died out in Theravadin Buddhist countries and was never introduced into Thailand, the country with the strongest contemporary resistance to reviving the nuns' order. Chatsumarn Kabilsingh, now a fully ordained nun named Dhammananda, has argued that Thai women's lack of the nuns' *sangha* is at least partially responsible for the flourishing sex trade in Thailand. See *Thai Women in Buddhism* (Berkeley, CA: Parallax Press, 1991), 67–86.

8. Trangu Rinpoche, *The Open Door to Emptiness* (Manila: Tara Publishing, 1983), 43–44.

9. See note 5 in this chapter.

10. Traleg Kyabgon, *The Essence of Buddhism: An Introduction to Its Philosophy and Practice* (Boston and London: Shambhala, 2001), 19–21.

11. See note 4 in this chapter.

6

Touched by Suffering

American Pragmatism and Engaged Buddhism

Judy D. Whipps

The awareness of our human suffering—either through empathic realization of others' suffering, or the painful experience in one's own life
is motivation for both philosophy and activism, for contemplation
and engagement. In my own work, as someone interested in both
philosophy and community work, I began my philosophic studies
looking at the interaction between philosophy and activism. When
does one retreat to the hills to contemplate, and what causes one to
come back from pure contemplation to take on activist roles in public life? I have wondered why so many philosophers and religious
figures left the world of action for the life of the mind.

In my own work, I found inspiration for social engagement
through the work of American pragmatist Jane Addams in the Progressive Era (1890–1920), and in the lives and works of Engaged
Buddhists, particularly Thich Nhat Hanh and Chan Khong. Investigating the biographies of these thinkers and activists demonstrates how
they have transformed traditions of disengagement, of philosophic
and religious withdrawal, to bring thinking and contemplation into
the world of public action. This essay investigates three similarities in
the philosophies of pragmatism and Engaged Buddhism: the focus on
compassion, interdependence, and community, noting especially how
these ideas have been influenced by feminist thought and the result
of this world engagement in the peace movements they started.

Western philosophy has a history of placing theoretical thinking as a higher "good," denigrating action as a lower function. In ancient Greek thought Pythagoras compared philosophers to men who came to a festival as observers only, distanced from others to only observe, to "admire the beautiful works of art as well as the fine performances and speeches."[1] As Hannah Arendt says in "Love, Work, and Action," the classical Greek assumption was that "all action actually is but a means whose true end is contemplation."[2] Contemplation occurred only in silence, when "every movement, the movements of the body and soul as well as of speech and reasoning, must cease before truth."[3] Action in the history of philosophy was often considered necessary only in order to clear the space for contemplation.

The traditional hierarchy that valued thinking and contemplation over action also valued nonphysical rational thought over the physicality of bodily life, both of which had disastrous implications for women and lower economic classes. Women, because of their connection to physical birth and childrearing, as well as being objects of sexual desire, were sometimes categorized as unable to achieve the highest contemplative states. Likewise, the slaves and laboring classes were seen by Aristotle as incapable of the "good life" due to their association with physical work. The traditional study of philosophy, as that which moves us away from the physical and particular to the abstract and theoretical, also moves us quickly away from the experience of human suffering. As thinkers, philosophers had most likely seen that unreflective action, without contemplation, often had disastrous effects and looked for the permanence of reflection and absolutes to transcend the impermanence of everyday reality.

Buddhism shares with Western philosophy a traditional history of withdrawal to a contemplative life in monasteries (although this is, of course, not universally true). Yet, as told in the stories of Siddhartha, the origins of Buddhism come directly from engagement with the world. According to tradition, the encounter with suffering is the motivation for Siddhartha Guatama's search for enlightenment. Outside of the palace, Siddhartha encountered several manifestations of suffering, among them poverty in a meeting with a homeless beggar; the pain of death when he saw a dead person prepared for cremation by mourning relatives; and sickness in a diseased and handicapped person. Siddhartha came back to the palace full of anxiety, burning with a desire to somehow alleviate the burden of suffering. During this time of anxiety and confusion, having a desire to understand and eradicate suffering but not knowing how, he met a wandering ascetic monk who seemed serene and detached. Siddhartha thought denial and detachment was a possible answer to the question of suffering, and so he left the palace for years of meditation, fasting, and discipline. After learning both physical and mental discipline through meditation and physical deprivation, Siddhartha discovered that although the ascetic practice had taught him much, he was no closer to answering the question of suffering than when he started on the quest. He then left the ascetics, bathed, ate, and sat down for days of meditation, after which he finally achieved enlightenment, and an understanding of the oneness of all of life. He rose from meditation and began the life of the *bodhisattva*,[4] one who stays on the planet to help others find the enlightenment that releases us from suffering through the "truths" described herein.

As told in this story, Siddhartha's direct face-to-face encounter with suffering was the beginning of his process of enlightenment. This is true even though he himself was not physically suffering. The direct empathetic realization of another human being in pain forced Siddhartha to take action; once he had this experience he could not once again assume a life of luxury. Suffering started the search for action, and became the drive for contemplation and philosophy. As the First Noble Truth, the realization of suffering plays an essential role in Buddhist thought, primarily as the impetus that makes the seeker look for spiritual freedom to alleviate the suffering.

We saw a similar impact from seeing human suffering in Jane Addams' life. As a young woman from an upper-class family in the 1880s, she was struck by the suffering around her. She lists as the motivating factors in her decision to start Hull House her experience of seeing the starving people at a London market; women broken down and scarred from carrying vats of steaming beer in Europe; and the physical deformations in young girls who worked with dangerous chemicals in a match factory. These experiences, along with her own sense of uselessness, spurred her to social action and enabled her to be a creative force in the development of American pragmatism. Hull House was situated in a poor immigrant neighborhood where children were sent to work in factories at the age of five, where the garbage could be eight inches deep in the streets, where mothers sometimes had to tie their children to the kitchen table leg to go to work because there was no child care. In this age there was very little charitable backup system—people could starve to death if they lost their jobs. In her work, Addams hoped to unite academic theories with action "to learn of life from life itself."[5] This approach to learning mirrors in some ways what Buddhist Thich Nhat Hanh has said: "Truth is found in life and not merely in conceptual knowledge."[6]

At Hull House, in the ghetto where people wore the signs of poverty and of mistreatment by industry, Addams was continually confronted with suffering, and she kept trying to find a method to change conditions as well as a way to understand life. Her travels in Europe at the end of World War I[7] brought her into direct contact with the starvation of thousands of European children, which drove her back again to philosophy; as she said, it "drew us back to an examination of ultimate aims, to an interpretation of life itself."[8]

As horrendous as the results of war was, Addams was not in Europe during the actual war. In contrast, for Chan Khong and Thich Nhat Hanh the suffering they observed in the villages of Vietnam was more immediate and intense. Bombs were falling, whole villages of people were being killed or injured, and the government was imprisoning and executing political and religious dissidents. When Engaged Buddhism began gathering adherents in the United States in the 1960s and 70s, the Vietnam War, the proliferation of nuclear weapons, and the realization of environmental problems were points of crisis that motivated caring people to look for spiritual alternatives, which included social justice activism.

As one might expect from movements involved in social justice, both Addams's pragmatist-feminism and Engaged Buddhism share a strong antiwar philosophy. From its origins in activism opposed to the war in Vietnam, much of the political action of Engaged Buddhists here in the United States had been directed toward peace work, first through the Fellowship of Reconciliation and later resulting in the Buddhist Peace Fellowship, which was started in 1978. Jane Addams was a founder of the global Women's International League for Peace and Freedom, and was awarded the Nobel Peace Prize in 1931. Thich Nhat Hanh was nominated for the Nobel Peace Prize by Martin Luther King, Jr., in 1967.

The History of Engaged Buddhism

Engaged Buddhism is a rebirth of Buddhist ideas in an activist social justice framework, born as a response to suffering. It is most often tied to the teachings of Thich Nhat Hanh, a Vietnamese Buddhist monk who was college-educated in Vietnam, studied in the United States, and lived in Vietnam during part of the American-Vietnam War. Engaged Buddhism is a phenomenon that has had widespread popularity in the United States and Europe, as well as in Asia. In the United States its origins were mostly in the Vietnamese antiwar peace movements, but could also be traced to Cold War realizations that at any time nuclear war could destroy all human civilization. (Joanna Macy has written powerfully on this latter aspect of Engaged Buddhism in *Despair and Personal Power in the Nuclear Age*.[9]) Many observers, both in this movement and outside of it, see Engaged Buddhism as a collection of social liberation movements without precedent in the Buddhist tradition.[10] Buddhist scholar Sallie B. King says of Engaged Buddhism, "These movements represent something new, engendered by modern historical conditions. This being the case, it is no surprise that we find throughout our subjects conscious attempts to formulate a Buddhist justification for social action."[11]

In the origins of the Engaged Buddhism movement, human suffering was the motivation for both action and philosophy, as we will see in the lives of Thich Nhat Hanh and Chan Khong. Chan Khong, a Vietnamese nun, directly encountered suffering imposed on innocent people in the Vietnam-American war. Living as a peace activist in Vietnam during the war, she lived under the fear of imminent imprisonment and death. Chan Khong's activism grew out of her work with the Vietnamese villagers who were injured in war. She describes some of the suffering in the villages:

> ... bombs had just fallen as we arrived at a very remote hamlet. ... There were dead and wounded people everywhere. ... I remember so vividly carrying a bleeding baby back to the boat in order to clean her wounds and do whatever surgery might be necessary. I cannot describe how painful and desperate it was to carry a baby covered with blood, her sobbing mother walking beside me, both of us unsure if we could save the child.[12]

The Engaged Buddhism movement has multiple origins,[13] but among those are the thirty-seven Buddhist monks and nuns who immolated themselves for the cause of peace in Vietnam, starting with the televised self-burning of Thich Quang Doc in Saigon in 1963. These Buddhist monks and nuns found themselves caught between the communist National Liberation Front and American and French armies. The common people felt powerless while they watched their homeland being destroyed by bullets and bombs, and they turned to their religious leaders, the Buddhists monks, for help but found that many of the established Buddhist orders in Vietnam advocated noninvolvement in the political situation. In the face of the peoples' protests against the silence of the religious leaders, many younger Buddhist monks and nuns felt compelled to act, and did so through nonviolent protest. Thich Nhat Hanh locates Vietnamese citizens' requests at the base of Engaged Buddhist in Vietnam:

> In a river current, it is not the water in front that pulls the river along, but the water in the rear that acts as the driving force, pushing the water in front forward. The image may serve to explain the engagement of the Unified Buddhist Church in worldly affairs.[14]

> This turn to action on the part of the monks and nuns was based in their Buddhist training, but was also partially influenced by both Gandhi and the American non-violent civil rights protests.[15]

Thich Nhat Hanh was born in Vietnam in 1926 and entered a Zen Buddhist monastery at the age of sixteen; after three years of monastery training he continued his education at a Buddhist school in Hue. He and four other Buddhists left that school after the staff rejected his suggestions that more liberal arts (philosophy, literature, and language) be included in their education. After then attending and graduating from Saigon University, where he studied philosophy and literature, he founded a new monastic community.[16] In an interview with Daniel Berrigan, a Catholic priest known for his antiwar activism during the Vietnam War, Nhat Hanh speaks longingly of that original community:

> A number of friends and I tried a new community . . . there was absolutely no rule, no discipline . . . we accepted non-monks—writers and artists—to be residents for months or years. Everyone still remembers the community, although the community is no longer there because of the war. . . . We established ourselves far away from the village, on a mountain in the deep forest. And we spent years there in order to heal ourselves. Because we were together, we created a kind of relationship that exists to this day . . . we feel the presence of each other.[17]

In 1960, Nhat Hanh left Vietnam to study religion and to lecture on contemporary Buddhism at Princeton University, but he returned after the successful 1963 revolution against tyrannical Vietnamese president Diem. Back in Vietnam, he began to plan a Buddhist institution of higher learning, Van Hanh University, and an affiliate organization, the School of Youth for Social Service (SYSS).[18] Both organizations grew out of a proposal that Nhat Hanh submitted to the Unified Buddhist Church (UBC)[19] in Vietnam. According to Chan Khong, this 1964 proposal called for an institute to train the country's leaders "in the practice of 'engaged' Buddhism," and "develop a center for training social workers to help bring about nonviolent social change based on the Buddha's teachings."[20] The SYSS, perhaps the first Engaged Buddhist organization, trained young people to work directly with villagers to improve the quality of their lives, primarily through better health care, improving farming, and building schools. Thich Nhat Hanh invited Chan Khong[21] (who at that time was in Paris completing her doctorate in biology) to come back to Vietnam to assist in creating the SYSS. The teaching staff for the SYSS was unpaid, and Chan Khong went from house to house raising money for the school.

Chan Khong was born in 1938, one of nine children in a struggling middle-class family in Vietnam. Her mother and father had accepted the Five Precepts of Buddhism, and encouraged her to do the same. As a teenager, she was already using her own money to feed children in the slums, so she was well aware of the many social problems in Vietnam. As she studied to become a Buddhist, she was puzzled by the lack of social action by the Buddhists. She brought her questions to a local monk:

> "The Buddha left his palace to find ways to relieve suffering of people. Why don't Buddhists do anything for the poor and hungry?" Thay Thanh Tu answered, "Buddhism changes people's hearts so they can help each other in the deepest, most effective ways, even without charitable institutions." ... Usually when I talked with him about social work, he expressed the folk belief that it was just "merit work" that could never lead to enlightenment. He said work like that was only a means to get reborn into a wealthy household ... "You need to study scriptures more and work to become enlightened. After you are enlightened, you will be able to save countless beings."[22]

Chan Khong eventually accepted the Five Precepts, but did not heed the monk's warning about social work. She continued to bring rice to families in the ghetto, and to buy supper for children on the street.

Chan Khong met Thich Nhat Hanh in the late 1950s[23] when she attended his three-month course at a temple in Saigon and thereafter

began a correspondence with him about Buddhism and social change.
Nhat Hanh encouraged her in her social work, telling her she did
not have to divide her time between this "merit work" and enlightenment work. She could be enlightened, he said, by the work she
loved, and through the contribution that Buddhism can make to social
change. Chan Khong continued her social work in the ghettos, while
Nhat Hanh was engaged in educational reform, and in the formation
of communities of Buddhist thinkers and writers. Thich Nhat Hanh
describes his early aspirations for monks and nuns:

> In the future I wanted to see monks and nuns operating
> high schools, taking care of kindergartens, and running
> health care centers, practicing meditation while doing the
> work of helping people—not just talking about compas-
> sion, but expressing compassion through action.[23]

Thich Nhat Hanh saw this expression of compassion in social activism
as a way to "infuse life into the practice of Buddhism" and to keep
Buddhism relevant to the changes in society and politics.

In February 1966, Thich Nhat Hanh created the Tiep Hien Order,
the Order of Interbeing, and ordained six members into the order,
all of whom were board members of the SYSS and at the time were
laypeople. Chan Khong was one of the original six members of this
new order, which was to "bring Buddhism directly into the arena
of social concerns during a time when the war was escalating and
the teachings of the Buddha were most sorely needed."[24] Nhat Hanh
wrote new precepts (the Fourteen Precepts) for this order, updating
the original Buddhist precepts written 2,500 years ago. No additional
members were allowed to join the order until 1981; by 1993 there were
"more than 150 members of the core community and thousands of
others worldwide who regularly recite the Fourteen Precepts."[25] The
members of the Order of Interbeing were asked to practice with a
community of friends, and to observe at least sixty days of mindfulness each year.

As the war progressed, after founding the Order of Interbeing,
in 1966 Thich Nhat Hanh left Vietnam for a speaking tour arranged
by the American Fellowship of Reconciliation, and was then not able
to return to Vietnam for fear of assassination or imprisonment. In the
1960s young Americans who were disillusioned with the nuclear arms
race, the war in Vietnam, and worldwide environmental crisis were
seeking out Buddhism. During Nhat Hanh's 1966 tour he met with

heads of state, spoke to large audiences, appeared on television, and met with both Martin Luther King, Jr., and Thomas Merton.

In 1968 Thich Nhat Hanh asked Chan Khong to meet him in Hong Kong to discuss future plans of the UBC and the SYSS. Chan Khong had a difficult time obtaining an exit visa because of her peace work, but was finally allowed to leave Vietnam for five days. While in Hong Kong, Thich Nhat Hanh asked her to go to France and become his assistant in the Vietnamese Buddhist Peace Delegation, to continue fund-raising and activism for peace. Chan Khong had already been imprisoned once in Vietnam, and had on several occasions narrowly escaped further persecution or execution. Believing that she could do more to help the people of Vietnam by publicizing their suffering and by raising money, she moved to France. Both Thich Nhat Hanh and Chan Khong have continued their social activism since leaving Vietnam. Chan Khong travels with Thich Nhat Hanh, organizing his tours and speaking engagements for universities. She started an organization to benefit the orphans in Vietnam, raising money from sponsors in the West and sending the money to the children through the SYSS. After the war ended, she continued to send aid to Vietnam in the form of medical supplies, using a series of fake names. Vietnamese friends have told Chan Khong that in 1992 and 1993, her photo was on display at the War Museum in Ho Chi Minh City, where she was listed as a "war criminal."[26]

For some Buddhist practitioners, Engaged Buddhism represents both a departure from and a re-creation of traditional Buddhism, a "turning of the wheel." According to Bardwell L. Smith, enlightenment as a Buddhist goal is individual and spiritual, not social or political. As he says:

> The primary goal of Buddhism is not a stable order or a just society but the discovery of genuine freedom (or awakening) by each person. It has never been asserted that the conditions of society are unimportant or unrelated to this more important goal, but it is critical to stress the distinction between what is primary and what is not. . . . Even the vocation of the bodhisattva is not as social reformer but as catalyst to personal transformation within society.[27]

Yet many Engaged Buddhists such as Thich Nhat Hanh, Chan Khong, and Joanna Macy apparently *do* see themselves as social reformers. What is new in the Engaged Buddhist view is a reinterpretation or reconstruction of some traditional Buddhist ideas, such as understanding the traditional doctrines of compassion, dependent co-arising (interbeing/interdependence), and *sangha*/community, as resources for world-changing political action.

The precepts of the Order of Interbeing that Nhat Hanh founded warn against a physical or psychological detachment from those who are suffering. It suggests that the members should "not avoid contact with suffering, or close your eyes before suffering," but rather stay in contact with suffering, "to maintain an awareness of the reality of suffering."[28] And in contrast to many monastic orders, the members of the Order of Interbeing are required to "take a clear stand against oppression and injustice and should strive to change the situation without engaging in partisan conflicts." This philosophy seeks a balance between the engagement and retreat, while encouraging mindfulness *during* engaged work.

Compassion

> The Buddha was once asked by a leading disciple, "Would it be true to say that a part of our training is for the development of love and compassion?" The Buddha replied, "No, it would not be true to say this. It would be true to say that the whole of our training is for the development of love and compassion."[29]

All Buddhists would agree on the importance of compassion, indeed the Mahayana Buddhist tradition is founded on the concept of the *bodhisattva*, an enlightened being who stays on the planet out of compassion for others. Traditionally, however, compassion has meant helping others toward enlightenment, and thus compassion has had very little meaning in the realm of social work or activism. In traditional Buddhism, the focus is not on the suffering caused by living under an unjust or corrupt political state or by living in discriminatory social environments. Rarely in traditional Buddhist thought is there any idea of lessening suffering by changing social conditions, since social conditions are part of the illusion that must be seen through to obtain enlightenment. Engaged Buddhism radically changes this tradition.

In both Addams's life and the lives of the founders of Engaged Buddhism, the motivation for social activism can be traced to a personal and empathetic realization of suffering. Pragmatists like John Dewey and William James understood philosophy as embedded in and emerging from social issues and were involved in public causes. However, in choosing to live in the tenement house neighborhood and to connect individually with her neighbors' lives, Addams's philosophical work is based in relational compassion and a personal experience of suffering. Her philosophical writing grows out of her need to understand and interpret these experiences. Addams was also concerned with the internal suffering of the upper-class woman who had been carefully educated and socialized for caring, and who wanted to help others, yet was allowed no productive work. She calls this "apparent waste of herself" the "subjective necessity" for the settlement house movement.

According to Buddhist thought, compassion directly results from an understanding of the First Noble Truth; the realization of the suffering of self and others leads one to compassionate action.[30] As in the story of the Buddha's life, the realization of suffering through actual or empathetic experience leads to action, to finding a way to change the conditions that cause the suffering. Yet there are different understandings of the type of action to take when confronted with suffering. When Chan Khong first spoke with her teacher about relieving the physical suffering of the poor and hungry, he replied in the traditional Buddhist way, "Buddhism changes people's hearts so they can help each other in the deepest, most effective ways."[31] This is a spiritual form of compassion, liberating them from *samsara*, rather than freeing them from hunger or sickness.

Given the Buddhist belief in *karma* and the ultimate unreality of the physical world (in some schools), this form of compassion makes sense. Since compassion and assistance on the spiritual level can only be given by an enlightened person, the compassionate person is advised to place top priority on her own spiritual exercises. As Chan Khong's teacher told her, "You must wait until you are enlightened to be of real help to the poor." Addams too encountered what she called the "snare of preparation" when she looked for ways to help others. Many thought the way should be through higher learning, but she was dismayed at the thought of staying longer in school, which she worried was only "lumbering our minds with literature that only served to cloud the really vital situation spread before our eyes."[32] Likewise, Chan Khong says of academic and spiritual preparation, "The enlightenment my friend described was a kind of Ph.D. we could seek endlessly while refusing to help those right in front of us."[33]

Engaged Buddhists rely on Buddha's teachings on compassion as a foundation of their social involvement, but in doing so they revise the traditional expression of compassion to an outward, world-changing focus. The monk who advised Chan Khong to search for enlightenment rather than feed the poor has significant Buddhist scriptural support for his advice. Deep compassion for all sentient beings is an acknowledged part of the path to enlightenment, since "generating this deep compassion . . . is a completely life-transforming experience; one ceases to be an ordinary being and becomes a 'Son or Daughter of the Buddhas.' " However, this compassion must "result from a very specific and sustained series of meditations" that begin with renunciation of the world, since "it is necessary to have renunciation before one can truly begin to generate compassion."[34] This approach to compassion can lead one in a circular fashion to absorption in one's own spiritual state, with a focus within rather than performing any outwardly helpful action.

But "within" may be the necessary place to start any useful social action. According to Robert A. F. Thurman in "Nagarjuna's Guidelines for Buddhist Social Action," the "first principle of Buddhist social ethics" is "individualist transcendentalism," or individual enlightenment as opposed to social good. He says,

> Nagarjuna proclaims the supremacy of the individual, starting with the king himself. . . . The best thing the king can do for his nation is, finally, to perfect himself . . . for which purpose he may renounce the world and enter the monastic discipline of spiritual virtuosity.[35]

Here we see the inherent conflict between being in the world as a Buddhist activist, and retreating from the world for self-perfection. The "higher" or best path has always been the retreat to the monastery. It makes sense that the enlightened person would offer better help to the suffering person, but since enlightenment is a process that takes "eons,"[36] the practitioner may, for all practical purposes, never come back out of the monastery into the suffering of the world.

Pragmatists and Engaged Buddhists share an understanding of compassion that is more than philosophical or contemplative. As Nhat Hanh says elsewhere,

> Ideas about understanding and compassion are not understanding and compassion. Understanding and compassion must be real in our lives. They must be seen and touched. The real presence of understanding and compassion will alleviate suffering and cause joy to be born. But to realize

does not only mean to act. First of all, realization means transforming ourselves.[37]

There is a balance here between introspective understanding and action; the work toward enlightenment continues while one is active in the world. Members of the Order of Interbeing, he says, "change themselves in order to change society in the direction of compassion and understanding by living a joyful and mindful life."[38]

Interdependence and Interbeing

Both pragmatism and Engaged Buddhism share an understanding of the interdependence with all living things in the world, which provides a philosophic platform for community engagement. Rather than "Truth" as that which is learned from distanced observation, for pragmatists "truthing" occurs in process, through "experience" in interaction, acting and being acted upon by our environment. Pragmatists see each of us as threads woven into the fabric of life, deeply meshed into a thick historical, cultural, and physical continuum. Understanding this interdependence creates a mandate for action; the healthiest environment creates the most possibilities for each of us, culturally and personally. Addams understood this interdependence in personal and social terms. Living in an era of industrialization, she saw that meaningful existence for individuals or groups in complex industrial and technological societies is dependent on fruitful interaction with other individuals and groups. Pragmatist interdependence expresses a mutual dependence not merely for survival but for full human development and creativity, as well as the possibility of epistemological understanding. Addams was hopeful that understanding interdependence could hold the promise of civilization, cooperation, and coexistence; she saw that it creates an imperative to act. She started working for peace decades before World War I: when she saw the suffering caused by war, she came to understand the global nature of our national and individual interdependence.

For Engaged Buddhists also, an understanding of interdependence or interbeing has resulted in social activism. Engaged Buddhists have reconstructed the traditional Buddhist concept of "dependent origination." One of the basic tenets of Buddhism is that phenomena result from a series of causes, which means that all sentient beings, including of course humans, are the result of a group of causes. Our existence is conditioned by, or dependent upon, other causes. This is the essence of nondualism in Buddhism, the fact of dependent origination, the weaving together of physical and nonphysical causes and effects.[39] According to the twelve links in the chain of dependent origination, the major cause of suffering is ignorance about the nature of physical self as illusion. This may mean to some thinkers that the physical world doesn't exist at all—it is all illusion—a common concept in some Buddhist schools of thought, which could, of course, cause one to abandon attempts to change the physical and social world.[40]

Thich Nhat Hanh explains dependent origination by asking us to consider how our existence is contingent on the existence of other living beings and nonliving substances. He explains this in the concept of interbeing:

> Genesis in Buddhism is called interbeing. The birth, growth, and decline of things depend upon multiple causes and conditions and not just a single one. The presence of one thing (dharma) implies the presence of all other things.[41]

Or in a more metaphoric way, he says:

> If you are a poet, you will see clearly that there is a cloud floating in this sheet of paper. Without a cloud, there will be no rain; without rain, the trees cannot grow; and without trees, we cannot exist. If the cloud is not here, the sheet cannot be here either.... Everything coexists with this sheet of paper.... 'To be' is to inter-be. We cannot just *be* by ourselves alone. We have to inter-be with every other thing. This sheet of paper is, because everything else is.[42]

In their understanding of co-dependence, Engaged Buddhist thinkers continue to affirm the reality of the world, and as such, understand the implications that interdependence has for social activism. As we are all related and part of each other, through compassion and our own interests, interdependence requires that we relieve suffering wherever we find it. Every person's suffering is related to our suffering. As Sallie King says of Nhat Hanh's philosophy, "A mindful awareness of interdependence creates, on the one hand, an imperative to act to relieve the suffering of anyone who suffers and, on the other hand, the necessity to resolve conflict without acting 'against' the welfare of anyone, including those who have caused pain."[43]

For Engaged Buddhists spiritual practice occurs while being in the world; the contemplative life goes on while helping those who are suffering. Addressing one aspect of reality addresses the other aspect simultaneously. In helping others, we help ourselves; practicing compassion leads to increased understanding. As Thich Nhat Hanh says:

> It has become clear that the fate of the individual is inextricably linked to the fate of the whole human race. . . . In order to make peace within the human family, we must work for harmonious co-existence. If we continue to shut ourselves off from the rest of the world, imprisoning ourselves in narrow concerns and immediate problems, we are not likely to make peace or survive.[44]

Nhat Hanh continues in this essay to explain that depending on one's interests, each of us may decide to start at a different place in improving the individual, society, and nature, as all have an effect on the others.

Understanding interdependence can be the basis also for nonviolence and peaceful reconciliation, knowing that violence toward anyone is violence toward oneself; understanding the links between causation and suffering promotes nonjudgmental understanding of others. According to the Engaged Buddhists, we should not separate from those who are suffering, but instead we should find ways to be in relationship with them, which helps us realize our interdependence.

Engaged Community

In both pragmatism and Engaged Buddhism the move from retreat to engagement, from philosophy or religion to activism, required a foundation of community life. The success of Jane Addams's work at Hull House in Chicago, as well as her later peace work, depended on the community of women that she was surrounded by. As a settlement house, the residents lived together and formed strong personal bonds. The women of Hull House were remarkably talented, socially committed, and hard-working individuals; together they formed a strong and effective movement for social change. Most of these women never married, and they drew from their relationships with each other the support they needed to continue their commitments to larger social reforms. Florence Kelly, Julia Lathop, Ella Flagg Young, and Ellen

Gates Starr were among the many female Hull House residents who brought their energy and care together to support each other and each other's community projects. Addams attempted to duplicate this same synergy and support in her national and international peace work and was successful to some extent. Addams rarely wrote or talked about the important roles that these women played in her life, focusing instead on the work they accomplished, but given the ways that their individual social projects came together in support of each other's projects, it is easy to see that community was essential to Addams's successes and provided life-sustaining support when her efforts failed, as in her peace work.

The *sangha*, or the Buddhist religious community, is one of the Three Refuges of Buddhism. For Thich Nhat Hanh and Chan Khong, being part of a community is a requirement for spiritual as well as active lives. As Nhat Hanh says,

> Taking refuge in the Sangha means putting your trust in a community of solid members who practice mindfulness together. You do not have to practice intensively—just being in a Sangha where people are happy, living deeply the moments of their days, is enough. . . . A good community is needed to help us resist the unwholesome ways of our time. Mindful living protects us and helps us go in the direction of peace. With the support of friends in the practice, peace has a chance.[45]

Practicing in a community, a *sangha* is a requirement for joining the Order of Interbeing, and according to Chan Khong, one of the first steps to take as a Buddhist. "I always advise those who wish to practice the precepts to organize a sangha, a community of friends, around them, to recite the precepts every month, and share their experiences of living the precepts."[46] In their emphasis on the importance of the *sangha*, Engaged Buddhists have not deviated from traditional Buddhism. However, in the Order of Interbeing, the *sangha* is composed of monks, nuns, and laypeople, all equal participants in the *sangha*.[47] Such equality continues and extends the spirit (although not the usual practice) of Mahayana Buddhism.

The members of the order continue to practice sixty days of meditative mindfulness each year, just as they did in the busy days of social work in Vietnam. In *The Miracle of Mindfulness*, Thich Nhat Hanh justifies this time away from busy work:

Every worker in a peace or service community, no matter how urgent its work, has the right to such a day, for
without it we will lose ourselves quickly in a life full of
worry and action, and our responses will become increasingly useless.[48]

These days are ideally spent with the *sangha*, the community that one
practices with. Chan Khong says that this one day each week spent in
mindfulness enabled her to carry on cheerfully in the busiest time of
her life. Effective action requires this time of centering and retreat.

Feminist Interpretations

In many traditional religions, as well as in historical philosophic traditions, women's voices and lives were ignored or marginalized. The
origins of both American pragmatism and Engaged Buddhism share
an increasingly active feminism; both Engaged Buddhism in Asia and
America and early pragmatism arose in a time when women were
beginning to have a voice in social matters, and were beginning to participate in higher education. Without engaging in an unfounded essen-
tialism, without applying any conclusions about *all* women or *all* men
to particular individuals, we can note the convergence of generally
detached intellectual traditions with the female traditions of individualized caring that occurred at the foundation of these movements.

Feminist Buddhists have had reason to critique the patriarchy
in the tradition of Buddhism. According to Nancy J. Barnes in "Buddhist Women and the Nuns' Order in Asia," ancient Buddhist texts
tell of the women's *sangha*, the *bhikshuni*, established by the Buddha
just a few years after the men's *sangha*. Yet, the women's *sangha* was
based from its inception on a permanent hierarchical relationship
that placed the men's *sangha* in a position of power in relationship
to the women's *sangha*. (For example, one of the eight rules of the
women's order says that a monk, no matter how new to the order,
may admonish a *bhikshuni* (nun), but no *bhikshuni* may ever admonish
a monk.[49]) The women's orders were never supported financially or
culturally in terms of respect at the level of the men's orders, and in
many cases the women's orders completely disappeared from some
Asian countries over the centuries. The disappearance of the orders
has presented a problem of establishing a lineage, since monks and
nuns can only be ordained by ordained others—if there is no one

in the order to ordain them, ordination is impossible. The Order of Interbeing ordains both women and men equally in the same order, a departure from traditional Buddhism.

But while the Order of Interbeing laid the foundation for equality in the *sangha*, even these very mindful people can fall back in traditional roles of men and women. When Maxine Hong Kingston went with American Vietnam veterans to Plum Village in France in the 1990s, she noted that while Thich Nhat Hanh was generally absent from community life at Plum Village and spent most of his days writing poetry or in his garden, as a nun Chan Khong did most of the everyday work of the village. According to Kingston, "she [Chan Khong] is the necessary, ubiquitous one who gets the world tasks done—drives everywhere in her little car, deals with the French authorities for building permits, does the business of the community."[50]

Buddhist traditions are not without resources for feminists. American Buddhist writer Joanna Macy finds comparisons between the Mediterranean/Christian female figure of Wisdom with the female Mother of All Buddhas, Perfection of Wisdom. This teaching entered Buddhism about five centuries after the Buddha, and represents a time when "the world, no longer feared or fled, is re-entered with compassion."[51] And as Anne C. Klein points out in *Meeting the Great Bliss Queen*, "Buddhist perspectives can be a resource for Western feminist theory partly because they are for feminists a completely fresh perspective,"[52] one that does not carry with it into Western culture all of the patriarchic tradition of Western religions and culture. The Order of Interbeing as a new Buddhist order also offers the possibility of a fresh start with equality. Due to its contemporary beginnings, in the Order of Interbeing we can see the real influence of female founders such as Chan Khong. In the same way, the American pragmatist movement is recent enough that we can readily trace the contributions of women.

Without claiming any definite correlation between the leadership of women in the Engaged Buddhism movement and the stress on activism rather than retreat, it is significant to at least note the contemporary concurrence. From their own autobiographical records, it is evident that Thich Nhat Hanh's and Chan Khong's social activism arose independently of each other. However, it is also apparent that Chan Khong's activism was from the beginning more concerned with nurturing issues (food, children's well-being, and providing emotional support), while Nhat Hanh at that time was primarily interested in the also significant, while less individually nurturing, issues of higher education and politics.

The expansion of feminism around the turn of the century coincided with the transformation of pragmatism into a socially active philosophy; the influence of Jane Addams and other women certainly contributed to this transformation. Charlene Haddock Seigfried's work, particularly her 1996 book *Pragmatism and Feminism*, has been central in the effort to bring these women back into the philosophical discussion, as well as to bring feminist perspectives to the field of pragmatism.

Peace Work

For the Engaged Buddhists and for Jane Addams and her colleagues, compassion has meant more than individual caring; they have worked for larger systemic social change. Nowhere is this more apparent than in their peace activism. Addams and other pragmatist-feminists in her time saw peace activism as radically connected to social reform work and to the struggle for women's rights. The movement toward social justice, toward egalitarian economic structures, and away from competitive hierarchies necessitated a social structure based in cooperation and peace, not on war. Peace was a necessary foundation in order to alleviate suffering and work toward justice.

Engaged Buddhism, having its origins in a time of war, also has a commitment to peace. The movement has spoken directly to the suffering of American veterans of the Vietnam War. As Thich Nhat Hanh said to Claude Anshin Thomas and other veterans, "You veterans are the light at the tip of the candle. You burn hot and bright. You understand deeply the nature of suffering."[53] Thomas's life was transformed by Engaged Buddhist practice, encountered first at a retreat organized by Thich Nhat Hanh and American Vietnam veterans at the Omega Institute in New York. Maxine Hong Kingston has carried on that work with Vietnam veterans by combining Buddhist contemplation and writing at retreats and workshops (described in a recent book, *The Fifth Book of Peace*.)

As we have seen, philosophically Engaged Buddhism comes from a tradition that emphasizes detached withdrawal from the world, yet Thich Nhat Hanh and other Engaged Buddhists found that they could go back to basic teachings of the Buddha to reconstruct and recover some older aspects of Buddhism. Engaged Buddhists see their work as the true expression of Buddhism, as a movement for liberation.[54] As King says, "To speak of social issues in a Buddhist context is . . . to return to Buddhism in its original wholeness."[55]

The pragmatists, in a similar way, responded also to social suffering through understanding the nature of interdependence; they reconstructed the contemplative, detached-observer aspect of philosophy and returned it to a social engagement.

Engaged Buddhists and pragmatists share some common experiences and understandings in their movements to activism, such as in the nature and extent of suffering in the world around them, and the influence of women. While there is no reason to think that either of these movements had an influence on each other, looking at both of them together is instructive in thinking about the relation between philosophy and social action. The Engaged Buddhists have a lot to teach us about being ethically in the world. In their lives and philosophies we can see contemplation as useful, and even necessary, but not sufficient as a way of being in the world. From Jane Addams and the American pragmatist movement we can see the effect of philosophizing in the world, through action. From both, we know that participation in our social and political world is necessary when we understand ourselves as being in an interdependent relationship with all others and the environment. Mindfulness and reflection combined with activism is essential if our efforts in the world are to be meaningful.

Notes

1. Nicholas Lobkowicz, *Theory and Practice* (Notre Dame, IN: University of Notre Dame Press, 1968), 5.

2. Hannah Arendt, "Labor, Work, Action," in *Amor Mundi: Explorations in the Faith and Thought of Hannah Arendt*, ed. J. W. Bernauer (The Hague: Martinus Nijhoff, 1987), 29.

3. Arendt points out that this priority on contemplation and on stillness shows up in the Christian as well as ancient Greek philosophers, from Plato through Augustine and Aquinas. See her discussion in the first chapter of *The Human Condition* (Chicago: University of Chicago Press, 1958).

4. According to Chan Khong's book, *Learning True Love: Practicing Buddhism in a Time of War* (Berkeley, CA: Parallax Press, 2007), *bodhisattva* literally means "enlightened being" or "one who works to relieve the suffering of others and bring them to enlightenment." The Avalokitesvara Bodhisattva is one who "listens to the cries of the world and offers the gift of non-fear" (xi). In Tibetan Buddhist beliefs, the Dalai Lama is the reincarnation of the Avalokitesvara Bodhisattva.

5. Jane Addams, *Twenty Years at Hull-House* (Champaign, IL: University of Illinois Press, 1990), 51.

6. Thich Nhat Hanh, *Interbeing* (Berkeley, CA: Parallax Press, 1993), 17.

7. Addams and Alice Hamilton were the first American civilians allowed into Germany after the war ended, and Addams saw women and children living in desperate conditions. See her book *Peace and Bread in Time of War*, introduction by Katherine Joslin (Champaign, IL: University of Illinois Press, 2002).

8. Jane Addams, *The Second Twenty Years at Hull-House: September 1909 to September 1929* (New York: Macmillan, 1930), 14

9. Macy is both a Christian and a Buddhist. She is a scholar of Buddhism and of general systems theory. She has published several books on Buddhism; the latest is *World As Lover, World As Self*. Her essays are often reproduced in collections on Engaged Buddhism.

10. See Christopher S. Queen, "Introduction: The Shapes and Sources of Engaged Buddhism," in *Engaged Buddhism: Buddhist Liberation Movements in Asia*, eds. Christopher S. Queen and Sallie B. King (Albany: State University of New York Press, 1996).

11. *Engaged Buddhism*, 404.

12. Chan Khong, *Learning True Love: Practicing Buddhism in a Time of War*, rev. ed. (Berkeley, CA: Parallax Press, 2007), 69.

13. Queen and King in their book *Engaged Buddhism* include in their list of Buddhist activism movements the work of Aung San Suu Kyi in Burma, the mass conversion of Untouchables starting with the work of Dr. B. R. Ambedkar of India, the Sri Lanka movement, the movements among several Asian countries to restore women's full right of ordination, and the Dalai Lama's work for his homeland, Tibet (2–3).

14. Thich Nhat Hanh, *Vietnam: Lotus in a Sea of Fire* (New York: Hill and Wang, 1967), 3.

15. In 1963 interviews with Vietnamese monks, they acknowledged to Marjorie Hope and James Young that they were influenced by Gandhi and "the American Negroes' silent protest," saying "Everything in this world has relations—it is the law of interdependent causes." Several of the monks involved with the peace work in Vietnam in the 1960s had been educated in America, such as Thich Quang Lien and Thich Nhat Hanh. See Marjorie Hope and James Young, "The Third Way: Thich Nhat Hanh and Cao Ngoc Phong," in *The Struggle for Humanity: Agents of Nonviolent Change in a Violent World* (Maryknoll, NY: Orbis Books, 1977.)

16. Ibid., 193–94.

17. Thich Nhat Hanh and Daniel Berrigan, *The Raft Is Not the Shore: Conversations Toward a Buddhist/Christian Awareness* (Maryknoll, NY: Orbis Books, 2000), 119, 125.

18. Hope and Young, *The Struggle for Humanity*, 195.

19. The Unified Buddhist Church (UBC) was formed as a result of a four-day conference held in 1963, during which the Theravada and Mahayana Buddhists joined forces. Thich Nhat Hanh was closely associated with this

organization, although he did not agree with all of their actions. See Sallie B. King, "Thich Nhat Hanh and the Unified Buddhist Church," in *Engaged Buddhism*.

20. Chan Khong, *Learning True Love*, 47.

21. At that time Chan Khong was still named Cao Ngoc Phuong, her birth name. She received the name Sister Chan Khong—True Emptiness—when she was ordained as a nun. For the sake of clarity, I will use the name Chan Khong throughout this essay.

22. Chan Khong, *Learning True Love*, 15–16.

23. There is some confusion about the dates here. Chan Khong's autobiography says she met Thich Nhat Hanh in 1960 and then corresponded with him at the Phuong Boi Monastery "deep in the rainforest" (*Learning True Love*, 25). However, Hope's biographical essay on Thich Nhat Hanh says that he was in the United States, teaching and studying at Princeton and Columbia, from 1960 to 1963 (*The Struggle for Humanity*, 194). According to King, Thich Nhat Hanh went to the United States. in 1961 and lectured at Princeton in 1963 (*Engaged Buddhism*, 322).

24. Thich Nhat Hanh, *Cultivating the Mind of Love: The Practice of Looking Deeply in the Mahayana Buddhist Tradition* (Berkeley, CA: Parallax Press, 2006), 32.

25. Chan Khong 79.

26. Fred Eppsteiner, editor's introduction, in Thich Nhat Hanh, *Interbeing* (Berkeley, CA: Parallax Press, 1993), viii.

27. Bardwell L. Smith, quoted in Christopher S. Queen, "Introduction: the Shapes and Sources of Engaged Buddhism," in *Engaged Buddhism*, 17.

28. Nhat Hanh, *Interbeing*, 17.

29. This story is told by Christina Feldman in "Nurturing Compassion," in *Engaged Buddhism*, 19. She does not give a Buddhist scriptural citation.

30. See Robert Thurman's introduction to tape four of *The Four Noble Truths*, lectures given by His Holiness the XIV Dalai Lama, 1997, Mystic Fire Audio.

31. Chan Khong, *Learning True Love*, 15.

32. Addams, *Twenty Years*, 43.

33. Ibid., 16.

34. *Bodhicaryavatara* 1:9, quoted in Williams, 199.

35. Robert A. F. Thurman, "Nagarjuna's Guidelines for Buddhist Social Action," in *The Path of Compassion: Writings on Socially Engage Buddhism*, ed. Fred Eppsteiner (Berkeley, CA: Parallax Press, 1985), 122.

36. The Dalai Lama recently said the process of enlightenment may take "eons and eons." Tape four, *The Four Noble Truths*.

37. Nhat Hanh, *Interbeing*, 5.

38. Ibid., 10.

39. This concept of nonphysical cause separates Buddhists from pragmatists. Pragmatists generally choose to ignore metaphysical philosophizing.

40. This way of thinking only affirms dualism, by choosing to believe in the nonphysical aspect of reality. Ignoring our interdependence on others, and on social and political realities, also leads to ignorance.

41. Thich Nhat Hanh, *Zen Keys* (New York: Three Leaves, 1994), 41.

42. Thich Nhat Hanh, *Peace Is Every Step: The Path of Mindfulness in Everyday Life* (New York: Bantam, 1992), 95–96.

43. King, conclusion in *Engaged Buddhism*, 407.

44. Nhat Hanh, "Individual, Society and Nature," in *The Path of Compassion*, ed. Fred Eppsteiner, 41–42.

45. Nhat Hanh, *Cultivating the Mind of Love*, 72.

46. Chan Khong, *Learning True Love*, 82.

47. The emphasis on equality is an interesting aspect of Engaged Buddhism. The charter for the Order of Interbeing says it "does not recognize the necessity of a mediator and lay disciples, between humans and ultimate reality. It considers, however, the insight and experiences of ancestral teachers, monks, nuns and laypeople, as helpful to those who are practicing the Way" (Nhat Hanh, *Interbeing*, 73).

48. Thich Nhat Hanh, *The Miracle of Mindfulness* (Boston: Beacon, 1999), 28.

49. This and seven other rules establishing the male orders over the female orders are listed in Barnes's chapter in *Engaged Buddhism*, 261.

50. Maxine Hong Kingston, *The Fifth Book of Peace* (New York: Vintage International, 2004), 377.

51. Joanna Macy, "Mother of All Buddhas: The Second Turning of the Wheel," in *World As Lover, World As Self*, 106.

52. Anne Carolyn Klein, *Meeting the Great Bliss Queen: Buddhists, Feminists, and the Art of the Self* (Boston: Beacon, 1996), xvi.

53. Claude Anshin Thomas, *At Hell's Gate: A Soldier's Journey from War to Peace* (Boston: Shambhala, 2004), 42.

54. In the introduction to *Engaged Buddhism* Christopher S. Queen notes that not all Engaged Buddhists are people who have been "oppressed, disadvantaged or marginalized." He rewrites the definition of a liberation movement as one that is a "voluntary association guided by exemplary leaders and a common vision of a new society based on peace, justice and freedom" (10). Under that definition he includes Engaged Buddhism as a liberation movement.

55. Kingston, *The Fifth Book*, 408.

7

Identity Theft

Simulating *Nirvana* in Postmodern America

John Kitterman

This essay will look at how contemporary American life might affect the understanding and practice of Buddhism. It has become a commonplace that in less than fifty years, beginning with the interest in Asian religions among the 1960s counterculture and the increase in Asian immigrants because of relaxed immigration rules, Buddhism has been adapting to American culture, and the debate has been ongoing as to whether the process has been good for the *dharma*; that is, can Buddhism, with its conceptions of *anatman* (no-self), *anitya* (impermanence), and *maya* (illusion), find a home in a culture that has historically privileged individuality, Manifest Destiny, and realism?[1] These questions are certainly not new. In his discussion of The World's Parliament of Religions in Chicago in 1893, Richard Seager delineates the same problems confronting Buddhists in America over a hundred years ago: "Could the teachings of the Buddha about the nonexistence of the self be reconciled with American individualism? Could a tradition emphasizing contemplation thrive in a culture known for its extroversion and activism? . . . Wasn't a religion based on the premise that human life is characterized by suffering too negative and world-renouncing to appeal to a nation known for its optimism?"[2]

But for the purposes of this essay I would like to turn the question around and ask not *should* Buddhism adapt to America, but is

Buddhism a religion that by its nature *can* adapt to postmodern American culture, especially given that America possesses the dominant culture in a kind of global imperialism? At the core of Buddhism there exists a contradiction, I would argue, that cannot be modified to fit the status quo that in contemporary America is largely determined by what many economists refer to as global capitalism. This contradiction obviously has to do with the terms just mentioned: It defies common sense to say that my own sense of self is not real and that the everyday world before me is an illusion. I would suggest that it is much easier for the human mind to wrap around a narrative of God's intervention into human affairs, of man's fallen state, of a savior, and of a heaven, than it is to understand the inherent paradoxes and atheism of *nirvana*. Be that as it may, there is one Western philosophical tradition that, despite some differences, does theorize the inherent problem of adaptation: psychoanalysis—not the ego-centered kind often practiced in America, but the French kind, the so-called return to Freud as developed by Jacques Lacan in the 1950s and 60s and promulgated by his followers like Julia Kristeva, Shoshana Felman, and especially the Slovenian psychoanalyst and Marxist philosopher Slavoj Žižek, whose work from *The Sublime Object of Ideology* (1989) to *The Puppet and the Dwarf* (2003) has dissected American popular culture and its global influence by exposing the pathways of unconscious desire.[3] Lacanian psychoanalysis posits a divided self, an ego that is an illusion, and a therapeutic praxis that seeks to expose the imaginary nature of the self, but it is not a theory or practice that lends itself to HMO-driven managed care; you can't realize no-mind in six to eight office visits.

Later in this essay I will go into more detail about the structure of Lacanian psychoanalysis, how Žižek understands postmodernist culture, and what these findings imply for Buddhism in America. But for the meantime I want to emphasize that I am not so concerned about the ways in which Buddhism can adapt as I am about how certain elements of postmodernism might problematize the contemplation of Buddhism in this country. While I agree that the problems of whether the laity need to support or participate in some form of monasticism or whether chanting or meditation—at home or in a temple—is the best way to continue the *dharma* while allowing Americans to go about their normal routines, are interesting, complex, and important, to some extent I would like to suggest that such concerns are liable to miss the forest for the trees. Postmodern America is in such a rapid state of change due mainly to the hegemony of late capitalism and the influence of media technologies that these local problems may seem almost trivial by comparison. America can be seen as an increasingly strange place to nourish Buddhism because America at the present moment is where late capitalism is reaching a kind of crisis by producing a simulation of selfhood diametrically opposed to the Buddhist search for an authentic, empty self.

The problem for Buddhists in America is more insidious than whether American practices are "watered down" traditional forms or materialistic versions for the laity of a monastic spirituality, because the problem of postmodern changes in reality on a global level is so large, nearly universal, that it is therefore almost invisible. Local issues can be discussed and corrected, but the cultural effects of global capitalism become naturalized by their very ubiquity. What I am demonstrating in this chapter is that the very fabric of postmodern life has been so altered that, especially for the generations who have come of age in the late twentieth century, in a philosophical sense everyday life experiences are completely different. Unless Buddhists take account of these profound changes produced by the globalization of American culture, they will not fully understand how a postmodern *dharma* can be conceptualized. Some may argue that Buddhism itself is as much a philosophy as it is a religion and it can thereby evade changes to its core while its form mutates to its surroundings, but what I am suggesting is that the very distinction between surroundings and core are collapsing. In another hundred years perhaps the differences between Indian and American Buddhism will seem as archaic as the differences between a McDonald's in New Delhi and New York.

The history of these postmodern changes cannot be properly understood without knowing something about the history of modernism. The early chapters of Habermas's *The Philosophical Discourse of Modernity* describe the breakdown of the medieval European religious worldview with the rise of reason, science, and technology and the consequent formation and mobilization of capital.[4] Ego-centered reason and market capitalism subsequently produce a stable, bourgeois subjectivity that injects itself into the political process through revolutionary democratic reform. Reason, technology, capitalism, democracy, and identity are thus linked during the modern period, beginning roughly around 1500 with global exploration, the Reformation, and the Renaissance.

One of the most significant characteristics of modernity that Habermas focuses on—we might almost call it the foundational identity of modernity—is the idea of newness, of what is modern. The concept of time itself goes through a radical transformation: "Whereas

in the Christian West the 'new world' had meant the still-to-come
age of the future, which was to dawn only on the last day . . . the
secular concept of modernity expresses the conviction that the future
has already begun: It is the epoch that lives for the future, that opens
itself up to the novelty of the future." He goes on to say that historical
events begin to accelerate so fast during the modern period that the
feel of time also begins to change; people begin to experience what
Habermas calls the "pressure of time." The result of this pressure
is that modernity becomes a thing in itself, a continual renewal of
the present moment, radically broken with the past and open only
to the future: "Modernity can and will no longer borrow the criteria by which it takes its orientation from the models supplied by
another epoch; *it has to create its normativity out of itself.* Modernity
sees itself cast back upon itself without any possibility of escape"
(italics Habermas's).[5]

This "pressure of time" means that human beings living in the
industrialized West begin to feel like they have to keep up with the
latest technological products, and consumption slowly but surely
becomes less a utilitarian means to an end and more a necessary end
in itself. In the late twentieth century the very fabrication of the new
through advertising associated with late capitalism and the compul-
sion of consumers to have whatever is new coincide with what many
theorists see as postmodernism's break with modernism. This break
includes of course the assault on subject-centered reason by Nietzsche
and his successors Derrida and Foucault, and the consequent "death
of the subject," which we will discuss in a moment in its relationship
to the Buddhist concept of no-self.

But the economic and social effects of what Fredric Jameson
calls the third wave of global capitalism—after the first market wave
and the second imperialistic wave—concern us here in their centering of desire on a new form of living in the moment: "We must
therefore also posit another type of consumption: consumption of
the very process of consumption itself, above and beyond its content
and the immediate commercial products. It is necessary to speak of a
kind of technological bonus of pleasure afforded by the new machin-
ery and, as it were, symbolically reenacted and ritually devoured at
each session of official media consumption itself."[6] If we think about
the consumption of products as being a symptom of an individual's
attachment to the world of appearances, to his immersion in *samsara*, and to the Buddha's Four Noble Truths about the rise of attachment and the need to understand how desire works and how it can
be extinguished, then we can begin to understand the tremendous

change that is occurring in the human condition. Individual identity in postmodern America, I would argue, is largely a product itself of this late capitalism. That is to say, individual identities are created as subjectivities simply to consume other products that other subjectivities (let's call them CEOs) have marketed. (Marxists like Althusser call this process "interpellation"—the response of human consciousness to the "hailing" by often invisible forces in society largely controlled by the prevailing ideology.) The process is self-referential, self-consuming if you will, a kind of Möbius strip (one of Lacan's favorite images) of capitalistic *nirvana*—the perpetual business machine.

However, it is the "technological bonus of pleasure," as Jameson calls it, that is especially critical for us when thinking about the influence of postmodernism on Buddhism, because in Lacanian psychoanalysis what attaches the subject to the object of his desire is the notion of "surplus pleasure," a term that Lacan modeled on Marx's idea of "surplus profit," thereby linking capitalism inexorably to the subject's excessive desire. Lacan theorized that human identity is always divided, that it is always lacking something, because human identity is formed when a child breaks away from its identification with its mother, from the Imaginary Order (or with a significant Other, a process Lacan whimsically referred to as "castration") and finds its separate existence in the realm of language, in the Symbolic Order. That is, the child becomes an autonomous person through the Symbolic Order, through using language; it is what distances him from the rest of the world, just as the Imaginary Order, the order of fantasy, had connected (and in many ways still connects) him to others. For the rest of his life a person is perpetually looking for this former fusion with the (m)other, this piece of the Real, in every other Other that the person encounters, whether it is a human being, a car, God, or the "star" of a reality TV show. Lacan calls this missing piece *objet a*, the object that represents the other (*autre* = other in French), and Žižek calls it "the sublime object of ideology" because it is what we are looking for in ideology, something more in the ideology than the ideology itself, whether the ideology is communism or capitalism, Christianity or Buddhism.

That is to say, all belief systems are forms of false consciousness insofar as they participate in this illusion that they are supplying some missing otherness to the individual who holds them. Thus, the "technological bonus of pleasure" that consumption in postmodern society secretes is the ideological heroin, if you will, that keeps us coming back for more. Capitalism, through its technological media representation, has found a way not only to tap into an obsessive desire for completion, for oneness with the other, but also to deliver a bonus thrill of surplus pleasure (Lacan calls it *jouissance*) that other pleasures can hardly match.

I think we can begin to see the implications for Buddhism. It must compete in the global marketplace with tremendous pressures on human beings to consume, running the risk of itself becoming reified into another product to purchase. What's more, because capitalism keeps producing new products through the discoveries of technology, this process becomes, as we have seen, self-referential, so that the consumer is caught in a loop of desire and fulfillment the likes of which has never existed before on the planet, as Western economies quickly go global. Technology can also supply a "bonus of pleasure" that simulates the *jouissance* that the individual would feel in recovering some of the lost feeling of oneness that he owned before becoming individuated. Human beings become even more removed from their spiritual roots when they discover in the consumption of products a kind of ideological bliss that replaces the bliss (admittedly still ideological) that they found in religion.[7]

Jameson describes the rise of the media image as "the final form of commodity reification":

> But here I think a profound modification of the public sphere needs to be theorized: the emergence of a new realm of image reality . . . becomes semiautonomous and floats above reality, with this fundamental historical difference that in the classical period reality persisted independently of that sentimental and romantic "cultural sphere," whereas today it seems to have lost that separate mode of existence. Today culture impacts back on reality in ways that make any independent and, as it were, non- or extra-cultural form of it problematical (in a kind of Heisenberg principle of mass culture which intervenes between your eye and the thing itself), so that finally the theorists unite their voices in the new doxa that the "referent" no longer exists.[8]

Reality, that is, can no longer be found except through the culture, or reality and culture are separate sides of the same Möbius strip, and this change in the postmodern environment is often invisible to human beings because the confusion seems so normal. Ask any twenty-something whether or not what he sees on TV is real, and he will not know how to respond. Lacan makes a distinction that might be useful here: Along with the Imaginary and Symbolic Orders mentioned here, he posits a Real Order in the human psyche, a realm that is both fascinating and terrifying but largely evaded or unrealized because the Imaginary Order conceals it and the Symbolic Order conceptualizes it into what we commonly refer to as normal reality. That is to say, the Real is always mediated by fantasy, on the one hand, and language, on the other, into everyday reality so that we never have to confront it in all its impossible *jouissance* except in small doses that rise from the unconscious in the form of symptoms.

Therefore, the quest for the Buddha mind, in Lacanian terms, would be the quest for the Real in reality, a quest to understand how the Real gets "symbolically reenacted and ritually devoured" in the era of late capitalism. Similarly, we could say that the quest for newness has reached its apotheosis in this autonomy of the media image: The need for new objects to fulfill seemingly new desires means that time keeps shrinking to the point when it no longer exists, or more precisely, it shrinks to the fifteen minutes of fame or the five-second sound bite, the barest quantum of time that desire needs to fixate on an object. This reduction or retraction of linear time, of the opening into futurity from the closest approximation to the present, I would suggest, is the postmodern equivalent or simulation—along with the confusion between appearance and reality—of Buddhist *nirvana*: a perpetual present. What I am suggesting then is that the third phase of capitalism has been able to figure out how to simulate *nirvana* so that the quest for Buddha mind, for the Real, can be contained within our normal human existence, through supply and demand.

Nishitani talks about the significance of the present moment in Buddhism in terms of Nietzsche's conception of Eternal Recurrence and the home-ground of the Real: "at the home-ground of the present—directly beneath the present that penetrates vertically through the stratified accumulation of endless numbers of lesser and greater cycles of time—nihility opens up as the field of the ecstatic transcendence of world and time. It means that the abyss of nihility on which this endless recurrence takes place appears as an infinite openness directly beneath the present."[9] If my analysis of the influence of capitalism on modern and postmodern identity is valid, then what we are approaching is a time when any sense of historicity becomes lost to an absorption in the present moment, a moment-by-moment "lifestyle" that to a human being has the feel of "the ecstatic transcendence of world and time," that is, because he cannot think about the past or the future when he is so caught up in the moment, the absolute demand for newness that marks postmodernity. Each moment is drained of the Real as soon as it becomes past; "It's history," to use a revealing phrase of dismissal from the 1980s.

That postmodern Americans lack a sense of history is a common-place; Jameson makes this point on the first page of his book when he says that postmodern theory attempts to restore a sense of history to an era that has forgotten it: "Modernism also thought compulsively about the New and tried to watch its coming into being . . . , but the postmodern looks for breaks, for events rather than new worlds, for the telltale instant after which it is no longer the same."[10] But added to this immersion in the present is a kind of addiction to it, a feeling that the present moment is a kind of home-ground of experience: Enjoy what you have now by not becoming too attached to it because something better is sure to come along in just a moment.

How else to explain, for example, the contemporary depen-dence on camera/cell phones, Instant Messaging, and the pressure constantly to stay in contact with others, as if the present moment must be extended in all directions to encompass the whole lifeworld? Buddhist doctrine suggests that the desire for liberation may be dis-guised in other desires, that being inserted into the capitalist moment bears some resemblance to *satori*, but the difference of course is that the big Other of the economic system has constructed a semblance of the eternal present, not the real thing. In Nishitani's vision the individual is confronted with the nihility of his own being in the present, and when he does so the present opens up, or the bottom falls out, revealing an infinite emptiness, the Nietzschean abyss. The cell phone addiction indicates the extent to which the simulation of this abyss terrifies the postmodern individual: he cannot confront his own lack of being in the present, his own silence becomes boredom, and therefore he must communicate with others in a simulation of Eternal Recurrence.

The abyss in human identity is of the same order as the "death of the self" that I spoke about earlier. Jameson describes it as the death of "the autonomous bourgeois monad or ego or individual—and the accompanying stress, whether as some new moral ideal or as empiri-cal description, on the *decentering* of that formerly centered subject or psyche" (italics Jameson's). He goes on to say that there are two ways of looking at this death: "the historicist one, that a once-existing centered subject, in the period of classical capitalism and the nuclear family, has today in the world of organizational bureaucracy dis-solved; and the more radical poststructuralist position, for which such a subject never existed in the first place but constituted something like an ideological mirage."[11] Although Jameson inclines toward the first position, I believe Buddhism has more in common with the second. That is, the separateness that constitutes an individual ego is an illusion caused by attachment to the phenomenal world.

This is essentially the same position that Lacanian psychoanalysis takes. Unlike other forms of Western psychology that put the strengthening of the ego at the center of therapeutic practice, Lacan's return to Freud indicates that the ego is an illusion created when a child at about a year and a half old goes through the "mirror stage," a phase when he sees himself reflected in the gaze of a mirror or another person as a coherent, whole human being and not as a disordered collection of fragments.[12] At this moment a human develops an ego, a sense of identity, to make himself feel whole, when in fact he is always already a divided self, which is largely determined by his unconscious fantasies and his historical place in the signifying chain, by the Imaginary and Symbolic Orders. Because the ego is a misidentification of an individual's real nature, Lacanian psychoanalysis ends when a client is able to see how his identity is fundamentally empty but has been socially constructed by his place in the Symbolic Order. He is able to recognize and traverse his imaginary identifications, which formerly kept him chained to a misleading image of himself. This quest eventually leads him to some sense of the Real that always fails to be accounted for in either the Imaginary or Symbolic Orders, the piece of the Real that constitutes the *objet a* or the "sublime object."

The psychoanalyst remains essentially passive in this therapy; in his silence he forces the client to seek to understand the emptiness of the master position, of the subject-supposed-to-know, and thereby to see his own emptiness. In other words, the analyst's position of knowledge and the client's position of ignorance are merely points on a signifying chain that has been entrenched in the social order (the social construction of identity), and once one sees how his identity is thereby configured he is liberated from those confines. Obviously, the similarity to the disciple/sage relationship is clear: the master knows more than the follower only because the follower believes that he does. The disciple must recognize his own emptiness as reflected back from the emptiness of the master.

Žižek describes this process in the following passage from the end of his first book:

Now, perhaps we are able to locate that radical change which, according to Lacan, defines the final stage of the psychoanalytic process: "subjective destitution." What is at stake in this "destitution" is precisely the fact that *the subject no longer presupposes himself as subject*; by accomplishing this he annuls, so to speak, the effects of the act of formal conversion. In other words, he assumes not the existence but the *nonexistence* of the big Other; he accepts the Real in its utter, meaningless idiocy; he keeps open the gap between the Real and its symbolization. The price to be paid for this is that by the same act he also *annuls himself as subject*, because—and this would be Hegel's last lesson—the subject is subject only in so far as he presupposes himself as absolute through the movement of double reflection.[13]

For Žižek, "subjective destitution," like the Christian "dark night of the soul," occurs when the subject stops being the subjectivity formed by the double reflection of how he sees himself as part of the social order. As the mirror stage formed his sense of himself originally, so now the mirror stage is as if it were reversed and he sees that his former identity was an illusion created through his interpellation by the big Other. Nishitani's reading of Nietzsche describes a similar process in the realization of one's nihility: "infinite openness as transcendence beyond world and time takes on the character of eternity. It is not, however, the eternity of a transcendent *being*, but something that might be called the eternity of a transcendent *nothingness*, or the eternity, so to speak, of Death itself" (italics Nishitani's). This "Great Death," as he calls it, a sense of personal death that is also the death of everything, "occurs en route to what Nietzsche has in mind when he says, 'When you gaze long into an abyss, the abyss starts gazing back into you.' This is the self-presentation of nihility, what has been called above a participation in nihility."[14]

In other words, the sense of nihilism comes from the dawning realization that the object, the abyss, is staring back into the emptiness of the subject. However, Nishitani continues by explaining that in Buddhism this experience of a Great Death is followed by an inexplicable conversion to a "Great Life": "It is something of which we cannot ask why. There can be no conceivable reason for it, and no conceivable basis for it to take hold of. That is to say, this conversion is an event taking place at a point more elemental than the dimension on which events occur that can be spoken of in terms of reasons and bases."[15] This description of Great Life, of *satori*, is probably what Žižek was getting at when he discussed accepting "the Real in its utter, meaningless idiocy." The Real is always impossible to deal with because it is outside the ordinary human realms of fantasy and language; therefore, it is by definition idiotic—meaningless in human terms. Psychoanalysis has no way to describe this realm because it is beyond symbolization; in Buddhist terms we should say that it is "not this, not that." But Nishitani draws a distinction between Nietzschean nihilism, or what he calls relative nothingness, and the absolute nothingness of emptiness, thus taking the next step beyond the despairing dead end of so much of the Western metaphysical tradition.

The "death of the subject" coincides in postmodern culture with the rise of the power of the image to duplicate and, eventually, even to do away with reality. Jean Baudrillard, who may rightfully be called the father of simulation theory, argues that simulations, as the apotheosis of media representations of the image, develop as identity disintegrates. Eventually the subject and the object become indistinguishable. He discusses the evolution of representation and the postmodern crisis that occurs when images begin to replace reality. Beginning in 1970 with his essay "Consumer Society," Baudrillard sketches the way that people start to identify with the objects they are consuming. In effect, the objects also begin to take on the life of the individual consuming them, floating free as signifiers of desire. In "Symbolic Exchange and Death" he continues this semiotic analysis of postmodern society by positing the emergence of what he calls the "hyperreal" and by arguing that nothing can escape the exchange values of this code of signs elaborated by late capitalism except death itself.

These two ideas need further elaboration: first, the hyperreal, and later the escape from the matrix of images through death. In his seminal essay "Simulacra and Simulations" Baudrillard describes the image as evolving through four stages: reflection of reality, masking of reality, masking the absence of reality, and finally replacing reality altogether.[16] In the fourth stage the simulation of reality actually covers the same space as reality so that the two are indistinguishable: Baudrillard alludes to the famous story in Borges of the map that so exactly details every point of the landscape of an empire that it eventually replaces the deserts of that landscape. According to Baudrillard, this is what is happening in the present stage of media-driven capitalism: "Simulation is no longer that of a territory, a referential being or a substance. It is the generation by models of a real without origin or reality: a hyperreal."[17] Elsewhere he says that the hyperreal goes farther than the goals of surrealism because it completely erases the differences between reality and fantasy that artists were demonstrating by confusing the two. We can take an example that Jameson uses to demonstrate how simulations work in everyday reality. The extreme of photographic realism in painting and sculpture causes a "derealization" in one's perception of the world. When you encounter the scrupulously detailed simulations of a museum guard or tourist standing in the gallery of an art museum you are visiting, "your moment of doubt and hesitation as to the breath and warmth of these polyester figures . . . tends to return upon the real human beings moving about you in the museum and to transform them also for the briefest instant into so many dead and flesh-colored simulacra in their own right. The world thereby momentarily loses its depth and threatens to become a glossy skin, a stereoscopic illusion, a rush of filmic images without density. But is this now a terrifying or an exhilarating experience?"[18]

The question is a good one because it speaks to an encounter with the Lacanian impossible Real in which "normal" reality loses some of its substance, but the simulation Jameson describes here is still on the third order of Baudrillard's hierarchy, the image that points to a lack in reality itself. In the fourth stage the simulation transcends extreme realism or surrealism and assumes its hyperreal status—that is, it no longer needs the real to function as image:

> In fact we must interpret hyperrealism inversely: today, *reality itself is hyperrealistic*. The secret of surrealism was that the most banal reality could become surreal, but only at privileged moments, which still derived from art and the imaginary. Now the whole of everyday political, social, historical, economic reality is incorporated into the simulative dimension of hyperrealism; we already live out the "aesthetic" hallucination of reality. The old saying, "reality is stranger than fiction," which belonged to the surrealist phase of the aestheticization of life, has been surpassed. There is no longer a fiction that life can confront, even in order to surpass it; reality has passed over into the play of reality. (Italics Baudrillard's)[19]

No doubt everyone living in twenty-first-century America or portions of its far-flung empire of so-called cultural imperialism can come up with his own examples of the simulation that replaces its referent, which floats free and redoubles itself, everything from "Reality" TV with its "Average Joes" who go on to become "stars" on other reality shows to video games with "real" product placements to Serbian television showing the film *Wag the Dog* during the recent war in Yugoslavia, a movie about the U.S. government simulating a war with Albania to hide a president's sexual escapade with a teenage girl. Or consider the late comic Andy Kauffman: Does anyone really know if he was faking those wrestling matches or not—and wasn't that the point? What is the TV show *Survivor* but a romantic simulation of Third World suffering with First World participants, that is, without real danger? Does anyone know for sure if that toppling of the statue of Saddam Hussein, that celebrated image exactly the reverse of the Iwo Jima memorial, was staged or real?

When the questions about simulations become life-and-death issues, people start to take notice of the transformations of everyday reality that have become so normalized over roughly the last quarter century that they have become all but invisible. Ironically, Michel De Certeau makes the case that simulations are the last refuge for a belief that the Real is something that is visible. He relates this idea to a change in paradigms from a premodern belief that the Real is invisible (in spiritual or Platonic forms), to a modern faith in facts and proofs. But this empirical interpretation of the world is pushed to its tipping point in the simulation, as the following passage poetically suggests:

> In short, the contemporary simulacrum is the last localization of the belief in sight. It is the identification of the *seen* with what is to be *believed*—once we have abandoned the hypothesis that holds that the waters of an invisible ocean (the Real) haunt the shores of the visible and create the effects, the decipherable signs or the misleading reflections of its presence. The simulacrum is what the relationship of the visible to the real becomes when the postulate of an invisible immensity of the Being (or beings) hidden behind appearances crumbles. (Italics De Certeau's)[20]

Perhaps the most striking point here for our purposes in thinking about Buddhism's relationship to simulacra is that invisible Being is "crumbling" behind appearances in our everyday world. It seems a paradox that in some way simulations bring people closer to the invisible Being, because they are the "last localizations" of the visible.

That is to say, a simulacrum is almost completely abstract; at the same time that it can create in every detail the material world, it also relies very little on that world. It is as far as Western technology can push representation without falling into the invisible itself.

This situation is similar to what I was arguing before, that time has so collapsed that the perpetual now of late commodity capitalism imitates a kind of "Be Here Now" *nirvana*. The apotheosis of sight in De Certeau's theory of simulations adds the dimensions of space to the dimension of time. Someone playing a video game can experience the surplus enjoyment of being not only in an infinite present but in infinite space, a time and space that is somehow more fascinating, more real, than reality itself.

Baudrillard ventures farther than anyone in discussing the purposes behind the evolution of the image to its present hyperreal form and the advantages that the simulation possesses over "normal" reality. He traces its history back to the Old Testament prohibition against representations of the divine and the consequent history of iconoclasm:

> [Iconoclasts'] rage to destroy images rose precisely because they sensed this omnipotence of simulacra, this facility they have of erasing God from the consciousness of people, and the overwhelming, destructive truth which they suggest: that ultimately there has never been any God; that only simulacra exist; indeed that God himself has only ever been his own simulacrum. Had they been able to believe that images only occulted or masked the Platonic idea of God, there would have been no reason to destroy them. One can live with the idea of a distorted truth. But their metaphysical despair came from the idea that the images concealed nothing at all, and that in fact they were not images, such as the original model would have made them, but actually perfect simulacra forever radiant with their own fascination. But this death of the divine referential has to be exorcised at all cost.[21]

This seems to be Baudrillard's own position: Simulations not only mask a nothingness behind themselves, but they are more "radiant" even than the Real itself. This notion is similar to Žižek's argument that all ideology serves as a "sublime object" that covers the constitutive lack in the self. It would seem that Baudrillard, De Certeau, and Žižek are suggesting that we have reached a kind of final stage in secular, post-industrial Western society when representations of reality, which have been indebted to the material world, are now trembling on the brink of their own limitlessness as simulations. That is to say, the idea that images served to mask the absence of a divine, big Other might flip once again in another paradigm shift that privileges the virtual rather than the visual as a way to mask the Real, assuming that the Real is always that which cannot be confronted in human terms.

Privileging a virtual world, which seems even more real than "normal" reality, would mean that simulations would become everyday reality. And not only more real, but better. To paraphrase an advertisement so old that it seems almost mythic, not only do we not care whether it is real or it is Memorex, we have found that Memorex is better than the Real! The fact that simulations provide a semblance of immediacy in time, an infinity in space, and, we could add, an imperishability because of the first two characteristics, means that a simulated world seems better than everyday reality. The Old Country at Busch Gardens in Williamsburg, Virginia, is superior to the European villages it imitates, because it is here in the States, the experiences are all consistently the same and guaranteed (the beer is always cold and the villagers are always smiling), and they can be infinitely repeated, not to mention the greater paradox that The Old Country is more popular than the "real" old country next door, the historic district of Williamsburg itself, the seat of the first Virginia legislature.

In an interesting article on *The Matrix*, a film many theorists of simulations (and students of Buddhism) refer to, philosopher David Weberman discusses whether the construct that Neo and his colleagues want to destroy is not only preferable to ordinary reality but perhaps "is as metaphysically real as unsimulated reality, if not more so." Weberman remains skeptical that simulations will replace reality anytime soon, for metaphysical reasons, but he does conclude with this claim: "If our future experience turns out to be such that simulated reality has a greater causal impact on our lived experience and actual behavior than nonsimulated reality, then, in one sense, a pragmatic sense, it will be more real."[22] Some theorists of course believe that simulations of reality might prove to be a liberating experience from the restrictions of the human body and human prejudice.

Donna Haraway, for example, in her important "Cyborg Manifesto," argues persuasively that technology offers us a kind of "post-human" world in which old boundaries—like those between man/woman and human/machine—get broken down, thereby uniting people against oppression. She sees simulations as a transition from the "old hierarchical dominations" of representation, and writes that cyborgs "are as hard to see politically as materially. They are about consciousness—or its simulation."[23] Haraway's position reminds me that I don't want to suggest in this essay that there is something inherently wrong with modern science and technology or that simulations of material reality or of consciousness should be forbidden. That would be as impossible as overcoming ideology; but like ideology, modern technology can become so pervasive and invisible that we need to be able to think critically about how these shifts in "normal" reality are affecting us, particularly in our metaphysics and our search for the Real.

The fact that eBay is the fastest growing company in America demonstrates that the global economy, the Internet, and worldwide consumption are all linked in a heretofore unimaginable way, yet even conservatives have to express some astonishment at how late capitalism has drastically altered society, initiating cultural wars and identity politics. After all, Arnold Schwarzenegger does return in *Terminator II* to help save the world from machines like himself, but he also becomes governor of California. Who knows whether Timothy Leary's experiment to have his head surgically removed from his body at his death (captured on film) and then frozen so that in the future his thoughts could be downloaded into a better, more permanent body will be successful, but the fact that Americans are representing these issues now in their science fiction narratives indicates that they are becoming so normalized that we are already living in our own simulated empire.

The *Matrix* movies owe a debt to William Gibson's cyberpunk novels, which first illustrated the possibilities of virtual adventures to a wide audience. In *Neuromancer*, for example, where people who live in their bodies instead of cyberspace are referred to as "meat," the protagonist, Case, encounters a human being who has died and now lives completely in the virtual world: he has become a construct, part of a "ROM personality matrix." Case feels uneasy about the ontological status of this character, and the character himself, realizing that he is nothing but a construct, asks Case to "erase" him.[24] But there is every reason to speculate that in the not-too-distant future someone will come up with a virtual construct for enlightenment: an encounter with a sage in the Tibetan mountains with all the special effects of a Hollywood movie, something like a cross between *The Razor's Edge* and *Little Buddha*. Or better, a simulation of everyday reality is so lifelike that it becomes "the copy for which there is no original," thereby answering the perennial question of how the supreme reality fell into human consciousness. Would it work, or are the effects of such media narratives already becoming an obstacle against such a thing happening? Where is the Real in a simulation?

Baudrillard believes that simulations speak to a desire for the Real in postmodern society and that late capitalism seeks "the restoration of the real which escapes it,"[25] but this "restoration" is a misleading one. The term is a reminder of the current passion in American media for "makeovers": cars, homes, bodies—ultimately identities—as if the postmodern subject had some hint that his selfhood was under assault and he needed something authentic to verify it. Baudrillard concludes that simulations ultimately imitate what Žižek, after Alain Badiou, refers to as the "passion for the Real," and this point, I believe, takes us to the heart of the problem for Buddhism: The search for some kind of ultimate reality has been subverted in American culture into a paradoxical quest for the Real, on the one hand, and a simultaneous avoidance of the Real, on the other hand, often at one and the same time through the simulating of a *nirvana*-like experience with its characteristic eternal time and space and "technological bonus of pleasure." Simulations take countless forms, like the phenomenal world outside the simulation, but their ultimate function in the postmodern global village is to "seduce" the consumer, to use another of Baudrillard's terms, by the play of surfaces, and in doing so to hide the Real and annihilate it, thereby keeping people contained as subjectivities within the big Other of capitalism. As in Buddhism when a student's very belief that he can transcend the world may block that transcendence, so in late capitalism a desire for the hyperreal that simulations offer may actually block access to the Real itself.

In his controversial book *Welcome to the Desert of the Real: Five Essays on September 11 and Related Dates*, Žižek discusses this contemporary phenomenon.[26] He points out that people in First World America want to have their cake and eat it too: they want the real thing but without any of the pathological properties that come with the Real, without any sacrifice. As examples Žižek mentions coffee without caffeine (in an earlier version of this chapter he called this way of thinking "Passion in the Era of Decaffeinated Belief"), war without bloodshed (i.e., video game war, as we saw in Operation Desert Storm. And isn't the American public's increasing reluctance to support a bloody war in Iraq the logical outcome of this concept?), virtual sex without bodies, the other without his otherness, and so on. He carries these observations to his point about 9/11:

Virtual Reality simply generalizes this procedure of offering a product deprived of its substance: it provides reality itself deprived of its substance, of the hard resistant kernel of the Real—just as decaffeinated coffee smells and tastes like real coffee without being real coffee Virtual Reality is experienced as reality without being so. What happens at the end of this process of virtualization, however, is that we begin to experience "real reality" itself as a virtual entity. For the great majority of the public, the WTC explosions were events on the TV screen, and when we watched the oft-repeated shot of frightened people running towards the camera ahead of the giant cloud of dust from the collapsing tower, was not the framing of the shot itself reminiscent of spectacular shots in catastrophe movies, a special effect which outdid all others, since—as Jeremy Bentham knew—reality is the best appearance of itself?[27]

We have been so conditioned by media effects that in a sense we can no longer look at reality objectively. Of course one could argue that we have never been able to do this, that the whole problem for religion as well as for science is to see reality, like Zen, which strives to directly point at reality. However, as this essay has described, the situation is not only getting worse in our global culture, it has reached a kind of apotheosis. The inability to distinguish between the real and the illusion has progressed to the privileging of the illusion over the real. America has always been a land of illusion, even at the same time that it was a material wilderness that had to be struggled with to be mastered. Before the Europeans colonized the New World it was described by the early explorers as a paradise; Columbus even thought he had found the fabled Garden of Eden.

The early dream of America as a perfect place, a land of infinite freedom and opportunity, underlies the illusion that simulations today offer that same ideal refuge both for and from the Real, as recent movies like *Pleasantville* and *The Truman Show* have suggested, in that the perfect society is an impossible dream (there is always a snake in the garden) that must nevertheless be pursued, or that it should be pursued *because* it is impossible and therefore we are in no danger of ever having what we wish for. The irony works in the everyday details of postmodern reality. Take for example the surge in couples taking pre-engagement tests to see if they are compatible. The media described one case in which the couple had dated for six months before they signed up to take the PREPARE Relationship Inventory. The woman recounted the moment: "This is real, we're going to take this step to see if we want to get engaged."[28] As Žižek observes, the pathological element so inherent in relationships has been removed: the couple can now have a happy marriage because they believe what the psychological tests reveal about themselves. If they took a test to see if they were compatible with Buddhism, would they join a temple? Living in such a media-saturated environment, postmodern Americans have become—for good or bad—the recipients and purveyors of the phenomenon of the "death of the subject." Their quest for authenticity, their passion for the Real, like middle-class suburban white kids dressing like incarcerated ghetto hip hop heads, points to an inner emptiness that cannot be acknowledged because that would throw into doubt the reality of the big Other that supposedly gives life meaning. This double bind is endemic to the human condition, no doubt, but in America we can see the problem most clearly in the masquerade of twenty-first-century simulations, and Buddhism in America needs to recognize the paradoxes just as clearly if it is to do any good.

Buddhist teachers in America need to think critically about the changing metaphysics inherent in twenty-first-century global capitalism, in which human beings become more alienated than ever from the decision-making processes that influence their everyday lives through the commodification of desires and the masking of the Real through hyperreal simulations. At the same time the passion for the Real indicates there is an increasing feeling that human beings—for better or worse—are losing some substance; the "death of the subject" can be experienced on a practical level as ideas about what it means to be human go through a metamorphosis. The recent emphasis on "identity theft" is a striking example of this process. Of course the term refers to the effects of having someone swipe your credit card number or password so that he can have access to your accounts and buy products with your money, but ironically the real identity theft of postmodern subjectivity seems to be hidden in this concern with the material thing. We are so commodified that we can only think of ourselves as part of the economic code, especially in the virtual world of online accounts.

What I think is crucial is to keep asking ourselves: What is Real? And how is the Real different from mediated reality? As a materialist in the Marxist tradition, Žižek suggests that the Real doesn't really exist, that human beings live in an atheistic universe. He believes that the idea of the Real is simply another way to avoid confronting the Absolute, to postpone the realization that we can live without the consistency in the Other that confers relative meaning on our existence:

Here, we should abandon the standard metaphorics of the Real as the terrifying Thing that is impossible to confront face to face, as the ultimate Real concealed beneath the layers of imaginary and/or symbolic Veils: the very idea that, beneath the deceptive appearances, there lies hidden some ultimate Real Thing too horrible for us to look at directly is the ultimate appearance—this Real Thing is a fantasmatic spectre whose presence guarantees the consistency of our symbolic edifice, thus enabling us to avoid confronting its constitutive inconsistency ("antagonism").[29]

In other words, enlightenment consists in giving up our belief that there is such a thing as enlightenment, that there is a difference between "normal" consciousness and Buddha consciousness. Žižek also argues in his most recent book, *The Puppet and the Dwarf*, that the popular idea of Buddhism's alleged indifference to the phenomenal world prevents it from acknowledging this pathological inconsistency or emptiness in the big Other that is found in the phenomenal world, that the Buddhist's act of renunciation is another kind of escape from the Real. However, although I think this hard, materialist kernel of truth speaks to the impossibility of "finding" enlightenment, I would disagree and argue that Nishitani's and Baudrillard's theorizing about death—the second point of Baudrillard's, which I have held in suspension for half this essay—do provide the only way out of the capitalist system of exchange. Baudrillard's answer to how to live in a thoroughly mediated world is—silence. Don't respond—a kind of death. Like Lacan's notion of "subjective destitution," the death of the self is the only legitimate act that one can perform without being contained in a symbolic exchange, and once this transformation has occurred, there is no attachment to the phenomenal world. But this "Great Death" must be authentic: the simulation of *nirvana* such as we find in postmodern America, with its possibilities for infinite vistas of time and space and infinite identities, is not real. If you encounter the Buddha on the road, kill him—he just might be a simulation!

Notes

1. See, for example, Amy Edelstein, "Is Buddhism Surviving America? An Interview with Helen Tworkov," *WIE* 14 (Fall/Winter 1998): [journal online] available from http://www.wie.org/j14/tworkov.asp?pf=1.htm (accessed 15 June 2005), and "Tensions in American Buddhism," *Religion and*

Ethics Newsweekly 445 (6 July 2001): [journal online]; available from http://www.pbs.org/wnet/ religionandethics/week445/ buddhism.htm (accessed 23 June 2005).

2. Richard Hughes Seager, *Buddhism in America* (New York: Columbia University Press, 1999), 37.

3. A recent title on Lacanian psychoanalysis bears out my point: Philippe Van Haute's *Against Adaptation: Lacan's "Subversion" of the Subject* (New York: Other Press, 2002) argues that unlike ego-centered psychology, Lacanian therapy does not want the client to adapt to the reality principle.

4. Jürgen Habermas, *The Philosophical Discourse of Modernity* (Cambridge: MIT Press, 1990), 1–50.

5. Ibid., 5–7.

6. Fredric Jameson, *Postmodernism, or, The Cultural Logic of Late Capitalism* (Durham: Duke University Press, 1991), 276.

7. A similar point is made by Thomas Frank in *One Market under God: Extreme Capitalism, Market Populism, and the End of Economic Democracy* where he argues that global capitalism has become identified with the spread of democracy as an inherently moral enterprise, almost as if capitalism had finally replaced the deity lost when a secular modernism supplanted the medieval religious worldview.

8. Jameson, *Postmodernism*, 276–77.

9. Keiji Nishitani, *Religion and Nothingness*, trans. Jan Van Bragt (Berkeley: University of California Press, 1983), 229.

10. Jameson, *Postmodernism*, ix.

11. Ibid., 15.

12. Although the dialogue between psychoanalysis and Buddhism goes back at least as far as D. T. Suzuki's and Erich Fromm's lectures at the University of Mexico in 1960, it has not been until recently—and largely fueled by the Internet—that the relationships between the two have begun to be deeply explored. It is striking that the French Lacanian version of psychoanalysis has not been as prominent as the American versions, this despite the fact that Lacan posits that the ego is an illusion. For example, in Seth Robert Segall's collection, *Encountering Buddhism: Western Psychology and Buddhist Teachings* (2003), the only reference to Lacan in the whole book is in an essay by Jeffrey B. Rubin where he states, "Most analysts—with the exception of Lacanians—claim that strengthening the self is crucial to the psychoanalytic process." Likewise, in *The Couch and the Tree: Dialogues in Psychoanalysis and Buddhism* (1998), edited by Anthony Molino, only one essay makes specific mention of Lacan in its title: Anthony Molino's "Zen, Lacan, and the Alien Ego." The omissions are especially striking considering that Lacan begins his first seminar in 1953 with the following allusion: "The master breaks the silence with anything—with a sarcastic remark, with a kick-start. That is how a Buddhist master conducts his search for meaning, according to the technique of *zen*. It behoves [*sic*] the students to find out for themselves the answer to their own questions. The master does not teach *ex cathedra* a readymade science; he supplies an answer when the students are on the verge of finding it."

On the other hand, Buddhist scholars and practitioners seem to be much more familiar with Jungian psychology and psychotherapy, which, in its totalizing narratives of a hero with a thousand faces questing into his unconscious, covers up the subject's constitutive lack. That is to say, the hero remains an individual throughout the narrative; in Lacanian terms there is no such thing as a hero because his individuality is already an illusion. The subject recognizes the nothingness that he already always is, thereby more closely resembling, I would argue, the no-self in Buddhist doctrine.

13. Slavoj Žižek, *The Sublime Object of Ideology* (London: Verso, 1989), 230–31.

14. Nishitani, *Religion and Nothingness*, 230–31.

15. Ibid., 231.

16. Jean Baudrillard, "Simulacra and Simulations," in *Jean Baudrillard: Selected Writings*, ed. Mark Poster (Stanford: Stanford University Press, 1988), 170.

17. Ibid., 166.

18. Jameson, *Postmodernism*, 34.

19. Jean Baudrillard, "Symbolic Exchange and Death," in *Jean Baudrillard: Selected Writings*, ed. Mark Poster (Stanford: Stanford University Press, 1988), 146.

20. Michel De Certeau, "The Jabbering of Social Life," in *On Signs*, ed. Marshall Blonsky (Baltimore: The Johns Hopkins University Press, 1985), 153.

21. Baudrillard, "Simulacra and Simulations," 169.

22. David Weberman, "*The Matrix* Simulation and the Postmodern Age," in *The Matrix and Philosophy: Welcome to the Desert of the Real*, ed. William Irwin (Chicago: Open Court, 2002), 236, 239.

23. Donna Haraway, "A Cyborg Manifesto: Science, Technology, and Socialist-Feminism in the Late Twentieth Century," in *Contemporary Literary Criticism: Literary and Cultural Studies*, eds. Robert Con Davis and Ronald Schleifer (New York: Longman, 1998), 705, 699.

24. William Gibson, *Neuromancer* (New York: Ace Books, 1984), 79, 106.

25. Baudrillard, "Simulacra and Simulations," 180.

26. The title refers to the greeting Morpheus gives Neo in *The Matrix* when he shows him what the construct hides—a wasteland after some holocaust. Clearly, the Real in this case is not something all that desirable. Nevertheless, Neo and his comrades persist in desiring it. However, the phrase comes from Baudrillard in "Simulacra and Simulations" when he claims that the Borgesian map that once exactly covered the Empire has now been replaced by the "precession of simulacra" so that "it is the map that engenders the territory. . . . It is the real, and not the map, whose vestiges subsist here and there, in the deserts which are no longer those of the Empire, but our own. *The desert of the real itself.*" In effect, he is saying that today the Real is no longer a fruitful plain as it has been replaced by the hyperreal simulation.

27. Slavoj Žižek, *Welcome to the Desert of the Real: Five Essays on September 11 and Related Dates* (London: Verso, 2002), 11. This effect of course does not have to be so spectacular. On a much more mundane level, a recent trip on a gurney through the hallways of a hospital to the operating room reminded me of all the TV shows and movies where the camera views what the patient on the gurney sees. The experience was quite unsettling as I started imagining all the tragic and comic operations that followed the simulated journey, as if I were not real anymore, or never had been.

28. Ellen Barry, "Couples Take Tests before They Take the Plunge," *Roanoke Times*, 22 June 2005, A8.

29. Žižek, *Welcome to the Desert of the Real*, 31–32.

Part III

Sangha: Who Is an American Buddhist?

8

Family Life and Spiritual Kinship in American Buddhist Communities

Charles S. Prebish

Introduction

One of the most quoted summary phrases concerning Buddhism's growth in countries beyond its Indian birthplace is Michael Carrithers's remark: "No Buddhism without the *Sangha* and no *Sangha* without the Discipline."[1] For Carrithers, Buddhism's growth and survival in countries beyond India required and was predicated upon the establishment of the *sangha*, and its implementation, as the basis for Buddha's spiritual family. Early on in Buddhist history, the original Buddhist *sangha*, initially conceived as consisting only of monks, was expanded to include nuns, and then lay followers of both genders, thus rather quickly including of all Buddha's disciples and being identified as "the *sangha* of the four quarters." In a very real way, this *sangha* of the four quarters was envisioned as a universal order, transcending both time and space, and encompassing all geographical areas.

Within Buddha's spiritual family, the most overarching model for familial propriety, and paternity, is that of the *kalyanamitra*, or the spiritual friend. In a famous passage from the *Saṃyutta Nikāya*, Buddha is questioned by his disciple Ananda regarding the status of the state of spiritual friendship, and Ananda suggests that this state is *half* the holy life. He is immediately reprimanded by Buddha for his faulty understanding, who instructs: "Not so Ananda; not so Ananda.

This association with spiritual friendship, association with virtuous companionship, association with goodness *is the whole of the holy life.*"[2] Without delay Buddha goes on to suggest that he himself is the highest *kalyanamitra*, and it is because of his function in this capacity that beings subject to birth and rebirth are able to free themselves from old age, sickness, and death; and indeed, from suffering (*duhkha*) itself. With Buddha established as the highest spiritual friend, he necessarily becomes the archetypal model for all subsequent spiritual kinship relationships in his spiritual family. Within a short while, it becomes quite clear from Buddha's initial preaching that his spiritual family is modeled on the ideal secular family, and he is exceedingly explicit on both the nature of, and relationships within, that ideal secular family. The remainder of this chapter examines that model, as well as its application to modern America.

The Ideal Family Life

Although the primary models for the most effective religious lifestyle in Buddhism are the celibate monastic or the committed *bodhisattva*, members of the laity have always constituted the great majority of Buddhist practitioners. As such, the interpersonal familial social relationships of the laity are especially important, and were occasionally the focus of Buddha's most pointed and specific instructions. Hammalawa Saddhatissa, in his classic volume *Buddhist Ethics*, notes that "The duties of children to their parents were stressed in India from a very early date." He goes on to point out that the "*Rukkhadhamma Jātaka* expressed the value of the solidarity of a family, using the simile of the trees of a forest"; these are "able to withstand the force of the wind whereas a solitary tree, however large, is not."[3] Perhaps the most famous and important of Buddha's family-oriented sermons is the *Sigālovāda Sutta* of the *Dīgha Nikāya*, in which Buddha provides explicit instructions to the layman Sigala, who is trying to honor his father's dying wish that he honor the six directions.[4] Buddha likens worshipping the six directions to proper actions toward six different categories of persons. The six directions—east, south, west, north, nadir, and zenith—respectively correspond to parents, teachers, wife and children, friends and companions, servants and workpeople, and religious teachers and Brahmins. Before expounding on the specific requirements of proper social and familial relating, Buddha encourages Sigala, generally, to keep the precepts, and to avoid acting from impulse (*chanda*), hatred (*dosa*), fear (*bhaya*), or delusion (*moha*).

The first relationship addressed by Buddha is that of parents and children. On the relationship between parents and children, Buddha's instructions are straightforward and explicit. As the *Sigālovāda Sutta* proclaims:

> In five ways a child should minister to his parents as the eastern quarter: "once supported by them, I will now be their support; I will perform duties incumbent on them; I will keep up the lineage and tradition of my family; I will make myself worthy of my heritage; I will make alms offerings on their behalf after they are dead." In five ways parents thus ministered to, as the eastern quarter by their child, show their love for him: they restrain him from vice; they exhort him to virtue; they train him to a profession; they contract a suitable marriage for him; and in due time they hand over his inheritance.[5]

These relational expectations are maintained throughout the Buddhist tradition, and especially so in East Asia, where filial piety plays an outstanding role as the foundational basis of ethical life. Kenneth Ch'en even notes that one Chinese rendering of the aforementioned text translates one of the child's duties as "not to disobey the commandments of the parents."[6]

The *Sigālovāda Sutta* also offers a similar dyadic pattern of husband-wife relational expectations:

> In five ways should a wife as western quarter be ministered to by her husband: by respect, by courtesy, by faithfulness, by handing over authority to her, by providing her with adornment. In these five ways does the wife, ministered to by her husband as the western quarter, love him: her duties are well performed, by hospitality to the kin of both, by faithfulness, by watching over the goods he brings, and by skill and industry in discharging all her business.[7]

Because, as noted here, most marriages in early Buddhism were arranged, Buddha occasionally offered advice to a man's daughters on how to conduct themselves in marriage. Peter Harvey summarizes one of these passages, from the *Aṅguttara Nikāya*, this way: "(1) Regarding her husband 'she gets up before him, retires after him, willingly does what he asks, is lovely in her ways and gentle in speech,' not being one to anger him; (2) she honours all whom her husband respects, whether relative, monk or brahmin; (3) she is deft and nimble in her husband's home-crafts, such as weaving; (4) she watches over servants and workpeople with care and kindness; and (5) she looks after the wealth her husband brings home."[8] It should also be noted that divorce, although generally infrequent in early Buddhism, was permitted.

In other words, all familial relationships, like interpersonal relationships throughout Buddhism, are steeped in the ethical values and standards typified by the four "divine abodes" (brahmaviharas) of lovingkindness (metta), compassion (karuna), joy (mudita), and equanimity (upekkha). These qualities remain a powerful benchmark against which Buddhist family life throughout the world, including modern America, is invariably measured.

Coming to America

The very first comprehensive book on Buddhism in America, Emma Layman's Buddhism in America, written in 1976, devoted an entire chapter to the question "Who are the American Buddhists?" She focused on how Asian American Buddhists compared to American "convert" Buddhists. What she did not consider was just how one determines who is an American Buddhist.[9] Three years later, when I wrote my own book called American Buddhism, I suggested that one of the traditional ways of identifying Buddhists in Asian countries—taking refuge and accepting the five vows of the laity—was probably an inadequate and even misleading approach when applied to the American scene.[10]

It shouldn't be surprising that a quarter century ago, American Buddhists defined themselves in a variety of radically different ways. Asian American Buddhists—who are sometimes called "cradle" Buddhists—brought a complex of identity problems to their involvement in Buddhist practice in America. "Convert" Buddhists found themselves struggling with potential multiple affiliations. Could one be Jewish and Buddhist? or Christian and Buddhist? If so, how did this so-called ism-crossing translate into individual religious life? What seems clear is that the issue of religious identity is complex for both cradle and convert Buddhists, and this impacts enormously with respect to the interpenetration of family and religious life.

In the search for establishing some sort of "orthodoxy" in determining who is, and is not, a Buddhist in America, the problem is exacerbated by the fact that all forms of Buddhism, from every Asian

Buddhist culture, are present on American soil *at the same time*. This is the first time in more than 2,500 years of Buddhist history that this has occurred. In other words, what works as the defining characteristic for the American convert followers of a Chinese Buddhist sect might not work for the American convert practitioners of a Buddhist tradition imported from Sri Lanka or Thailand; and neither of those sets of characteristics might work for the Asian American followers of those same traditions.

My solution in 1979 tried to simplify the problem as much as possible. I am convinced that it remains correct and workable today, although some additional problems can now be noted. If a Buddhist is defined as someone who says "I am a Buddhist," when questioned about *their most important pursuit*, we not only abandon our attachment to ritual formulas that are neither workable nor even uniformly followed, but we also provide more than a little freedom for American Buddhist groups—a freedom in which they can develop a procedure that is consistent with their own self-image and mission. What appears initially as an outrageously simplistic definition of Buddhist affiliation serves the double purpose of providing a new standard and a simple method of professing Buddhist commitment while at the same time imposing a renewed sense of seriousness on all Buddhist groups.[11]

The yardstick of self-identification does not compromise any specific tradition, but rather augments and accommodates the specific requirements of each. What the definition does not provide is some means for determining an "official" membership, which becomes a problem when one tries to actually count the numbers of Buddhists in America. More recently, new interpretations have sought to improve on earlier attempts to establish some sense of Buddhist identification in America. The most persuasive, by Thomas Tweed, simply changes the titles. He calls the cradle Buddhists "adherents"; and divides the convert Buddhists into one of two groups: self-identifiers and "sympathizers" (or sometimes, and more creatively, "night-stand Buddhists," in view of the Buddhist books that are often placed next to their beds). In the end, virtually all the investigators and interpreters of American Buddhism affirm the hybrid nature of all religious commitments, and then conclude that Buddhists are those people who simply say they are Buddhists.[12] It is both obvious and true. What is not so obvious is what religious choice the children of convert Buddhists will make in the future, and what religious choices the children of third-, fourth-, and fifth-generation Asian American Buddhists will make as the recollection of their original practice dims and is replaced by their immersion in American culture.

We will probably never have a completely accurate total of the current number of Buddhists in America. The January 9, 1970 issue of *Life Magazine*, for example, suggested that 200,000 Americans had joined a sect of American Buddhism known as Nichiren Shoshu. Around the same time, another group called Buddhist Churches of America estimated around 100,000 members. Both figures were almost certainly inflated exaggerations. The unreliability of membership estimates does not mean that the number of Buddhists in America was not growing, and growing rapidly at that time. In 1965 a number of amendments were added to the Immigration and Nationality Act of 1952, making it significantly easier for individuals from war-torn Asian countries to find new homes in America. The impact was dramatic. The Chinese population, for example, increased by over 400,000 by 1985, and surpassed 921,000 by 1990.[13] Moreover, similar results can be seen in the Vietnamese, Cambodian, Thai, Burmese, Sri Lankan, Laotian, Korean, and Japanese American communities. In addition, a phenomenon known as the counterculture was sweeping the American landscape, and especially so among young people. The counterculture sought to create a saner reality based on meditative reflection, social change, the elimination of personal suffering. Moreover, the American religious panorama was changing because of increasing secularization on the social front. Traditional religious groups within Christianity and Judaism were losing members fast, and many of these disenchanted members turned to alternative religions like Buddhism in their search for human fulfillment.

It wasn't until 1990 that figures based on actual research began to appear. In 1990 a general survey on religious affiliation was conducted by Barry Kosmin and Seymour Lachman that suggested that American Buddhists constituted about .4 percent of the adult population in America. By also factoring in the non-adult population, a figure of around one million Buddhists in America was proposed.[14] In 2001, Barry Kosmin teamed with Egon Mayer to produce a new survey called the American Religious Identity Survey (ARIS). It was based on interviews with 50,281 people (slightly less than half the number of the 1990 survey). The preliminary results were reported in the December 24, 2001 edition of *USA Today*, and the overall result suggested there are fewer than 1.5 million Buddhists in America. It remains unclear whether these figures really are accurate.

Scholars of Buddhism have come to very different conclusions about the number of Buddhists in America. In the mid-1990s, Robert Thurman, a Buddhist studies professor at Columbia University and a former Buddhist monk himself, told Peter Jennings on *ABC Nightly*

News with Peter Jennings that there were five to six million Buddhists in the United States. Thurman was probably guessing, but by 1997, a German scholar named Martin Baumann postulated three to four million Buddhists in America, based on his own surveys and extensive research. Utilizing the comprehensive current research on immigrant Buddhist communities in the United States, it is quite likely that Baumann's figure was correct for its time, and there now may well be many more Buddhists on American soil.[15] That makes American Buddhism as large as many prominent Protestant denominations.

Having explored who can be considered a Buddhist in America, and how many Buddhists there might be in the United States, it is certainly appropriate to ask how they all got here. Most scholars agree that about 75 to 80 percent of the Buddhists in America are of Asian American descent, with the remainder being composed of American converts who are primarily of European American ancestry. African American and Hispanic American converts to Buddhism remain a small part of the overall convert community. The easiest way to conveniently identify all these groups is under the two broad headings of Asian immigrant Buddhists and American convert Buddhists. Unfortunately, these two main groups have not always communicated well with one another.

Most recently, it has been suggested that a far more fruitful approach is to focus not on the ethnic/racial divide between the two Buddhisms, but rather on the function Buddhism plays in their respective lives.[16] In that respect, in the Asian immigrant community, Buddhism serves an important function in maintaining the ethnic group's sense of family life and heritage. On the other hand, in the American convert communities, Buddhism provides an alternative religious identity, offering a worldview shift from the religion of their parents.

Because these various American Buddhist communities practice different forms of Buddhism, it is important to understand the lines of transmission from Asia, and there seem to be three distinct procedures by which this has happened.[17] In one circumstance, Buddhism is imported from one country to another, in this case, from Asia to America. The catalyst for this is a "demand-driven" transmission: The host or new culture wants this tradition, and thus it is often called "Import" Buddhism. Sometimes it is called "Elite" Buddhism because its proponents have often discovered Buddhism through travel or education. And they have sufficient leisure and funds to indulge their interest. Import Buddhism is usually associated with Tibetan Buddhism, Zen, and Vipassana. A second line of transmission is called "Export" Buddhism. It reflects the intent of an Asian Buddhist parent community to share its Buddhist teaching with individuals in other parts of the world. This sort of Buddhism moves throughout the world via missionary activities sponsored by the parent Buddhist community. As a result, it is often called "Evangelical" Buddhism. The best known Export Buddhist group is Soka Gakkai International, but a number of Chinese Buddhist groups also sponsor extensive activities. Finally, there is "Ethnic" Buddhism, or that form of Buddhism brought to America by Asian immigrants. One Buddhist scholar has identified this form of Buddhism as "Baggage" Buddhism, although the term has proved offensive and insensitive to many Asian American Buddhists.

To summarize, we have seen two Buddhisms—Asian immigrant Buddhism and American convert Buddhism—and three lines of transmission from Asia: Elite Buddhism, which is imported to America; Evangelical Buddhism, which is exported to America; and Ethnic Buddhism, which arrives in America with the ongoing Asian immigrant population.

Family Life and Practice in American Buddhism

Of the eight leading comprehensive, scholarly books on Buddhism in America,[18] only Layman's *Buddhism in America*, Prebish and Tanaka's *The Faces of Buddhism in America*, and James Coleman's *The New Buddhism* even mention American Buddhist family life, and none of these includes more than a half-dozen pages on the topic. To make matters worse, Layman's volume unfortunately misconstrues the role of family life in Buddhism in both its ancient and American expressions when she says, "Buddhism has never placed much emphasis on the concept of family, or the concept of the specific roles of parents and children as determined by their Buddhist identity. . . . Hence, although Sunday Schools were established in some of the Jodo Shinshu churches of America around the turn of the century, most Buddhists of Oriental ancestry did not regard Buddhism as contributing too significantly to a sense of 'family.' "[19] Coleman's volume deals with family issues exclusively in the context of gender equality for women in convert communities and the problems encountered by parents with children in maintaining a rigorous meditation practice schedule.[20] And *The Faces of Buddhism in America* doesn't move beyond a few cursory comments confined to the Pure Land and Zen traditions. So where does one look to find information about Buddhist family practice in American communities?

In 1998 Judith Simmer-Brown, Professor of Buddhist Studies at Naropa University and a longtime student of Chögyam Trungpa Rinpoche, delivered one of the keynote addresses at the second annual Buddhism in America conference in San Diego. An article adapted from her address was eventually posted on the Shambhala International Internet site, and titled "American Buddhism: The Legacy for Our Children."[21] To be sure, Simmer-Brown's article is an important manifesto for convert practitioners of Buddhism, but practical concerns for children and family life are almost totally absent from the text.

A careful search of the Internet yields precious little in the way of family-oriented Buddhist sites. Ron Epstein has compiled a useful little reference file titled "Buddhism and Respect for Parents" with links to some classic Buddhist sources, but these are general and without specific reference to America.[22] Of the few sites that offer specific information aimed at American Buddhists, one of the very best—if not the best—is a composite picture developed by a woman simply identified as "Vanessa."[23] She has assembled a tidy list of materials under the rubric "Family Dharma Connections," including "Dharma lessons & Daily Practice," "Buddhist Holidays," "Children's Books," "Book reviews," "Children's Videos," and "Mindful Divorce." The last item on the list is especially useful, not simply because it emphasizes the necessity for placing children first, but because it suggests how to utilize the Four Noble Truths as a primer for understanding and explaining divorce. There is even a Buddhist Parents' Discussion group to which one may subscribe.

Occasionally, some individual convert Buddhist communities establish programs for children, such as Zen Mountain Monastery's Zen Kids' Sunday Program. This program is a monthly, three-hour play practice in which children are exposed to a number of aspects of Buddhist and Zen training, such as the liturgy and meditation practice. In so doing, "By participating in the Zen Kids Program, children and parents of the sangha create their own personal relationship to the Monastery."[24] John Daido Loori Rōshi, abbot of Zen Mountain Monastery (ZMM), frequently publishes his teachings, or *teishos*, on the ZMM webpage. One of these is called "Caoshan's Love Between Parent and Child," and provides Daido Roshi an opportunity to weave together the parent-child and student-teacher relationships in a fashion that harkens back to Buddha's original teachings. He says:[25]

In the beginning, the teacher-student relationship is very similar to a parent-child relationship. The student is in a completely new territory, unsure. There is a need for a lot of fundamental instructions from the teacher. After a while that changes and the teacher becomes a guide, fine-tuning the assessment of the student and pointing appropriately. Still the student is dependent on the guide. The next phase is characterized by the teacher being more like a spiritual friend. That evolves into spiritual equality between the teacher and the student. Still, the relationship continues.

At the time of the transmission of the Dharma, the parent becomes the child, the child becomes the parent; the teacher becomes the student, the student becomes the teacher. That fact is concretely expressed in the ceremony of transmission. First, the student circumambulates the teacher sitting on the high seat. Then the teacher steps down so that the student can sit on the high seat and the teacher circumambulates the student. The differences between the two become blurred.

A student can see the teacher because they are the teacher. A teacher seeing the student is meeting himself. My teacher meeting me is my teacher meeting himself, just as it is me meeting myself. Isn't this the same as the Buddha meeting the Buddha?

We often say that to realize oneself is to be really intimate with oneself. Isn't being intimate with oneself also the same as Buddha meeting Buddha? That's what the transmission of the Dharma is about. It doesn't go from A to B. It's realized within A, just as it was realized within B.

In birth, both parent and child transform; they become each other. We don't usually realize the full impact of that fact. It is fascinating when parents and their kids come to the Monastery for our Sunday programs. It is very clear which child belongs to which parent. Even if we scrambled the whole group, it would be straightforward to sort the families out. The kids are a perfect reflection of their parents. But we are not very conscious of that when we are raising our children.

When I look at my own children right now, I see myself the way I was twenty years back. I have a son who is forty-three and one who is forty. The things they struggle with are the things I was struggling with when

I was raising them. Our appreciations are similar. Both of my sons have a deep love of nature and a need to spend long days in the wilderness. And that sense of confidence in the wild is being passed on to their kids. My two grand-children are both avid hikers and canoeists who know their way around the back country. They also deal with anger much the same way I do.

As parents and teachers, we transmit our ways of life whether we realize it or not. What is most indelibly transmitted is what we do, not necessarily what we say. Master Dogen called this teaching through the whole body and mind. It's not just words. It's the actuality of our lives—our actions, our silence, our movements, the way we use our minds.

Teachings such as this are important in advancing rather than trivial-izing children's knowledge of the Buddhadharma. This latter problem is evident in popular magazines, such as *Tricycle*'s "Children Talking About 'Buddha' " in the Winter 1993 issue's version of the regular fea-ture "What Does Being a Buddhist Mean to You?" Prior to 1995, the only book I could find published by a member of a convert Buddhist group that focused on family life in American Buddhism was Sandy Eastoak's edited volume *Dharma Family Treasures: Sharing Mindful-ness with Children*, published by North Atlantic Press in 1994. More recently, two very helpful additional volumes have appeared: Myla and Jon Kabat-Zinn's *Everyday Blessings: The Inner Work of Mindful Parenting* (published by Hyperion in 1998), and *Kindness: A Treasury of Buddhist Wisdom for Children and Parents*, written by Sarah Conover and illustrated by Valerie Wahl (published by Eastern Washington University Press in 2001).

To date, there has been only one empirical study of a mostly convert Buddhist group in the United States: Phillip Hammond and David Machacek's study of Sōka Gakkai International USA (SGI-USA). Nonetheless, their study reveals some interesting data regard-ing family practice. Initially, membership in this organization was almost exclusively Asian. However, the percentage dropped from 96 percent in 1960 to 30 percent in 1970; and in the survey conducted by Hammond and Machacek in 1997, only 15 percent were Japanese.[26] In addition, according to their 1997 study, "SGI-USA members place significantly less emphasis on marriage and family life than do most Americans," and scored significantly lower than the General Social Survey on the importance of being married and having children.[27] It probably wouldn't be going too far in suggesting similar results for other convert Buddhist groups as well, largely precipitated by the convert focus on individualism and meditation practice rather than group- and community-defining activities. In fact, one well-known convert Buddhist teacher only half-jokingly referred to the famous Three Jewels of *Buddha, Dharma,* and *Sangha* as having been amended in America to Me, Myself, and I.

In Asian immigrant Buddhist communities, the situation is radically different, and in many cases, Buddhist family life defines the identity of the entire community. Yet only recently have scholars begun to point out the paucity of studies on Asian American Buddhism (and for reasons that extend beyond the scope of this chapter).[28] Moreover, a unit devoted to the study of Asian American religious communities has only been a fairly recent addition to the American Academy of Religion, and attendance at its sessions remains small. However, some fairly current books—such as Tetsuden Kashima's *Buddhism in America: The Social Organization of an Ethnic Religious Institution,* Paul Numrich's *Old Wisdom in the New World: Americanization in Two Immigrant Theravada Buddhist Temples,* and Janet McLellan's *Many Petals of the Lotus: Five Asian Buddhist Communities in Toronto*—provide ample documentation of how Buddhism functions in these immigrant communities.

Quite recently, Dr. Kenneth Tanaka, a scholar-practitioner who maintains a ministry in the Jodo Shinshu Buddhist Churches of America organization, has written a remarkable tract entitled "Parents Sharing the Nembutsu Teachings with Their Young Children," which addresses all the core issues of Buddhist family life in American ethnic Buddhist communities.[29] Tanaka's pamphlet includes considerations of parenting and sharing in the context of Buddhist values, handling difficult situations and questions, the fundamental outlook on life as stressed in Shin Buddhism, suggested daily activities, the testimonial of a Buddhist mother in San Francisco, and a useful bibliography of recommended books. Perhaps more than any other Buddhist organization in North America, Buddhist Churches of America has emphasized the Sunday School concept as a means of inculcating the importance of Buddhist family life in America. Nonetheless, despite the organization's efforts, the young adult population of its temples have begun to leave the organization at an alarmingly rapid rate. In an attempt to combat this trend, and to reinforce Buddhist identity in America, the organization has changed the name of their program from Sunday School to Dharma School. Presumably, this was done to "re-focus the goals and to re-establish the propagational, educational aspects of the program away from its Sunday day care image."[30]

To my knowledge, only one popular Buddhist publication addresses the issue of Buddhist family life in America with regularity: *Turning Wheel-Journal of the Buddhist Peace Fellowship*. For many years the journal has run a regular Family Practice column. Between 1995 and 1997 it was written by Patrick McMahon from the Spirit Rock community, and since 1997, it has been (mostly) supervised by Mushim Ikeda-Nash. The column regularly discusses marriage, intimacy, death, and even cooking from a Buddhist perspective. In addition, the journal occasionally devotes an entire issue to family-related matters. The Winter 1996 issue, for example, focused on "Family—What Is It?" This compelling issue discussed the full range of Buddhist lifestyle issues in America, from Buddhist marriage to children returning home to care for aging and dying parents. One article, "On Retreat for Twenty Years," even identified parenting as essential Buddhist practice. A number of years later—in Fall 1998—the journal identified an entire issue as the "Back-to-School Issue," discussing the Buddhist transformation of education . . . in the public schools, monastery, family, university, reform school, and the garden.

Summary and Conclusions

One of the most profound developments in the globalization of Buddhism is that the various traditions, once so distinct in their respective Asian homelands, now find themselves in close proximity for the first time in the history of Buddhism to one another in their new Western settings. It is not unusual for Theravada, Mahayana, and Vajrayana groups to find themselves neighbors in the same country, city, and even neighborhood. No doubt one can argue that this represents a great prosperity for the Buddhist tradition, but it also presents serious challenges and even liabilities as well. Is it possible to make some sense out of the seemingly conflicting emphases of these diverse Buddhist traditions and sects and schools? Is it possible to find some unifying principle or basis by which the huge diversity of global Buddhism might reestablish the sense of spiritual kinship among all Buddhists that prevailed in Buddha's original *sangha* of the four quarters?

Notes

1. See Michael Carrithers, " 'They Will Be Lords Upon the Island': Buddhism in Sri Lanka," in *The World of Buddhism: Buddhist Monks and Nuns*

in Society and Culture, eds. Heinz Bechert and Richard Gombrich (New York: Facts on File, 1984), 133.

2. *Saṃyutta Nikāya* XLV.2.2ff. See, for example, M. Leon Feer, ed., *Saṃyutta Nikāya*, Vol. 5, reprint (London: Luzac & Company, 1960), 2–3. I have added the italics for emphasis.

3. See Hammalawa Saddhatissa, *Buddhist Ethics*, 2nd edition (Boston: Wisdom Publications, 1997), 97. The passage in question reads: "Sādhu sambahulā ñāti api rukkhā arannajā, vāto vahati ekattham brahantam pi vanaspatiḥ."

4. See J. Estlin Carpenter, ed., *The Dīgha Nikāya*, Vol. 3, reprint (London: Luzac & Company, 1960), 180–93.

5. See Carpenter, *Dīgha Nikāya* III.189; verse 28 of the *Sigālovāda Sutta*. Translations from this text, here and throughout, are adapted from the those of T. W. Rhys Davids and C. A. F. Rhys Davids (published as *Dialogues of the Buddha*, Part 3, reprint [London: Luzac & Company, 1965]).

6. Kenneth Ch'en, *The Chinese Transformation of Buddhism* (Princeton: Princeton University Press, 1973), 19.

7. See Carpenter, *Dīgha Nikāya* III.190; verse 30 of the *Sigālovāda Sutta*.

8. Peter Harvey, *An Introduction to Buddhist Ethics* (Cambridge: Cambridge University Press, 2000), 101.

9. Emma McCloy Layman, *Buddhism in America* (Chicago: Nelson-Hall, 1976), 251–63.

10. Charles Prebish, *American Buddhism* (North Scituate, MA: Duxbury Press, 1979), 43–44.

11. Ibid., 188.

12. See Tweed's most recent chapter, "Who Is a Buddhist? Night-Stand Buddhists and Other Creatures," in *Westward Dharma: Buddhism Beyond Asia*, eds. Martin Baumann and Charles Prebish (Berkeley: University of California Press, 2002), 17–33.

13. See Stuart Chandler, "Chinese Buddhism in America: Identity and Practice," in *The Faces of Buddhism in America*, eds. Charles Prebish and Kenneth Tanaka (Berkeley: University of California Press, 1998), 17.

14. Barry A. Kosmin and Seymour P. Lachman, *One Nation under God: Religion in Contemporary American Society* (New York: Harmony Books, 1993), 3.

15. Martin Baumann, "The Dharma Has Come West: A Survey of Recent Studies and Sources," *Journal of Buddhist Ethics* 4 (1997): 198. See http://jbe.gold.ac.uk/4/baum2.html or ftp://scorpio/gold.ac.uk/pub/jbe/vol4/baum2.pdf (accessed 20 June 2002).

16. See Richard Hughes Seager's chapter, "Making Some Sense of Americanization," in his volume *Buddhism in America* (New York: Columbia University Press, 1999), 232–48.

17. A review of this topic can be found in Charles S. Prebish, *Luminous Passage: The Practice and Study of Buddhism in America* (Berkeley: University of California Press, 1999), 57–63.

18. Here I include Emma Layman's *Buddhism in America*, Charles Prebish's *American Buddhism*, Rick Fields's *How the Swans Came to the Lake: A Narrative History of Buddhism in America*, Charles Prebish and Kenneth Tanaka's *The Faces of Buddhism in America*, Charles Prebish's *Luminous Passage: The Practice and Study of Buddhism in America*, Duncan Ryūken Williams and Christopher S. Queen's *American Buddhism: Methods and Findings in Recent Scholarship*, Richard Seager's *Buddhism in America*, and James Coleman's *The New Buddhism: The Western Transformation of an Ancient Tradition*.

19. Layman, *Buddhism in America*, 198–99.

20. James Coleman, *The New Buddhism: The Western Transformation of an Ancient Tradition* (New York: Oxford University Press, 2001), 145–49.

21. See http://www.shambhala.org/member/simmer-brown.american buddhism.htm (accessed 24 June 2002).

22. See http://online.sfsu.edu/~rone/Buddhism/BuddhismParents/BuddhismParents.htm (accessed 24 June 2002).

23. See http://ourworld.compuserve.com/homepages/vanessa (accessed 24 June 2002). From there, all materials on the Buddhadharma for children are accessible.

24. See http://www.mro.org/zenkids/ (accessed 24 June 2002).

25. See http://www.mro.org/zmm/talks/teisho15.htm (accessed 24 June 2002).

26. See Phillip Hammond and David Machacek, *Sōka Gakkai in America* (New York: Oxford University Press, 1999), 43–44.

27. Ibid., 117.

28. See, for example, Irene Lin's "Journey to the Far West: Chinese Buddhism in America," *Amerasia Journal* 22:1 (1996): 107–32.

29. See http://www.fogbank.com/sbrc/library/webdocs/children.htm (accessed 9 July 2002).

30. See John Iwohara, "The Jodo Shinshu Ritual and Dharma School: A Proposed Rationale," *Hou-u: Dharma Rain* 1:2. See http://www.vbtemple. org/dharmarain/dr12_rit.htm (accessed 9 July 2002).

9

Buddha Loves Me This I Know

Nisei Buddhists in Christian America, 1889–1942

Lori Pierce

In the fall of 1939 two very interesting things happened to Tatsue Fujita, a Nisei[1] honor student at the University of Hawai'i. A talented and exceptionally bright young woman with a reputation as a particularly strong Buddhist, Tatsue won an essay contest sponsored by the Territorial Young Buddhist Association. The contest was meant to "stimulate interest in Buddhism" among young Nisei Buddhists. Junjiro Takakasu, a visiting Japanese scholar, was one of the judges. Fujita wrote an essay entitled "Buddhism as a Personal Experience." She argued that Buddhism was the best path to personal happiness because it acknowledged that intellect as well as intuition were necessary to achieve spiritual perfection. Quoting Ralph Waldo Emerson, William Blake, and the Dhammapada, she concluded that the truth of Buddhism lay in its transcendental nature. Further, she contended that Buddhism's compatibility with modern science verified its eminence as modern philosophy. "The light that shines immanent from the heart of Buddhism appears to me as being much stronger and more radiant than that of any other religion. . . . Today when modern science is turning from the objective accumulation of facts to the contemplation of mysteries, the teachings of Buddha which were expounded 2500 years ago are being increasingly substantiated by the latest pronouncements." Although this was not orthodox Shin theology, it was very much in accord with a growing sensibility about Buddhist modernism that was emerging in the West.[2]

Around the same time that Fujita won this contest, she also became the center of a community-wide controversy over her credentials as a potential teacher in the Hawai'i public school system. Fujita completed the required five years of training at the University of Hawai'i Teachers College (the former Territorial Normal School) with honors and the high praise of her teachers. Part of her training involved student teaching in the schools where she was observed by experienced teachers and supervisors. Although there is some dispute as to the actual facts of the case, what is known is that in spite of a spectacular academic reputation and the successful student training in the classroom, Fujita was denied her license to teach. It is suspected that one of her supervisors considered her too sympathetic to Japanese culture because of her heritage. According to Eileen Tamura, "Fujita agreed that she was interested in Japanese culture, but said it was secondary to her 'far greater interest and concern for the welfare of a democratic culture.' What she wanted to do . . . was 'to glean the best in both Oriental and Occidental culture,' as Nisei had 'repeatedly been urged to do."

Word reached the local Japanese newspapers and a public debate ensued. Had Fujita been denied her teaching license because she was insufficiently "Americanized"? Had her supervisors judged her more harshly based on her race and her insistence on maintaining a sense of her cultural integrity? Writing to Fujita, the dean of the Normal School, Benjamin Wist, said: "There is no direct charge of un-Americanness against you . . . [however] a question rose in my mind relative to your judgement in matters which might cast some reflection on an American public school teacher of American children. I did . . . ask you whether you are in the best position to judge what is best in terms of American democracy."[3]

In spite of appeals to the dean and the president of the university, and in spite of the power of the press that backed her cause, Fujita never realized her dream of being a school teacher. She returned to the University of Hawai'i and got a degree in philosophy. She subsequently moved to California and operated a small business. Apparently, she never spoke of the episode again.[4]

Eileen Tamura, who wrote about this episode in *Americanization, Acculturation and Ethnic Identity: The Nisei Generation in Hawaii*, did not mention Fujita's involvement in the Young Buddhist Association. Nor does she discuss the possibility that Fujita's Buddhism hindered her ability to convince the authorities at the normal school that she was no threat to the sound democratic education of "American" children.

Whether Buddhism was seen as too intimately tied to Japanese culture in the minds of the White Americans who judged Fujita is not known. What is known is that Buddhism was a suspect faith, an alien religion, often disparaged and nearly always misunderstood or misrepresented by Americans. But Buddhism, in spite of its ostensible foreignness and incompatibility with "American" virtues, was a primary means by which second-generation Japanese Americans forged their hybrid identities. Buddhism provided the most stable basis from which Nisei Buddhists could build an identity that comfortably bridged the gap between themselves and their Japanese parents. Although other cultural practices (family rituals, holiday celebrations, and language) were necessary frameworks of identity construction, Buddhism functioned both publicly and privately. It had the advantage of being a source of spiritual sustenance for individuals as they made their way through discriminatory institutions and racist incidents, but it also had the advantage of being a public, political expression of tolerance, democracy, and religious freedom. By claiming and publicly asserting their Buddhist identity, Nisei underscored their racial and religious difference as a challenge to the limits of White Christian American values of tolerance, democracy, and religious freedom. By refusing to adopt Christianity, Japanese American Buddhists made a public assertion of their identity that drew attention to the collapsed categories of White, Christian, and American.

Building Issei Buddhism

Both Hawai'i Hongwanji[5] and the North American Buddhist Mission (NABM) trace their origins in the United States to the very last years of the nineteenth century. By the 1890s Japanese immigration to the United States was beginning its ascendancy. Between 1890 and 1900, the number of Japanese in Hawai'i jumped from 12,610 to 61,111. The Pacific Coast states (California, Oregon, Washington, and Alaska) saw the numbers rise from 1,532 to 18,269. The illegal overthrow of the Hawaiian monarchy (1893) and subsequent annexation of Hawai'i to the United States (1898) had a significant impact on the pace and direction of immigration. Once the United States took control of Hawai'i, more emigrants began moving between Hawai'i and the Pacific Coast. Many used Hawai'i as a jumping off point, staying in Honolulu long enough to secure passage to the coast. In the wake of the Gentleman's Agreement of 1907, which required that

Japan further restrict its already restrictive emigration policies, the United States Congress prohibited the movement of Japanese from Hawai'i, Mexico, and Canada.[6]

Immigration to Hawai'i began slightly earlier than immigration to the Pacific Coast states. The first Japanese workers were recruited in 1868 to replace Chinese sugar plantation workers who refused to renew their short term labor contracts in favor of more lucrative opportunities. This first "crop" of laborers, however, proved to be unsatisfactory, and efforts to recruit Japanese workers for sugar and pineapple plantations did not resume until the late 1880s. The Hawai'i census recorded 116 Japanese in 1884; 12,360 in 1890; and 22,329 in 1896. The first American census of Hawai'i in 1900 reported a Japanese population of over 61,000.[7]

The first generation of Japanese immigrants to Hawai'i was older and larger than the first generation on the mainland. As was the case with Chinese immigration, men preceded women by many years. Japanese women did come to Hawai'i as workers, singly and as the wives of other laborers, but the vast majority of women who came as immigrants to Hawai'i and the Pacific Coast states arrived during Shashinkekekkon or the picture bride era of 1908–1921. The Gentleman's Agreement succeeded in cutting of the mass immigration of male laborers, but it left open a loophole that allowed those already in the United States or Hawai'i to send for their wives. Thus began a series of arranged marriages, which had the unintended (although entirely logical) consequence of facilitating the growth of the Japanese community. In spite of emigration restrictions, by 1920 the size of the community in the United States was more than double what it was in 1900.[8]

Most Japanese immigrants to Hawai'i and the United States were from provinces that had a reputation of being "heavily Buddhist" (Hiroshima, Yamaguchi, Wakayama, Okinawa, Kumamoto, and Fukuoka). Not only were they Buddhist, but they were provinces where Shin Buddhism—Pure Land Buddhism—was particularly popular. Pure Land Buddhist traditions developed in the twelfth and thirteenth centuries by Honen and his student Shinran. Pure Land Buddhism became popular in the countryside and rural farming communities because the rituals and practices were based on simple formulas that were easily memorized. In contrast to esoteric or meditation-based Buddhisms popular among the elite classes, Pure Land Buddhism was a simple expression of faith grounded in the daily lives of rural, working-class peoples. Eventually Soto Zen, Shingon, Nichiren, and Tendai Buddhism would also be transplanted to the

United States by Japanese immigrants. Pure Land Buddhist traditions became the largest and most popular because they were the tradition of the majority of Japanese immigrants to the United States.

Hawai'i Hongwanji marked the one hundredth anniversary of its founding in 1989, marking the genesis of Jodo Shinshu Buddhism in Hawai'i with the arrival of Soryu Kagahi in 1889. Kagahi was not an official representative of the *honzan* or headquarters of Nishi Hongwanji, but for the Japanese community in Hawai'i, his arrival signaled the emergence of organized religion in the tradition of their home country.

Kagahi arrived in Hawai'i to "investigate" the religious condition of Japanese emigrants, particularly their vulnerability to Christian conversion. Hawai'i had a long tradition of Christian missionary activity focused most acutely on Native Hawaiians, European and American sailors, and early Chinese migrants. These missionaries remained vigilant and constantly policed Hawai'i for signs of "reparganization." Although there was some effort to convert Japanese immigrants to Christianity, the isolation of the plantations from the major population centers and the language barrier between workers and missionaries hindered most serious efforts.[9]

In the absence of Buddhist clergy, immigrants improvised. In Japan, Buddhist priests were primarily called on to officiate at funerals. When a Japanese worker died in Hawai'i, the community relied on their own memories in order to recreate the proper rituals. Those who wished to recite texts or chant as part of their own spiritual practice gathered together in small informal groups, but the working and living conditions of most plantation workers made this nearly impossible.

In addition, Kagahi traveled throughout the islands, and when he returned to Japan, he reported on the dire religious needs of the Japanese community. Not only were they in need of clergy to oversee religious rituals, but Kagahi noted that they also needed pastoral and social care. Isolated and far from home, many took to gambling and drinking. It took several years, but eventually, in 1897, an official representative of the Nishi Hongwanji, Ejun Miyamoto, was sent to Hawai'i to establish a missionary outpost. Less than a year later Miyamoto was again dispatched to the West, this time to San Francisco to investigate the situation of Buddhist immigrants on the Pacific Coast. Miyamoto and Eryu Honda arrived in San Francisco and in 1899, two permanent missionaries, Shuye Sonoda and Kakuryo Nishijima, were sent to establish the North American Buddhist Mission (NABM), which during World War II became known as the Buddhist Churches of America (BCA).[10]

The growth of Buddhism in Hawai'i and the Pacific Coast states ran along parallel tracks and followed similar trajectories. In both cases the first official gathering of Buddhists resulted in the organizing of Young Buddhist associations. The Young Men's (and later Women's) Buddhist Association was founded in Japan in 1894. Christian missionaries and YMCA leaders had a great influence on young men and women in Meiji Japan, particularly those in urban areas and in the new, Western-style educational institutions. Yemyo Imamura, who would head Hawai'i Hongwanji for more than thirty years, and Sonoda and Nishijima in California were steeped in the religious, social, and political foment that was affecting Meiji Japan. In the case of Imamura, we know that he attended two progressively minded educational institutions, was a member of a temperance organization (*hanseikai*) and regularly wrote for their journal, exhorting young Buddhists to be independent in their thinking and throw off the old-fashioned religious leadership to which they had grown accustomed. As a young college student in the 1880s Imamura called for the formation of a young Buddhist organization and may have been one of the founding members of what became the International YBA.[11]

Paul David Numrich, studying Thai Buddhist temples in Chicago in the late twentieth century, coined the term "parallel congregations" as a way of describing the simultaneous existence of two groups within the same Buddhist temple. Thai Buddhists and White Buddhists were both members of the same temple, but participated in two very different sets of rituals and practices that rarely overlapped. Although they operated from the same institutions with the same teachers, Numrich found that the experience of Buddhism for the Thai immigrants was quite unlike what White converts were encountering. These parallel congregations served distinctive functions, often came together for common purposes, but most often moved alongside one another with little tension or sustained interaction.[12]

Issei and Nisei Buddhists in the early twentieth century operated in this same kind of parallel structure. The congregations functioned as one entity, but for Issei, Buddhism was expressed in terms of the customary practices, familiar language, and familiar rituals of their homeland and childhood. For the Nisei, who were often alienated from the "foreign" nature of the language and rituals, Buddhism took on a more activist and social orientation. As the first generation of American Buddhists, they needed to find ways to express American identity within a Buddhist context. This they did through their organizations and rhetorical assertions of American Buddhist identity.

Buddhist Americans: Nisei Buddhist Identity

The Nisei are perhaps the most written about and studied generation in Japanese American history. In Hawai'i and on the mainland they comprised the largest segment of the Japanese population and, as was the case with other immigrant communities, the second generation was the focus of discussions of assimilation and ethnic American identity.

In the Nisei generation we begin to see the distinctions between the Japanese community in Hawai'i and in the Pacific Coast states and the United States mainland. The Nisei in Hawai'i were slightly older than those in the United States, their parents having arrived in Hawai'i as early as 1885 (women arrived in larger numbers after 1900). Hawai'i Nisei were coming of age in the 1920s. Mainland Nisei were a few years behind; the WRA survey indicated that about 25 percent of the approximately 110,000 Japanese interned during World War II were Nisei born between 1918 and 1927.[13]

Other differences between the two communities were important; in Hawai'i, Nisei were more likely to have grown up in small, relatively isolated plantation towns among a multi-ethnic mix of immigrant workers from Portugal, China, Puerto Rico, Korea, and the Philippines. They would have gone to school with this eclectic mix of children and their Hawaiian neighbors and friends, but with a paucity of *haole* or White children. Their language was strongly influenced by the Creole that developed on plantations. Because of the greater number of Buddhist temples in Hawai'i, they were more likely than their mainland counterparts to have attended a Japanese language school and were also more likely to have been sent away to a boarding school in their adolescence because of the dearth of secondary educational opportunities in the rural areas of Hawaii.

Hawai'i born Japanese Americans in rural areas would have had greater access to Buddhist temples and missions. By 1918, less than twenty years after the official founding of the mission, there were thirty-three branch temples in plantation towns as small and isolated as Hana, Maui. In contrast, the NABM had built fewer temples that were dispersed over a wider region.[14] Simply put, Hawai'i Hongwanji was more successful at building Buddhist institutions, a fact that can be attributed to the greater size of the Hawai'i Japanese community and the concentration of communities on plantations. Statistically, however, the number of Buddhists reflects a great deal of movement and flexibility within the community.

An accurate number of Buddhists in the Japanese community
has been difficult to gauge. Part of the problem has been that historically Buddhist institutions enumerated their membership based
on families rather than individuals. Since the United States census
did not officially count religious affiliation, historians and sociolo-
gists have relied on self-reporting and a variety of surveys in order
to ascertain religious statistics.

Sociological surveys in the years before World War II consistently reported that the majority of Japanese, Issei, and Nisei were
affiliated with a Buddhist temple. This was true in Hawai'i and on the
United States mainland. Also true was the fact that urban residents
were less likely to be Buddhist than rural residents, and that the Issei
had a higher proportion of Buddhists than the Nisei. Additionally,
those employed in agricultural work were more likely to be Buddhist
than those in non-agricultural work.

David Yoo sums up the confusing statistics in this way: "Stanford professor Edward Strong's survey in the early 1930s found that
78% of the Issei claimed Buddhism while only 18% had taken up
the Christian faith. In a more comprehensive, if problematic, survey
taken by the War Relocation Authority in 1942, 68% of all immigrants
interned in World War II camps reported a Buddhist affiliation, compared to 21.9% Christian. The figures for the Nisei showed gains for
Christianity, but Buddhism still accounted for a greater percentage of
the second generation: 48.7% Buddhist and 35% Christian."[15]

The statistics for Hawai'i are equally unreliable—perhaps more
so because no systematic survey has ever been taken of the entire
Japanese community in Hawai'i. The 1896 census in Hawai'i indicated
that 96.9 percent of Japanese in Hawai'i were Buddhists, but since
the census asked about affiliation with Christian denominations, and
nearly all Japanese in Hawai'i at the time responded "no Christian
religion or no religion reported," this figure is worse than useless.
The General Superintendent of the Census resigned himself to a state
of "ignorance, unable to distinguish between Buddhists, followers of
Confusius, and those who refused to declare a preference."[16]

Statistician Robert C. Schmitt has also been unable to represent
accurately the number of Buddhists in the early years of the territorial period. The primary difficulty lies in the fact that when report-
ing church memberships, no consistent standard was used. Schmitt
noted that his figures "were based on information supplied by the
various denominations, which often used widely differing definitions
of membership and failed to adjust for duplications and overlap."[17]
Drawing on data first reported in *Thrum's Annual*, Schmitt recorded

40,000 Buddhists in 1905, and 33,900 in 1909.[18] A 1940 report to the Pan-Pacific Forum recorded a total of nearly 50,000 members of the six Buddhist sects and called this total "35 percent of the entire Japanese population in Hawai'i."[19] These numbers seem deceptively low given the proliferation of temples being built in Hawai'i during the early territorial period. Without the means to be precise, a measure of speculation will have to suffice. It is likely that in Hawai'i, the number of Nisei Buddhists was lower than the number of Issei Buddhists, as it was on the mainland.

Both Gary Okihiro and David Yoo have argued that Nisei Buddhist identity operated as a form of resistance to oppression and discrimination. Writing about Buddhism in World War II internment camps, Okihiro suggests that Buddhism grew stronger, especially among those who resisted internment (the so-called no-no boys) and that under the dire conditions of camp life, Issei and Nisei grew stronger in their faith.[20] In this Okihiro echoes the work of Tetsuden Kashima, who argued that after the passage of the 1924 Immigration Act, the number of Buddhists on the Pacific Coast actually rose.[21]

David Yoo contends that for the Nisei generation, Buddhism provided opportunities for leadership, networking, and community building. He also contends that "Buddhists forged a sense of self that embraced the very markers of racial and religious difference used against them. The faith of their mothers and fathers enabled the second generation to affirm their ancestry and at the same time lay claim to their status as Americans."[22] How did they accomplish this? By not converting to Christianity, by actively participating in Buddhist-sponsored activities and thereby choosing a public identification as American Buddhists, they used these social occasions to discuss their emerging sense of American Buddhist identity and critique the actions and politics of White Christian Americans in light of the discrimination they faced.

As we have seen, there was a relatively small number of Christians in the Japanese community before World War II. Many Japanese Christians had converted before emigration to the United States. Those who converted were more likely to have been employed in non-agricultural industries, to have lived in an urban environment. There were far more Nisei than Issei Christians.[23] However, conversion to Christianity did not seem to have been a major source of tension within families. In fact, conversion or joining a Christian church or group activity seems to have been treated fairly casually on the part of many Nisei. In some cases, especially in the absence of Buddhist-sponsored schools or churches, conversion was accidental or situational. One

Nisei reported: "Dad worked in the mill and mother did housekeeping. That's why they sent us all to kindergarten and later we became involved in Sunday school and all the clubs. It kept us out of trouble and off the streets. Religion didn't really have much to do with it at first."[24] In Hawai'i, students were often sent off to secondary education in Honolulu or other larger towns. Many of these were private Christian schools, so the choice of school necessarily had an impact on future religious affiliation. Even those attending public school often boarded in either the Christian or Buddhist boarding houses; religious affiliation was affected by these living arrangements.

Many Nisei reported that their parents did not discourage their interest in other religions. Even those who were "strong Buddhists" encouraged their children to find their own faith. Although many Issei wanted to raise their children as Buddhists, many conceded that Christianity may have been a more appropriate choice for their children. One Nisei summed it up rather concretely: "My parents are Buddhists but they have not made me one. Their opinion is that I choose my own religion. I chose the Christian religion because I knew it would help me in my future work."[25] He clearly recognized that, because it was the dominant religion of the country, Christianity would give him opportunities to meet those of a higher social class, or at the very least, mollify discrimination against him.

Nisei who chose Christianity, either casually because of a chance friendship or the opportunity to attend school, ended up in the awkward situation of embracing a religious institution that was having a very difficult time accepting them. This was more true on the mainland than in Hawai'i where Christianity was several generations old among Hawaiians.[26] Christian Nisei identity entailed an existential crisis; in order to identify as Christian and American, Nisei Christians had to either ignore or rationalize the fact that many White American Christians objected to their presence in the country. Nisei Buddhists could express an oppositional sense of American identity that took advantage of the marginal status of Buddhism and use it as a means of underscoring American values of tolerance and religious freedom and Buddhist values of accommodation and adaptation to surroundings.

Nisei Buddhists embraced the opportunities provided by Hawai'i Hongwanji and the NABM to participate in social, community-building opportunities. In Hawai'i and North America, Japanese communities were often dispersed over a wide area with few chances to gather. Although Japanese were nearly 40 percent of the population of Hawai'i, they often lived in dispersed communities among other ethnic immigrant groups. Boy Scouts, sports leagues, community outreach programs and, most notably, the Young Buddhist associations gave Nisei the opportunity to network with other Nisei, forming future personal and business alliances and creating opportunities for leadership. The members of the YBA were young adults, just out of high school or in college (there were "junior" YBAs for younger, high school–aged Buddhists) and were therefore well aware of their surroundings, of local, national, and international politics and their own responsibilities in the future.

Dobo, the newspaper of the Hawai'i YBA, often focused on the growing tension between Japan and the United States, and editorial writers and correspondents diligently worked to express both their loyalty to the parents and home culture and to the United States. In September, 1941, Ralph Honda, the president of the Hawai'i Federation of Young Buddhist Associations, expressed in no uncertain terms the attitude Nisei should take toward the coming confrontation. That he expressed his expectations in the form of the Eightfold Path illustrates the degree to which Nisei Buddhists used their faith to publicly assert their American identity. In adapting the Eightfold Path to the looming crisis of world war, Honda exhorted the delegates to the convention to redouble their efforts to be loyal Americans: "We are American citizens enjoying the rights and privileges that only a democracy can give. There remains but one view to take and that is to be loyal to our country, the United States of America." Right action entailed "gain[ing] the confidence of our fellow Americans . . . [to] show loyalty and dependability. This also implies that we should refrain from thoughtless actions which might cause misunderstanding." Right livelihood required "remain[ing] law abiding citizens of our community and our country. We have before us an unparalleled opportunity to prove that we are good and loyal citizens by living rightfully during this crisis, even at the expense of self-sacrifice."[27] Buddhism here became the mode of expression of the most deeply felt of American values, those which are expressed in the face of extreme crisis.

Periodicals like *Dobo*, *Bhratri*, and *Berkeley Bussei* also worked to educate Nisei Buddhists about the history, philosophy and practice of Buddhism. These journals reprinted the speeches and articles of scholars of Japanese religion, and took advantage of the number of White Buddhists who were expressing Buddhism in the Western idiom in a way to which the Nisei could more easily relate. Hawai'i Buddhists were able to take advantage of the services of Dorothy and Ernest Hunt, two British Buddhists who were ordained by Bishop Imamura and headed up the English Department of Hongwanji. Through the

English Department, Imamura and the Hunts ran Sunday School programs, community outreach, and special classes for Nisei on their
Buddhist faith. The result was an entirely unique expression of Buddhism that was neither fully Japanese nor fully European in its orientation. Tatsue Fujita's winning essay is one example, but many Nisei
expressed themselves in Buddhist journals and newspapers. Following the lead of modern Buddhist scholars—British, American, and
Japanese—they wrote about their faith in terms that often ignored
the specifics of Shin theology and faith and instead focused on what
might be called a pan-Buddhist Universalism. Nisei Buddhists who
were exposed to this nonsectarian Buddhism were attracted to its
progressive style and modern idiom.

It is these public expressions of their Buddhist identity that are
crucial in determining the salience of Buddhism in the construction of
Nisei as both American and Buddhist. The fact that the Nisei publicly
embraced, celebrated, and enriched Buddhism, offering it as a credible
alternative to Christianity, helped them to build a bridge to their parents in a way no other cultural practice could. Language often proved
too difficult to teach and sustain in the American context. Operating
for only an hour or two a day, it was nearly impossible for students
to learn enough Japanese to communicate fully and articulately with
their parents.[28] Children in Hawai'i communicated through a compli-
cated mix of Creole, English, and pidgin Japanese. Only those Kibei
who were sent back to Japan for their education could claim language
as a bridge between the Issei and Nisei generations.

The public assertion of Buddhist identity by the Nisei generation was also a direct challenge to the American values of religious
freedom, democracy, and tolerance. The claim that Japanese were
incapable of becoming "fully American" because they were "Mikado
worshippers" was a favorite red herring of race-baiters. It suggested
that no matter what their religious faith, Japanese were inculcated to
believe in the divinity of the emperor. Interviewing Issei women at
the YWCA during the war, Yukiko Kimura explored this question.
She surveyed nearly four hundred Issei women and found that over
90 percent did not believe in the divinity of the emperor. Their general expression was as follows: "Although we have never seen him,
we know that he is a human being just like us. . . . Of course we use
[the same term] for both worshipping Buddha or gods and for seeing
the emperor. We used the same term when President Roosevelt was
here . . . The president is the highest in this country, so we gave him
our highest reverence."[29]

Finally, Nisei Buddhists, by their existence and their public
exploration of the meaning of their existence, offered a direct challenge

to the forces of Americanization, especially those which suggest that the most direct path to American conformity was through religious identity. For those who believed that Christian values and American values were synonymous, there was no question that conversion to Christianity was a necessary step in the process of becoming fully American. These proponents, both Japanese and White, faced the challenge of convincing Nisei that conversion was not an expression of disloyalty to their families or that Christian values were compatible with Japanese cultural values. In spite of Christianity's universalism, this proved to be a much more difficult task than convincing the Nisei that they could remain Buddhist and still be loyal Americans.

In the end, for most Nisei before World War II, Buddhism provided the most stable bridge between the cultures that defined their self-consciousness. By remaining Buddhists, the Nisei could affirm their innate connection with their parents' homeland, their customs and traditions, language, food and values. Buddhism, especially the modern, progressive Buddhism that emerged from Meiji Japan in the late nineteenth century, was remarkably flexible and open to rhetorical and symbolic shifts that accommodated Japanese and American values. Other cultural practices and institutions, especially language, did not in the end provide the structure the Nisei needed to bridge the gap between themselves and their parents. Nisei regularly lamented having to attend language school; few, if any, achieved anything approaching fluency in the language and spoke to their parents in a functional, if not grammatically correct patois. This was especially the case in Hawai'i where a true Creole developed; Issei and Nisei were more likely to communicate in "pidgin" than in fluent Japanese or fluent English.

Buddhism, in the end, provided the most stable basis for the construction of a hybrid Nisei identity—one that was fully Japanese and fully American. The price, as we saw in the case of Tatsue Fujita, could be high. Growing up Buddhist in Christian America was, for some, a perilous journey. But for most second-generation Japanese Americans, Buddhism was a flexible presence that facilitated their ability to adapt to the United States and create a new American Buddhist identity.

Notes

1. Japanese immigrants are referred to by generational nomenclature: Issei refers to first generation or those who migrated from Japan to the United States. Nisei refers to the second generation, the children of the Issei. Sansei

is the third generation; Yonsei, fourth generation, and so forth. Nikkei can be used to refer to Japanese Americans as a whole; Kibei is used to refer to those born in the United States but sent back to Japan to be educated.

2. "YWBA of Hawai'i Girl, Miss Tatsue Fujita, wins YBA Essay Prize," *Dobo*, September 1939.

3. Eileen Tamura, *Americanization, Acculturation and Ethnic Identity: The Nisei Generation in Hawaii* (Philadelphia: Temple University Press, 1991), 47.

4. Tamura, *Americanization*, 49.

5. In Japan, the main temple of the Pure Land tradition is referred to as Hongwanji. Nishi and Higashi Hongwanji ("west" and "east" temples) are the headquarters of the two dominant sects of Shin Buddhism. The branches of these temples in Hawai'i, the United States, and Canada developed independently from one another and are, therefore, referred to in a variety of ways by local communities. In Hawai'i many Buddhist temples retain Hongwanji in their names. During World War II, however, the North American Buddhist Mission officially changed its name to Buddhist Churches of America, abandoning most of the Japanese nomenclature associated with the temples.

6. Paul Spickard, *Japanese Americans: The Formation and Transformations of an Ethnic Group* (New York: Twayne Publishers, 1996), 30.

7. Robert Schmitt, *Demographic Statistics of Hawai'i: 1778–1965* (Honolulu: University of Hawai'i Press, 1968), 75; 120.

8. The population grew from 85,000 to over 200,000. See Spickard, *Japanese Americans*, 163.

9. The most important exception to this rule would have been Reverend Takie Okumura who founded Makiki Christian Church in 1904. Okumura, who arrived in Hawai'i in 1894, was a tireless missionary among Japanese immigrants who worked against formidable odds and the rather more formidable presence of Yemyo Imamura, his Buddhist rival. For a perspective on their rivalry, see Louise Hunter, *Buddhism in Hawaii: Its Impact on a Yankee Community* (Honolulu: University of Hawai'i Press, 1971). For a completely different orientation to the same events, see Takie Okumura, *Seventy Years of Divine Blessings* (Honolulu: Takie Okumura, 1940).

10. For a brief discussion of the name change and other changes made during the war, see Tetsuden Kashima, *Buddhism in America: The Social Organization of an Ethnic Religious Institution* (Westport, CT: Greenwood Press, 1977), 47ff.

11. On Imamura, see Tomoe Moriya, *Yemyo Imamura: Pioneer American Buddhist*, trans. Tsuneichi Takeshita, ed. Alfred Bloom and Ruth Tabrah (Honolulu: Buddhist Study Center Press, 2000). On the founding of the YBA, see Judith Snodgrass, *Presenting Japanese Buddhism to the West: Orientalism, Occidentalism, and the Columbian Exposition* (Chapel Hill: University of North Carolina Press, 2003).

12. See Paul David Numrich, *Old Wisdom in the New World: Americanization in Two Immigrant Theravada Buddhist Temples* (Knoxville: University of Tennessee Press, 1996).

13. Spickard, *Japanese Americans*, 167; see also Dorothy Swaine Thomas, Charles Kikuchi, and James Sakoda, *The Salvage* (Berkeley: University of California Press, 1952), 580.

14. Kashima lists twenty-three Buddhist temples or branches built by 1918 on the mainland, seventeen in California. Most were located in larger metropolitan areas such as Fresno, Stockton, Los Angeles, San Francisco, and Sacramento. A very few were in small towns such as Watsonville, Florin, Hanford, and Guadalupe.

15. David Yoo, "Enlightened Identities: Buddhism and Japanese Americans of California, 1924–1941," *Western Historical Quarterly* 27 (Autumn 1996): 287.

16. Cited in Andrew Lind, "Religious Diversity in Hawai'i," *Social Process in Hawai'i* 16 (1952): 11–12.

17. Robert C. Schmitt, "Religious Statistics of Hawai'i," *Hawaiian Journal of History* 7 (1973): 45.

18. Schmitt, "Religious Statistics of Hawai'i," 44, table 3. This seems to suggest that only 40 percent of the entire Japanese population were members of the Buddhist church. Given the number of children enrolled in Japanese-language schools and the growth of the Young Buddhist associations, not to mention the explosive growth of the number of temples and branches between 1900 and 1935, this number seems incredibly low. But, if memberships are counted by households and registered in the names of the male head of the household, the percentage increases significantly. Membership was probably counted by the number of members of the *kyodan*, the group responsible for supporting the temple by making family contributions. If these men were generally older heads of households, over the age of thirty, for example, and we know that in 1910 there were 46,500 Japanese males over the age of thirty, Schmitt's figure of 33,900 "members" is perhaps low. But, if we could subtract from that the number of men in that age group who were members of the Young Buddhist Association, we might be able to derive a more accurate figure. According to Katsumi Onishi, men remained members of the Young Buddhist Association until their father passed away. Then the oldest son would be responsible for taking his father's place in the *kyodan*. Younger sons could join or remain members of the YBA. So, one number representing "Buddhists in Hawai'i in 1910," for example, would have to be calculated from a number of sources, most of which are not available. See Katsumi Onishi, "The Second Generation Japanese and the Hongwanji," *Social Process in Hawaii* 3 (1937): 43–48. Figures based on Eleanor C. Nordyke, *The Peopling of Hawai'i* (Honolulu: University of Hawai'i Press, 1989).

19. Kenju Ohtomo, "Buddhism in Hawaii," *Pan Pacific Forum* (January–March 1940), 21. The six sects are Nishi Hongwanji, Higashi Hongwanji, Jodo Shu, Soto, Shingon, Nichiern, and "others," probably meaning members of smaller sects and new religions such as Tenrikyo and Kempon Kokke Shu.

20. See Gary Okihiro, "Religion and Resistance in America's Concentration Camps," *Phylon* 45: 3 (1984): 220–33. Ironically, the interment provided

an interesting opportunity for pan-Buddhist affiliation. Many Japanese priests were deported; the few who were interred were pressed into duty for the entire community in spite of denominational differences. Furthermore, itinerant Buddhists like Sokei-an and Nyogen Senzaki who attracted a following among non-Japanese adherents and sympathizers were also an important presence in the camps. For fuller discussion, see Brian Masuru Hayashi, *Democratizing the Enemy: The Japanese American Internment* (Princeton, NJ: Princeton University Press, 2004) and *For the Sake of Our Japanese Brethren: Assimilation, Nationalism, and Protestantism among the Japanese of Los Angeles, 1895–1942* (Stanford: Stanford University Press, 1995). On Senzaki, see Rick Fields, *How the Swans Came to the Lake: A Narrative History of Buddhism in America*, 3rd ed. (Boulder, CO: Shambhala Press, 1995). On Sokei-an, see *Holding the Lotus to the Rock: The Autobiography of Sokei-an, America's First Zen Master*, ed. Michael Hotz (New York: Four Walls Eight Windows, 2003).

21. Ogura argued that in response to the blatant racism of the 1924 Immigration Act, many who had been reluctant to be actively Buddhist in a Christian country now became defiantly and self-consciously Buddhist. Kashima concurred, and noted that temple building had slowed after 1918, but picked up again after 1924. Of course, it could also be the case that temple building and Buddhist identity picked up in this era because of the number of children being born. Between 1910 and 1930 the number of Japanese on the Pacific Coast nearly doubled. The census of American internment camps indicates that the largest single group of Nisei was between fifteen and twenty-four years of age in 1942, born between 1918 and 1927.

22. Yoo, "Enlightened Identities," 281.

23. Thomas et al., *The Salvage*, 65–70.

24. Norman Knowles, "Religious Affiliation, Demographic Change and Family Formation among British Columbia's Chinese and Japanese Communities: A Case Study of Church of England Missions," *Canadian Ethnic Studies* 27:2 (1995): 65.

25. "Life Histories of Students," William Carlson Smith Papers, University of Oregon Special Collections, 1926–1927, Microfilm Reel 7, No. 198.

26. This is not to suggest that White Christians in Hawai'i did not share the paternalistic and sometimes bigoted, racist attitudes of Christians in the United States. Quite the contrary. The Hawai'i Evangelical Board regularly warned of the influx of pagan influence in Hawai'i and chastised Hawaiians for backsliding, allowing their heathen religious practice to creep back into the popular culture.

27. Ralph Honda, "Honda Advocates Eightfold Path to YBA Delegates," *Dobo*, September 1941, n.p.

28. On Japanese-language schools and education, see David Yoo, *Growing Up Nisei: Race, Generation and Culture among Japanese Americans of California 1924–1949* (Urbana: University of Illinois Press, 2000).

29. Yukiko Kimura, "A Study of the Pattern of Religious Concepts of the Japanese in Hawai'i," included in Japanese Evacuation and Resettlement Records, Bancroft Library, University of California, Berkeley, Reel 371, 136–38.

10

Analogue Consciousness Isn't Just for Faeries

Healing the Disjunction between Theory and Practice

Roger Corless

Buddhism and Christianity, although poles apart in their understanding of what is ultimately real, propose structurally similar ways of resolving the perceived division between the universal (or absolute) and the particular (or relative).[1] Both traditions profess a view of reality that is ultimately nondual, but in practice both are frequently dualistic, displaying world-denying features, opposing the body to the soul or mind, and often being sexist and homophobic. This essay will first review the worldviews of Buddhism and Christianity, the structural similarity of their respective goals, and the disjunction between theories of equality and the practice of inequality. Second, it will suggest that the cause of the disjunction between theory and practice is an unexamined, reified, heterosexist symbol system existing below the level of institutional consciousness. Because it is reified it assumes a real, rather than merely operational, split between subject and object, and it therefore compels the traditions to act in dualistic ways that contradict the nonduality of their publicly professed doctrines.

To heal the disjunction, an alternative, homophilic symbol structure will be proposed, based on Harry Hay's notion of the analogue or subject-SUBJECT consciousness. This symbol structure, it will be asserted, allows both Christianity and Buddhism to accept nonduality in practice as well as theory. The symbol structure can exist alongside the traditional models and is not intended to replace them. Both models can be understood as operational, and their interaction should prevent either Buddhism or Christianity from falling into the misplaced reification of hard dogma. If the alternative symbol structure is accepted along with the traditional symbol structure, the result should be more inclusive forms of Buddhism and Christianity in which their practice could be brought more effectively into line with their high teachings.

Since this chapter is appearing in a volume on Buddhism, a word in defense of the comparison with Christianity is perhaps necessary. It is no longer possible (if indeed it ever was) to study religions in isolation, as if they were static and lifeless, like dead butterflies in a display case. Religions are dynamic, interacting with each other and with the cultures in which they are embedded. This is especially true in the twenty-first-century United States, where all religions are accorded equal protection under the law, so that it is possible to have comparisons that do not privilege the truth of one tradition over another, and that permit each to illuminate the other. The comparison of Buddhism and Christianity is especially fruitful, since their worldviews are so different that the similarity in their disjunctions between theory and practice cannot be attributed to internal causes alone. There must be something about human consciousness in general that has allowed two such different systems to make the same mistake. Thus, we proceed first to lay out the differences.

Opposite Worldviews

When Christian and Buddhist worldviews are compared, the discussion often focuses on something called the "Absolute." The notion that a worldview has as a matter of course an Absolute is taken for granted, and God—or more exactly, "the Trinity"—is identified as the Christian Absolute. A search is then made for the Buddhist Absolute, and various candidates for this honor are proposed: the historical Buddha Shakyamuni; a cosmic Buddha such as Vairochana; the Dharmakaya; and even the law of *karma*. The search is spurious, however, since the Buddhist worldview does not have a placeholder for the "Absolute." This is one of its chief differences from certain forms of Hinduism. If we shift our investigation from the search for the Absolute to a search for the ultimate focus of concern, we would still come up with God for the Christian tradition, but the Buddhist tradition would yield "interdependent arising" (*pratityasamutpada*).

When we try to compare God and interdependent arising, we find it is worse than comparing apples and oranges. Apples and oranges, although very different, are not so different that they cannot be subsumed under the single term "fruit," but God and interdependent arising exist in different worldviews. And since worldviews are by definition autonomous absolutes, designed to find a place for and an explanation of everything, there does not seem to be any way that God and interdependent arising could be compared or contrasted. This is what makes dialog between Buddhism and Christianity so interesting: How can there be two proposals about the nature of reality that are so different that they do not seem to be speaking about the same reality? Is there, in fact, more than one reality?[2] The relevant question here, however, is the delineation of *God* and *interdependent arising* as ultimate foci of concern within their own worldviews.

God is such a common word in English that we might think we know what it means, although the mystics and theologians—being for once in agreement—insist that we cannot know God except partially and imperfectly. We can, however, get a pretty good handle on the *concept* of God. The God of the Christian tradition is eternal: that is to say, beginningless, existing before there was anything and then creating everything. Since creation includes time as well as space, it is a puzzle how God could have existed "before" creation. The puzzle is partially solved by understanding "before" in an ontological rather than a temporal sense. As Mother Julian says, God is the ground of our beseeching—that is, God is the ultimate given, absent which there would be nothing. The God of the Christian tradition is not a being inhabiting a preexisting karmic matrix. If that were so, the Christian God would fit into the Buddhist worldview as Ishvara (or equivalents such as Brahma and Shakra). Such a God could readily be understood by Buddhists, and as readily dismissed as a fantasy.

In contrast to the Christian tradition of an Absolute God, interdependent arising has been called "radical relativism," and so it may seem at first, since in this view everything is relative to everything else. Yet on the other hand, interdependent arising is not opposed to an Absolute and so it cannot be labeled "relative" in a colloquial sense. Some forms of Hinduism propose a subtle continuum in which events take place. Buddhism denies the existence of such a continuum, and when it has crept in it has been strongly challenged.[3] Interdependent arising is inarguable. It is seen to be the case by Buddha, and we are told that we shall see it when we become buddhas, but until then we must be satisfied with partial explanations and provocative experiences that allow us to accept that the teaching is reasonable and probable. Similarly, as we learned in Philosophy 101, God cannot be proved to exist, but God's existence can be shown to be reasonable (*rationabilis*) and probable.

If interdependent arising is the case, everything occurs because it is conditioned by everything else that occurs, and everything that occurs conditions the occurrence of everything else. In this world-view things don't go "back" to a beginning: the notion of *beginning* is meaningless. The conditioning of the conditioning goes "on" end-lessly rather than "back." Cyclic existence (*samsara*) is, like a complex iterative function, infinitely deep but bounded. It follows immediately that there is no way to understand, in a worldview of interdependent arising, the existence of the God of the Christian tradition. Buddhism is not atheistic, as the Christian missionaries to Asia thought, nor is it, as Heinrich Zimmer has proposed, "trans-theistic" (that is, bypassing the Christian God). Instead, Buddhism has no way of taking any posi-tion vis-à-vis the Christian God. The concept cannot be translated into the Buddhist universe of discourse. On the other hand, if the existence of God of the Christian tradition is the case, interdependent arising makes no sense. Things must go "back" to an uncaused Cause; they cannot merely condition each other.

Compared to the gulf between God and interdependent aris-ing, the other differences between the two worldviews seem minor. Christianity reports that a gap opened up between God and creation due to the disobedience, the sin, of humans, and that this gap is closed by Christ, who both incorporates the Christian and is incor-porated in the Christian, with the optimal result of participation in and divinization by the dying and rising Christ. Buddhism observes that life as experienced is suffering, and traces the suffering to the unskillful choices of the unaware mind (*avidya*), while affirming in both the Theravada and Mahayana traditions *mutatis mutandis*, that suffering is not the way reality ultimately is nor is unawareness the true state of mind. Buddhism, then, offers a series of tools, therapies, or medicines designed to help beings to become completely aware and to end their suffering.

So much for the differences. What is surprising is that, as is so often noticed in Buddhist-Christian dialog, there is a powerful reso-nance between these disparate worldviews. Their paths and goals, although mutually incomprehensible, are structurally similar, and the problems that they both have in fitting practice to theory appear to have similar causes.

Structural Similarities

Both traditions propose that reality as we find it is disconnected from reality as it truly is or truly should be.

The Christian story begins with the creation of the world as good, and humans as images or icons of God (Genesis 1: 27, LXX: *kat' eikona theou*). The disobedience of Adam and Eve in Genesis, chapter 3 is interpreted by Christianity as having cosmic, rather than—as Judaism usually interprets it—merely personal consequences, throwing the whole of creation into enmity with God. The gap between the creatures and the Creator is said to be unbridgeable from the side of the creature, and the whole of creation is thus condemned to futility and death. God's love is, however, so great that he builds a bridge in his own person as Jesus Christ, living a human life from birth to death, intimately participating in the suffering of humanity. Because the human Jesus is also God, he overcomes death, conquering it and sin once and for all. This so-called Work of Christ is taught by all Christian groups, although the mechanism by which it was brought about is discussed at length, and many different theories are advanced. After at least the First Council of Nicaea (325 CE), and in some ways before it, all theories on the Work of Christ are based on the doctrine of the simultaneous presence of full humanity and full divinity in Christ. The technical term that has become standard for this simultaneous presence of two forms of being normally considered to be opposite and mutually exclusive is the Greek *perichōr sis*, which went into Latin first as *circumincessio* and then as *circuminsessio*. In English it is known as circumincession, circuminsession, or co-inherence. The intent of these terms is to indicate that all of Christ's humanity is enclosed in his divinity and all of his divinity is enclosed in his humanity.

Co-inherence is a structure that resonates throughout Christian tradition. Charles Williams tells the history of the Church as the co-inherence of the physical with the Holy Spirit.[4] Meister Eckhart claims that co-inherence is a law of the spiritual world:

> There is a difference between spiritual things and bodily things. Every spiritual thing can dwell in another; but nothing bodily can exist in another. There may be water in a tub, and the tub surrounds it, but where the wood is, there is no water. In this sense, no material thing dwells in another, but every spiritual thing does dwell in another.[5]

When co-inherence is extended in this way to the incorporation of Christ in the Christian and the Christian in Christ (for example, John 15: 9–10) and the actual or potential divinization of all creation, the gap between creature and creator is not only closed; it is transformed into an intimate embrace.

Buddhism does not, as we have seen, begin with creation; rather, it teaches a gap between suffering (*samsara*) and liberation (*nirvana*) that is "without beginning." In Theravada this gap is usually regarded as real and in Mahayana as real but apparent—that is, it is the way things really appear to the unenlightened mind, but it is not the way things ultimately are. Even in Theravada, however, the reality of the gap is compromised by the teaching that mind in its true state is blissful. The path to liberation in both Theravada and Mahayana, then, is at least in part a becoming of what one is rather than a radical transformation. While Theravada prevaricates on this, Mahayana is quite specific. The Madhyamika school systematizes the Prajnaparamita literature by proposing that reality has both a superficial aspect called conventional truth (*samvrtisatya*) and a profound aspect called further truth (*paramārthasatya*).[6] Furthermore, reality as it truly is, is the simultaneity of the two aspects or truths in what is called the Middle Truth (*madhyamasatya*). Indian Madhyamika pictures the simultaneity as the coterminous presence of *samsara* and *nirvana*, while Chinese Mahayana goes further and speaks of the mutual interpenetration of the realm of *samsara* and the realm of *nirvana*. Mutual interpenetration is written in Chinese as *xiangru*, using the characters for "mutual" and "entering"; this term would do very well as a Chinese translation of co-inherence. Thus, the gap between suffering and liberation is not only closed, it is transformed into an intimate embrace.

The Schism between Theory and Practice

Since both traditions emphasize so strongly unity, wholeness, and nonduality in theory, it comes as something of a surprise to find how dualistic they are in practice. The dualism of Christianity is well known in the West, where Christianity is dominant, and the situation in the East, where Buddhism is dominant, is not very different. Both are seen by most of their detractors and many of their followers as acosmic (world-denying), with a pervasive anxiety about the body, sex, and women as full persons. Most mainline Christian dominations are explicitly homophobic, and Buddhism has only been prevented from explicit homophobia by ignoring the issue. Asian Buddhist teachers have been heard to say that there are no homosexuals in their country or in the Buddhist lineage.[7] For most Theravadins, *nirvana* is a distant goal that one reaches, if at all, in another realm. Mahayanists, despite being taught the value of the Bodhisattva path, frequently regard liberation as a postmortem departure to a kind of heaven. The acosmism of Buddhism in popular belief was put neatly to me by a friend who was brought up in China: if you did not drink alcohol, did not eat meat, and did not have sex, then you were a good Buddhist.

Why is practice and theory so at odds in Buddhism and Christianity? Because, I suggest, under the surface, in as it were the institutional subconscious, there is a reified heterosexism that compels the traditions to manifest as dualist.

Both Christianity and Buddhism give a privileged position to the male and to the celibate, but there does not seem to be any compelling doctrinal reason for this. Shakyamuni was male and after leaving home, celibate, but there is plenty of evidence in the Pali literature that laymen and laywomen were by no means unable to attain final liberation as *arahats*, provided that their roots of merit (*kusala-mula*) were strong enough and they had the time to practice. Jesus was male and celibate, but the New Testament is clear that for those who are "in Christ," there are no distinctions of gender (Galatians 3: 28), and its few commendations of celibacy are half-hearted and ambiguous.

Since the Buddha was a monk, it is not surprising that monasticism occupies an important place in Buddhism, but its supremacy needs to be explained. Since it cannot be explained with reference to doctrine, it is probably safe to assume a sociological, or shall we say sociobiological cause: first for the preeminence of the male and second for the preeminence of the monastic. The human is a sort of chimpanzee that wears clothes because it has lost its fur, and it forms troops dominated by alpha males who attain their position by making loud noises. It is only very recently that humans have become self-critical of this holdover from the simian past. There is perhaps a simple Marxist reason for this: The means of production in the twenty-first century have freed both men and women from their traditional work roles and permitted reflection on them. The conclusion is in, albeit only in theory: Men and women are, statistically speaking, equally competent. There is no reason why there should not be as many women as men in leadership positions, and yet any attempt by women to take leadership roles is met, in most Buddhist lineages and in all non-Protestant Christian denominations, with suspicion at best and suppression at worst.

Celibacy is a practical convenience for anyone who wants to concentrate on their job. The monastic is a kind of workaholic of the spirit. In Buddhism, the monastic receives the physical support (*artha*) of the Four Requisites (food, clothing, shelter, medicine) from the lay-people, while giving spiritual support (*dharma*) such as teaching and counseling in return. Celibacy is recommended as a spiritual practice by which one can subdue the passions more easily than if one were married. With all due respect, I wish to suggest that this venerable assumption is nonsense. Some people find celibacy a valid *ascesis*, many do not. Those who find it valuable might do just as well in a marriage or same-sex union in which both partners agree to refrain from sexual relations or to have them very occasionally because they find it helps their spiritual practice.[8] Those who cannot maintain their vows of celibacy either leave the monastery or are the subject of elaborate cover-up schemes that sometimes fail spectacularly.[9] Some Buddhist monks have privately confided in me that only a minority keep their vows of celibacy. The fact that a law is not observed is no argument for its abolition, but widespread nonobservance might lead us to ask about its presuppositions.

Path and Goal Symbolism

Both Christianity and Buddhism symbolize the path and its goal or fruit using male and female imagery that splits off certain supposedly ideal or typical qualities from the characteristics and personalities of real men and women: the male is symbolized as entirely active and the female is symbolized as entirely passive. In both traditions the virtues are those of the cartoon-book male hero vigorously fighting evil. The Church is "militant"; in the Middle Ages, the Christian monk was said to do battle with the enemies within the soul (the passions) as the counterpart of the knight who fought the external enemies of Christendom (the heathen). The Buddha, true to his birthright as a *kshatriya* (member of the warrior cast), overcame Mara with manly courage. The Bodhisattva path is one of combat; the word *bodhisattva* is interpreted as "spiritual warrior" and may be a corruption of *bodhi-sakta*, "powerful in [the practice leading to] enlightenment."

The end of the Christian path is frequently pictured as a spiritual marriage between Christ as male and the Christian as female (soul, *anima*, the feminine noun). The Church is the Bride of Christ, and while Christian nuns are (or were) married to Christ during their ceremony of monastic profession, Christian monks are not, despite the frequent references in medieval literature to Christ as female.[10] Although male imagery is also dominant in Buddhism, male-female imagery is uncommon except in Tantra, where the male practitioner visualizes actively penetrating the static female embodiment of wisdom. The symbolism is the mirror image of the Christian, but the partners are still reified and "ideal" and, contrary to Hindu Tantra, the male energy (*sakta*) is privileged over the female energy (*sakti*). The point of this discussion is that this reified heterosexist symbolism, which is implacably dualist, sleeps unchallenged in the collective unconsciousness of institutional Buddhism and Christianity. Institutions, like people, are controlled by their unconscious and unexamined assumptions; thus, I would argue, Buddhism and Christianity are forced to be dualistic in practice despite loudly maintaining nonduality in theory.

Analogue Consciousness and Non-Duality

Harry Hay, who is regarded as the founder of the modern gay movement, proposed that gays (or LGBT persons generally) see reality differently from straight persons. When a gay man falls in love with another man, the relationship is not that of subject to object but of subject to another subject, not of me to another but of me to another me:

> The Hetero monogamous relationship is one in which the participants, through bio-cultural inheritance, traditionally perceived each other as OBJECT. To the Hetero male, woman is primarily perceived as sex-*object* and then, only with increasing sophistication, as person-*object*. The Gay monogamous relationship is one in which the participants, through non-competitive instinctual inclinations, and *contrary to cultural inheritances*, perceive each other as Equals and learn, usually through deeply painful trials-and-errors, to experience each other, to continuously grow, and to develop *with* each other, empathically—as SUBJECT.[11]

Hay calls this gay consciousness subject-SUBJECT consciousness or *analogue consciousness* and proposes it as a solution to the problems brought about through the unthinking acceptance of patriarchal consciousness, or what he calls Hetero male consciousness. Hay regards the gay male as neither male or female at the level of consciousness, but as something else. He tells gay men that when they were young the boys told them that they threw a ball like a girl, but had they asked a girl about this, she would "have told [them] that [they] didn't throw a ball like a girl but like something *other*. You," he tells them, "were *not* a feminine boy, like the boys said, you were *OTHER!*"[12]

Hay describes how gays are other, living in what he calls a "new planet of Fairy-vision"[13] that, as his friend and collaborator Mitch Walker claims, overturns our conditioned views of reality: "Imagine, for instance, that the tops of the trees are really the roots."[14] Hay states: "Subject-SUBJECT consciousness is a multi-dimensional consciousness which may never be readily conveyable in the Hetero-male-evolved two-dimensional, or Binary, language to which we are primarily confined."[15] Analogue consciousness, then, challenges dualistic thinking and replaces it with nondual consciousness, and overturns, inverts, turns inside out, consensus reality. The inversion of consciousness is the way the Yogachara school of Mahayana Buddhism explains the transformation of deluded consciousness into clear wisdom. The inversion of society by the intervention of God is a common Biblical theme (for example, the Song of Hannah, I Samuel 2: 1–10, and its New Testament corollary, the Song of Mary, Luke 1: 46–55).

Analogue consciousness is, therefore, a tool that can be used to challenge the hegemony of the heterosexist models of the path and the goal in Buddhism and Christianity. There is certainly ample material for analogue consciousness in both traditions. The Buddha is said to have had a perfect body with glowing, golden skin, a mellifluous voice, and so on, and can certainly be the object of homophilic affection. Jeffrey Hopkins has shown that the symbolism of Tantric Buddhism can be changed from male-female to male-male (or female-female).[16] The homophilic, not to say homoerotic, possibilities of the scantily clad, well-muscled Jesus on the Cross are obvious to the unbiased observer.[17]

The reader's imagination can continue where this essay leaves off, but one caveat must be entered. Harry Hay's paean to analogue consciousness is so ecstatic that it is in danger of replacing male-female, subject-object duality with gay-straight duality. As the basis for "faerie" consciousness among groups that celebrate the gay spirit (Radical Faeries, Billy Club, Discovery, Gay Spirit Vision, and so forth), it is sometimes used to freeze a perceived rift between traditions such as Christianity and Buddhism on the one hand, and the neopagan traditions on the other, which are said to be more accepting of the body and sexuality. A Buddhist, however, would see that as deluded thinking, a dualism that has been thrown out of the front door has crept in through the back window. Analogue consciousness does not replace Hetero male consciousness; it offers itself instead as a partner, an equally valuable alternative, providing a check on the reification and dominance of both itself and Hetero male consciousness. It is not the exclusive possession of LGBT persons: It is a modality of the human spirit which has until now gone unrecognized.

If analogue consciousness is used to construct alternative models of the path and goal, and both they and the current heterosexual models are regarded as no more than helpful operational hypotheses, these new models will permit a certain relaxation of collective (institutional) and individual defenses. Operational hypotheses are nothing new to either tradition. In Buddhism they are called *upaya* (skillful means); Christians employed new models in Alexandrian Christianity as the principle of economy.[18] When this new symbol structure is in place, both traditions will be able to refresh and ennoble themselves as they begin, finally, to fit practice to theory.

Notes

1. This chapter is a revision of a paper present before the Gay Men's Issues in Religion Group of the annual meeting of the American Academy of Religion, Atlanta, Georgia, USA, 22–25 November 2003.

2. I have argued that there is, and I need not repeat that argument here. See Roger Corless, "Many Selves, Many Realities: The Implications of Heteronomy and the Plurality of Worlds Theory for Multiple Religious Belonging," *Pacific Coast Theological Society Journal*, 6 October 2002, http://www.pcts.org/journal/corless2002a/index.html.

3. Most recently, some Japanese Buddhologists, in a movement known as Critical Buddhism, have identified a creeping monism in Zen and have called for a return to the centrality of interdependent arising. See Jamie Hubbard and Paul L. Swanson, eds., *Pruning the Bodhi Tree: The Storm over Critical Buddhism*, (Honolulu: University of Hawai'i Press, 1999).

4. Charles Williams, *The Descent of the Dove: A Short History of the Holy Spirit in the Church* (Grand Rapids, MI: Eerdmans, 1980; reprint of 1939 edition), which bears the dedication "For the Companions of the Co-inherence."

5. Sermon 5, on I John 4: 16. *Meister Eckhart: Sermons and Treatises*, Volume I, trans. and ed. by M. O'C. Walshe (Shaftesbury, UK: Element Books, 1987; reprint of Watkins, 1979), 50.

6. This is often mistranslated as "ultimate truth," making it difficult to understand that it is only one aspect of reality as it truly is.

7. The Fourteenth Dalai Lama was neutral toward homosexuality until he found passages in the commentaries that he interprets as condemning it. Some other prominent Buddhist teachers, such as Thich Nhat Hanh, who

belong to a different commentarial tradition, take a positive view of homosexuality and Buddhism. There is no clear scriptural guidance for Buddhist laypeople since almost all the rules about sex are found in the Vinaya (monastic regulations) as lists of prohibitions addressed to celibates.

8. In the Middle Ages such an arrangement was called a "chaste marriage," and it has been the lifestyle of choice of persons who have been recognized as saints.

9. The recent "altar boy" scandal in the Catholic Church in the United States is well known. For the wider issue, see Eugene Kennedy, *The Unhealed Wound: The Church and Human Sexuality* (New York: St. Martin's Press, 2001). Buddhism has also had its difficulties. In *Traveller in Space: In Search of Female Identity in Tibetan Buddhism* (New York: George Braziller, 1996), June Campbell records how her illicit sexual relations with a highly respected Tibetan teacher were both denied and rationalized away by the institution.

10. Caroline Bynum, *Jesus as Mother: Studies in the Spirituality of the High Middle Ages* (Berkeley: University of California Press, 1983).

11. Harry Hay, *Radically Gay: Gay Liberation in the Words of Its Founder*, ed. Will Roscoe (Boston: Beacon Press, 1996), 210. Italics and capitals in original.

12. Hay, *Radically Gay*, 260.

13. Ibid.

14. Mitch Walker, quoted by Mark Thompson in "The Gay Tribe: A Brief History of Fairies," in *Gay Spirit: Myth and Meaning*, ed. Mark Thompson (New York: St. Martin's Press, 1987), 272.

15. Hay, *Radically Gay*, 260.

16. Jeffrey Hopkins, *Sex, Orgasm, and the Mind of Clear Light: The Sixty-Four Arts of Gay Male Love* (Berkeley, CA: North Atlantic Books, 1998).

17. Detailed suggestions for Christian meditation along these lines are made by Michael B. Kelly in "The Erotic Contemplative: Reflections on the Spiritual Journey of the Gay/Lesbian Christian," available online at www.eroticmassage.com or by writing to EROSpirit Research Institute, P.O. Box 3893, Oakland, CA 94609.

18. See my article "Lying to Tell the Truth—*Upāya* in Mahayana Buddhism and *Oikonomia* in Alexandrian Christianity," in *Buddha Nature: A Festschrift in Honor of Minoru Kiyota*, ed. Paul J. Griffiths and John P. Keenan (Reno, NV: Buddhist Books International, 1990), 27–40.

11

"A Dharma of Place"

Evolving Aesthetics and Cultivating Community in an American Zen Garden

Jeff Wilson

Enthusiasts of Japanese Zen gardens are used to juggling terms like *wabi-sabi* and *yugen*.[1] But how often do they find themselves talking about the use of red bricks to evoke a flowing stream, or contemplating an abstract Buddha figure made out of cement fondue? Such unusual approaches must be taken in investigating the Rochester Zen Center's Japanese-influenced garden, where Asian and North American traditions meet to produce an emerging American Zen aesthetic. This aesthetic, emerging from the fluid contact of two cultural, religious, and artistic spheres, can be seen in numerous Zen communities throughout the United States; examining the garden at the Rochester temple, one of the country's first and most influential convert Zen centers, provides a particularly clear window into this phenomenon.[2]

In America, where immigration has played a key role in shaping the religious landscape, scholars have often studied how Old World religions are transmitted and adapted to the New World situation by immigrant communities.[3] However, immigration plays a much smaller role in American Zen's history than in most American religions. Zen has mainly been transmitted by individual Japanese teachers to a Euro-American audience, presented as a therapy or spiritual practice rather than an ethnic, family-based traditional religion. Perhaps because of this peculiar American Zen emphasis on individuals rather than on communities, those few who have looked at Buddhism's transplantation have mainly explored abstract theological concepts such as enlightenment, or individualistic ritual practices such as meditation. Much rarer is the detailed study of material culture.

Yet Buddhist America is undeniably full of stuff, from homemade *zafu* cushions to plastic power beads to ancient imported statues. Careful attention to architecture and artifacts can provide useful information about American Buddhist groups and counteracts the tendency to look at convert American Zen as an atomized conglomeration of solitary sitters pursuing personal enlightenment. Religious spaces are expressions of a total community's self-identity: They offer members the chance to express themselves while at the same time subtly or overtly shaping the minds and bodies of the groups that inhabit them. In designing, constructing, maintaining, altering, and interacting with their communal space and the objects within it, religious practitioners are naturally moved beyond a personal perspective toward consciousness of being part of a group. And the spaces that result from these processes therefore reflect values and aesthetics that the community cherishes, providing clues as to how such groups are formed and maintained.

Three important points can be employed to analyze American Buddhist material culture. *Tradition*, encompassing forms used historically in Asia, is the starting point for all Buddhist lineages in the New World. *Adaptation* occurs when the new situation demands modifications to tradition, such as materials more suited to the new environment or the use of unusual objects because the traditional ones are unavailable. *Innovation* is a more radical response to the new surroundings—it involves actively seeking new expressions or methods of manufacture for the sake of expanding the range of possible forms.[4] Motivation is the most important distinguishing factor between the latter two categories: Adaptation is undertaken due to necessity and is practical in orientation (though often quite imaginative in execution), while innovation is pursued for its own sake, to creatively play with the untapped potential of Buddhist material culture. All three can be expected to appear in any given Buddhist space in America, regardless of the group's sectarian affiliation or ethnic composition. However, the degree of each phenomenon varies from group to group, and may provide information about how a particular American Buddhist community identifies itself: as staunchly traditional, progressively modern, or radically original, for instance.

History of the Rochester Zen Center Garden

It takes a certain kind of determination to live in Rochester, New York, where the average temperature is below freezing five months of the year, and winter typically dumps more than seven feet of snow on the city. At the same latitude as Sapporo, Rochester presents a very different environment from much of Japan, and it might seem like a strange place to find a garden designed along Japanese models. But in fact, for thirty years the students at Rochester Zen Center have been working on their large and distinctive garden, finding a middle path between the demands of Japanese tradition and the need to adapt to the realities of bleak Northeastern winters.

The center was founded in 1966 by Philip Kapleau, who studied Buddhism in Japan for thirteen years.[5] Kapleau actually viewed the unforgiving climate as a plus, believing it would help his disciples more readily direct their attention inward.[6] As he put it in his recollections of the center's founding, religiously sensitive people respond to their environments, acknowledging what he termed "a dharma of place."[7] By 1968 the group had purchased a house at 7 Arnold Park, but a disastrous fire soon after they moved in kept them busy with renovations for several years.[8] The back garden received some landscaping and a small pool with a fountain in 1972, but this was only the prelude to what was shortly to follow.[9]

In 1974 the center purchased 5 Arnold Park, and students began transforming the yard behind the Zen center's two buildings into a garden based on Japanese aesthetics. At that time, the center's community included James Rose, a famous landscape architect who studied design and architecture in Japan. The suggestion for a garden designed with Japanese Zen aesthetics came from Rose, and was quickly picked up by the other American students.[10] Casey Frank, a senior member of the community who was on the building committee at the time, explained:

> In the beginning, us young people were enamored with the Japanese aesthetic, more so than Roshi. He never, ever wanted the place to look Japanese. At the same time, he appreciated the beauty and practicality of the Japanese forms. That theme was in all our minds.[11]

Original center member and master gardener Audrey Fernandez echoed Frank's sentiment:

I've been very interested in Japanese gardens right from
the beginning. I read the original article in *House Beautiful*
on *shibui* and *wabi* and *sabi*, and oh! I was just thrilled, I
just couldn't imagine anything more beautiful. And I actually contributed a book on Japanese gardens to the library,
it's up there now. So I was very aware of this ... it just
seems natural to get some things that people also use in
Japanese gardens.[12]

Despite Kapleau's apparent reluctance toward the creation of the garden, other members of the community forged ahead.

The garden debuted on October 26, 1974. Drawing heavily on
the dry Zen garden tradition of *karesansui*, it featured long, curving swaths of white pebbles that swirled around islands of grass or
leafy ground cover.[13] Interesting rocks and trees rose here and there
from among the greenery, aligned in ways that suggested balance and
asymmetrical relationship. In his design, Rose relied on the traditional
Japanese aesthetic notion of *wabi*, which conveys a sense of distance,
age, quiet, and loneliness, like an abandoned fisherman's hut on a
gray, windy day.[14] Rose and his assistants drew upon the *wabi* aesthetic in choosing weathered rocks, and in designing the garden as an
interplay between gravel streams and grassy islands.[15] Several small
bridges, especially a miniature curved bridge, added to the sense of
scale by making the scene appear distant and unattainable. Irregu-
larly placed stones allowed people to move carefully along a few
prescribed paths, but as with many of the traditional Zen gardens of
Japan, the garden was primarily for contemplating, not exploring.[16]

However, the beautiful and traditional Japanese design soon
presented problems. The bridges became precarious; a former member of the Grounds Committee described the curved bridge as "a
wooden eyebrow that froze like Niagara Falls in winter to spill the
unwary to boulders underneath."[17] Meanwhile, space was at a premium, and the popular Zen center was already bursting at the seams,
creating a dilemma. The gravel river was not meant for walking on,
and the intrusion of human beings inevitably destroyed the sense of
scale, turning strolling Zen students into giant monsters marching
across the landscape.[18] Tradition was all fine and good, but necessity
demanded adaptation.

To remedy the Godzilla effect, in 1975 the Zen center hired David
Engel, another important architect. Like Rose, Engel was an American
strongly influenced by Japanese design aesthetics, and he quickly hit
upon an elegant solution. Directing teams of Zen center volunteers,

Engel removed the immaculate gravel flows and laid down 28,000 red bricks in their place.[19] The bricks were laid down lengthwise, providing a flowing sense to the paths, thus preserving the *karesansui* tradition of utilizing solid materials to evoke the fluidity of water. In some places they actually swirl into a circular pattern, creating an eddy or pool effect. Some trees and rocks were shuffled around as well and the miniature bridges were removed, eliminating the distant look of the garden to return it to a normal sense of scale.

The introduction of red brick into the garden, a building material absent from Zen gardens in Japan, was not such a departure for Rochester itself. Brick of this type is a staple construction material of the city—several of the Zen center's own buildings are made out it. Here we see the use of adaptation in the transformation of Zen in the West. Adding in brick, Engel and his helpers created a new look unfamiliar to Japan, yet tied to the aesthetic familiarity of the Rochester environment. Brick provided needed practicality. With the paths now fit for walking and with benches to sit on, the garden became a fully interactive space to be viewed from within, not without.

Engel further modified the garden by designing a new area, characterized by staggered box shapes and right angles, departing from the curving elements that Rose relied upon. Benches placed in this open, ordered space invited people into the garden for exploration and rest. While the garden continued to be used as a place for meditation, it lost its role as a tool for abstract contemplation.

People could now poke around in the garden, but Engel deliberately arranged trees and other elements so that visitors could still only see a portion at a time:

> One shouldn't be able to see the whole garden from one view. There should be some taller things in the foreground. Occasionally the view should be interrupted to increase the perspective. There shouldn't be all just one space— there should be some compartmentalization, a progression from narrowing down to opening up. It should have some strength and structure.[20]

The only way to discover the shape and character of the garden is to experience it directly, walking from area to area with attention to the changing surroundings. This simultaneous revealing and masking of the garden plays on the Japanese notion of *yugen*, which is characterized as dark, mysterious, subtle, and unknown, like the moon behind a veil of clouds.[21] In Japanese Zen gardens, *yugen* is achieved by arranging elements in such a way that they partially obscure each other, so that one cannot take in the entirety of the garden from any single viewing point. The *karesansui* at Ryōan-ji in Kyōto is a classic example—from no vantage point can all fifteen stones be seen.[22] Engel also added an important new element that drew on another feature of Japanese aesthetics, known as *shibui*. The notion of *shibui* is one of order, propriety, elegance, and refinement, like a formal tea ceremony.[23] The solid brick and right angles of the new resting area provoke a definite sense of *shibui* in the viewer. Compared with the rest of the garden, this section feels most civilized and ordered.

In 1976, a third architect further modified the Zen garden. Once again, the center was privileged to call upon the talents of a major artist, in this case George Nakashima, an architect and furniture maker whose woodwork is preserved in the Museum of Modern Art. The Zen community had decided to convert the 1896 carriage house in the back of the garden into a formal Buddha hall.[24] Nakashima supervised the renovation, adapting the old structure for its new use.[25] His most important contribution to the garden was the addition of a covered wooden walkway that runs along the outside of the Buddha hall and the main building, connecting them in a seamless flow that actually crosses through the garden itself. At the same point where this walkway crosses the garden, it is itself penetrated by the garden, as this is conspicuously the only section that lacks a waist-high wall of wooden planks, allowing movement into the garden, and creating a sense of spaciousness. Furthermore, the brick pathway that navigates the garden leads up to and under this nexus point, evoking the old *shinden* style of Japanese architecture, which included streams known as *yarimizu* that ran under and through the buildings of the estate.[26] Ever so subtly, the walkway actually rises at this point, as if it were a bridge spanning a flowing brook.[27]

The circumambulating manner in which the walkway snakes along the outside of the Buddha hall, rather than simply leading directly from door to door, mirrors the exterior walkways that surround Shinto shrines. The walkway is an intentionally interstitial space that belongs neither wholly to the inside, nor completely to the outside. Beneath its overhanging roof one is sheltered from precipitation, yet exposed to the temperature. The circuitous route invites walkers to pay attention to their journey, rather than simply hurrying along the straightest line between two points. This emphasis on attention to the present moment, free from wandering thoughts or preoccupations, is emphasized as the path to enlightenment among practitioners of American Zen. Here we see one of the ways in which architecture is marshaled to the cause of producing *satori*.[28]

Particularly interesting, wherever the walkway is fully open to the garden, as at the entrance to the Buddha hall, a further mediating element is introduced in the form of a strip of gravel bounded by small rocks, with larger flat stones providing diversion, and places for stepping into or out of the garden. The outer edge of the border is exactly aligned with the edge of the walkway's sloping roof, indicating that it is meant to further blur the distinction between interior and exterior. Such borders can often be found in both Zen gardens and traditional Japanese tea houses.[29] All of these techniques for diminishing the separation between the outer natural spaces and the inner human world point back to a key concept in Japanese aesthetics, the non-differentiation of nature and humanity.

Cleverly, Nakashima managed to suggest an alignment between the straight support poles of the walkway and the straight trunks of the trees in the *shibui* section, increasing the sense of order and relationship between the buildings and garden elements. The snaking, weather-beaten walkway, which is perpetually gloomy and suggestive, continues the theme of *yugen*, and the *okarikomi*, a type of clipped bush, obscure the path and buildings.[30] Yet the very mysteriousness of the walkway also serves to highlight the general cleanliness of the garden in the patio section it borders, enhancing that area's feeling of *shibui*.

All of these developments—the gravel paths, the replacement with bricks, the Asian foliage, the winding walkway, the carriage house turned into a Buddha hall—demonstrate the creative tension between tradition and adaptation seen at numerous Zen centers in America. But there is one more aspect of the contemporary Rochester garden that must be analyzed. And while it includes elements of tradition and adaptation, another concept, that of innovation, best describes this next feature.

Building the Universal Buddha

The heart of the garden is found toward the back, a little beyond the entrance to the Buddha hall. From a distance it appears to be a tall mountain, rearing up from the sea of green foliage like a classical *horai* stone, a type of vertical rock that suggests the land of the immortals. Up close, it resolves into a clear though abstract seated figure. This six-foot-high sculpture is known as the Universal Buddha, and it directly evokes the traditional images of Buddha seated in the full-lotus posture of *zazen* prized by Zen Buddhists. The full-lotus is the most stable seated configuration, good for long periods of intense meditation, and its triangular peaked shape replicates the feel of a mountain, a recollection that Zen teachers took frequent advantage of. Philip Kapleau makes use of this metaphor in *The Three Pillars of Zen*:

> According to Dogen, one must sit with a sense of dignity or grandeur, like a mountain or a giant pine. Moreover, since body is the material aspect of mind, and mind the immaterial aspect of body, to assemble the hands and arms, and the feet and legs, into a unity at one central point, where the joined hands rest on the heels of the locked legs, as in the full-lotus posture, facilitates the unification of mind. Finally, however intangibly, the lotus posture creates a sense of rootedness in the earth, together with a feeling of an all-encompassing oneness, void of the sensation of inner or outer.[31]

For Zen Buddhists, sitting in *zazen* like a mountain is ideal. As students approach the Buddha hall, the Universal Buddha silently manifests to them the proper form for *zazen*, acting as a mirror and model to aspire toward as it reveals the practice/attainment whose pursuit forms the core of their community. Note also the many horticultural allusions in this passage—trees, flowers, roots—that demonstrate an appreciation for the lessons of the living environment even in the context of inwardly focused meditation practice.

Despite the sculpture's allusion to elements of Zen tradition, it is in fact highly innovative in design. This sculpture draws more heavily on North American principles of abstract art than any Japanese precedents—it is neither purely symbolic like the *horai* stones, nor plainly representative like the fully articulated Buddha statues of Japan. Its prominent placement and size are also innovative, driven not by the practical need to adapt to different circumstances, but by a new imaginative conception and usage of space and balance absent from Japanese Zen gardens. Also innovative is a secret that this deceptive abstract Buddha holds. To all appearances it is a rough jumble of individual stones, artfully arranged to evoke the idea of a Buddha seated in meditation. But in fact, this Universal Buddha is a single piece, molded by the sculptor to look like discrete stones.

In the mid-1980s, Kapleau decided that there was an element that he would like added to the garden. He enlisted John Fillion, a Toronto-area sculptor, to create a Buddha without a face based on designs Kapleau had sketched out. Fillion decided to mold the Buddha out of a curiously named industrial construction material: cement fondue.[32] Cement fondue is actually a powder, which is mixed with water and massaged into whatever shape is necessary. The material is so plastic, in fact, that it can be used to take casts of individual fingerprints. Therefore the rough-hewn look of the Universal Buddha is a deception—rather than a gathering of venerable, weathered stones, it is actually a block of construction-grade cement fondue, deliberately crafted to disguise its true nature. And the sculpture does succeed—visitors are unaware that the piece is not in fact a rock statue.[33]

Also notable in the iconography of the statue, there is an elongated section on the left-hand side (when facing the sculpture) that can appear to stretch to the ground. There seems to be a suggestion here of the *bhumisparsa mudra*, the gesture of touching the Earth with his right hand that the Buddha performed at the moment of his enlightenment. This gesture signifies the Buddha's great awakening, and the intimate connection with the Earth that is a natural subject for any garden.

The awakening motif was further suggested by a magnolia tree (since removed due to disease) whose branches stretched out to shelter the Universal Buddha. The Buddha was born beneath a tree in the garden of Lumbini, which suddenly bloomed as he appeared. In springtime the magnolia burst with color like a nimbus of blossoms, visually recreating this mythic motif. Significantly, this blossoming usually occurred in April, the month associated with the birth of the Buddha in Japan. The Buddha also attained enlightenment under a tree, and he passed away between two trees. On the approach to the Buddha hall, the Universal Buddha appeared to be situated between two trees, the magnolia on the left and the Japanese maple on the right. Thus, this arrangement simultaneously evoked the birth, enlightenment, and death of the Buddha, as well as demonstrating the proper form of *zazen*, and suggesting a mountain with all the attendant associations in Zen.

At first, the Zen center's more Japanophilic students weren't quite sure how to take the introduction of this unusual figure into the garden. "I could never make up my mind whether it was a stroke of genius, or he was completely *meshuggeneh*," said Casey Frank.[34] Yet the Buddha did eventually win the community over. One reason was that the Universal Buddha manages to convey a range of interpretations.

As Frank explains, "The Buddha has no ethnicity; it is all humans, transhuman."[35] The name and shape point to the universal Buddha-nature of all beings, to which the practice of Zen is designed to awaken the practitioner.[36] Thus, the Universal Buddha lays out both the path and the goal to the Zen student who stops to contemplate its features. This aspect was intended by Kapleau, and points to innovation more than simple adaptation.[37] Kapleau sought to present a new, non-traditional look, not for purposes of adaptation to the environment, but to highlight an aspect of Zen thought he felt essential to communicate to his community. The Universal Buddha is a thesis advanced in cement fondue. That Kapleau succeeded in his plans can be seen by the prominent place that the Universal Buddha now occupies in Rochester Zen Center publications, demonstrating that it has become a focal point of community attention and identity formation.

In some ways, the creation of the non-ethnic Universal Buddha is a material representation of an intense debate that altered the course of the Rochester community, centering on issues of tradition, adaptation, and innovation. When Kapleau founded his center, he decided that much of the traditional Zen he had learned in Japan needed a more Western idiom and aesthetic in order to remain relevant to his American students. For example, contrary to his own training in Japan, Kapleau used English in the Rochester liturgy and advised members to wear Western clothes. This led to a strong reaction from Kapleau's strict teacher, Yasutani Hakuun, who objected to these adaptations. The rift eventually prompted Kapleau to end their relationship and withdraw the Rochester Zen Center from affiliation with Yasutani's organization, a major event in the history of the community.[38] The Universal Buddha is more than an object—it is a concrete expression of Kapleau's decision that his community would not be bound by any single ethnic tradition, a declaration that Zen transcends cultural boundaries and can be adapted as needed to any situation.

At the same time, the statue also quietly reflects another core principle that the Rochester Zen Center is formed around. While Kapleau wished to move beyond rigid adherence to Japanese forms, he still identified his teaching and practice as solidly Buddhist. This led to a schism with his first senior disciple, Toni Packer, who in 1981 decided that Buddhism had become too restrictive a label on her approach to spirituality. She left the community, taking many students with her, a key event perhaps even more important in the history of the center than the split with Yasutani.[39] Traces of that break linger in the cement fondue of the Universal Buddha, which while universal—and thus a repudiation of Yasutani and Yamada—is also clearly a *Buddha*, and thus a refutation of Packer's approach as well. Even within the innovation of the Universal Buddha tradition remains apparent, pointing the community toward their Buddhist identity that outweighs ethnicity but remains a cohesive binding power.

Conclusion

The proper understanding of a Zen temple garden includes not only its aesthetic appeal and evocative suggestions, but also an understanding of its role as a place of Zen practice. While *zazen* is emphasized in Zen, the true goal is to carry the attitude of meditation away from the cushion and out into the world. Thus Zen practitioners at the center also engage in mindful activities, such as sweeping, raking, shoveling, planting, and pruning.[40]

Other activities conducted in the garden include seated and walking meditation, public and semi-private ceremonies, picnicking, and relaxation.[41] Important additions to the garden are often celebrated with formal ceremonies. Major annual community-wide events are held in the garden, such as celebrations of the Buddha's birthday. It is also the site of significant community rituals. For example, Zen students undertaking formal precept vows have been led through the garden walkway past a series of images representing the unstable mental states they seek to leave behind.[42] The garden has become a cherished part of the life of Rochester Zen Center. As one member put it in the center's journal: "The garden hears the cries of the world. . . . It provides a setting, a locus, where all things can rest and be resolved."[43] For some, the garden is almost a living, nurturing entity that guides and awakens the community.

Finally, the garden now carries a particular resonance for the entire community. In his final hours, Philip Kapleau requested that he be taken out into the garden one last time. There he passed away on May 6, 2004, surrounded by softly chanting students and family members. A memorial garden for Kapleau is being planned for one corner of the grounds and is expected to become a focal point for the community.[44]

The *Sakutei-ki*, a classic manual of garden architecture written in the eleventh century, says: "When copying the gardens of famous masters of old, bear in mind the intention of your patron and design your version according to your own taste."[45] This illustrates that for more than one thousand years, both tradition and innovation have informed Japanese gardening, which allowed for a certain level of flexibility, spontaneity, and freedom of expression. Norris Johnson has suggested that careful observers can trace a phylogenetic lineage of Buddhist architecture from India, to China and Korea, and then to Japan.[46] Now it appears that the lineage has successfully made the transition to a new land, mixing with the native aesthetics and construction materials to produce unique offspring that nevertheless bear the stamp of the old forms. When fire is passed to a new torch, the flame is neither exactly the same fire as the original, nor is it entirely different. So too the transmission of Japanese Buddhist aesthetics to America has resulted in the creation of communities that express themselves through an aesthetic that is neither the same, nor altogether new. Through combining traditional, adaptive, and innovative elements, this blend of new and old, Asia and North America, defines the emerging American Zen aesthetic.

Notes

1. For example, see Lennox Tierney, *Wabi Sabi: A New Look at Japanese Design* (Layton, UT: Gibbs Smith, 1999).

2. An earlier version of this research appeared as Jeff Wilson, "Aesthetics of American Zen: Tradition, Adaptation, and Innovation in the Rochester Zen Center Garden," *Japan Studies Review* 9 (2005): 101–14. The author would like to thank everyone at the Rochester Zen Center for their assistance with this research, particularly Audrey Fernandez, Casey Frank, Scott Jennings, and Christopher Taylor.

3. For example, see Sydney Ahlstrom, *A Religious History of the American People* (New Haven, CT: Yale University Press, 1972).

4. While these terms are used here to analyze American Buddhist material culture, they could also be employed in other areas, such as analysis of theology or ritual. For example, *zazen*, the basic form of seated Zen meditation, is a traditional practice in Japan, usually performed by priests and monastics. The way in which it is widely performed by the laity at Rochester Zen Center is an adaptation to a new situation, where middle-class Euro-American laypeople are the primary group interested in pursuing meditation practice. Americans have begun to alter the practice in significantly innovative ways, such as the creation of "Zen driving": see K. T. Berger, *Zen Driving* (New York: Ballantine Books, 1988). Despite the presentation of three separate terms, it should be acknowledged that these are not static categories. Traditions are always in flux, adaptation can be quite innovative, and innovations may be pursued with the goal of reaching some state imagined to be more traditional or authentic. This typology is meant to suggest lines of investigation, not pronounce the final word on any phenomenon.

5. Audrey Fernandez, *American Zen Twenty Years* (Rochester, NY: Rochester Zen Center, 1986).

6. Bob Schrei, "Roshi Takes a Bow," *Zen Bow* 9:3–4 (1976): 53–57.

7. Philip Kapleau, "Coming to Rochester" *Zen Bow* 12:4 (1990): 5.

8. Casey Frank, "Arnold Park-ji," *Zen Bow* 18:2 (1996): 18–22.

9. Philip Kapleau, "Editorial," *Zen Bow* 5:3 (1972): 3–5.

10. Casey Frank, telephone interview with former Rochester Zen Center construction foreman. 29 September 2003.

11. Frank, telephone interview. Roshi is a term for a Zen master, applied here to Philip Kapleau.

12. Audrey Fernandez, personal interview with former Rochester Zen Center president. 14 May 2004. *Shibui, wabi,* and *sabi* are terms used in Japanese aesthetics. They will be defined in the course of this chapter.

13. Frank, "Arnold Park-ji." *Karesansui* is a Japanese gardening style that uses dry elements such as rocks and sand to suggest water.

14. Vincent T. Covello and Yuji Yoshimura, *The Japanese Art of Stone Appreciation: Suiseki and Its Use with Bonsai* (Boston: Charles E. Tuttle, 1984), 30.

15. Anonymous, "At the Center . . . ," *Zen Bow* 7:4 (1974): 22–23.

16. Christopher Tadgell, *Japan: The Informal Contained* (London: Ellipsis, 2000), 156–57.

17. Fernandez, *American Zen,* 18.

18. Frank, telephone interview.

19. Frank, "Arnold Park-ji."

20. David Engel, Casey Frank, Tony Caprino, and John Botsford, "Meeting: Afternoon, Trip to Stone Quarry," 6 May 1976 (minutes).

21. Covello and Yoshimura, *Japanese Art of Stone Appreciation,* 83–84.

22. Lorraine E. Kuck, *The World of Japanese Gardens: From Chinese Origins to Modern Landscape Art* (New York: Weatherhill, 1984), 258.

23. Covello and Yoshimura, *Japanese Art of Stone Appreciation,* 83.

24. Anonymous, "Work," *Zen Bow* 8:4 (1975): 22.

25. There is only space in this chapter to mention the most prominent designers who directly made their mark on the Zen center's grounds. However, this is not intended to slight the work of the many other architects, carpenters, gardeners, and volunteers who worked alongside Rose, Engel, and Nakashima. There is no room to go into detail about the contributions of such workers as Barry Keeson, Pat Simons, and John Botsford, but this should not diminish the reality that the garden arises from the visions and labor of many members of the Rochester Zen Center community.

26. Gunter Nitschke, *Japanese Gardens: Right Angle and Natural Form* (Cologne: Benedikt Taschen Verlag, 1993).

27. Frank, telephone interview.

28. *Satori* is the Zen experience of spiritual insight, the goal of practice at Rochester Zen Center. See Philip Kapleau, *The Three Pillars of Zen: Teaching, Practice, Enlightenment* (Boston: Beacon Press, 1965).

29. Masao Hayakawa, *The Garden Art of Japan,* trans. Richard L. Gage (New York: Weatherhill 1973).

30. William Morrow, *Japanese Gardens* (New York: Harper Collins, 1979).

31. Kapleau, *Three Pillars of Zen*, 10.

32. Frank, telephone interview.

33. Jason Martin, "Triple Specials: A Visit Celebrating Roshi's Birthday at the RZC," *Toronto Zen Center* (accessed 30 September 2003): www.torontozen.org/tzc_article_triple.htm.

34. Frank, telephone interview. *Meshuggeneh* is Yiddish for "crazy."

35. Frank, telephone interview.

36. Fernandez, *American Zen*.

37. Scott Jennings, personal interview with Rochester Zen Center archivist, 13 May 2004.

38. Robert H. Sharf, "Sanbōkyōdan: Zen and the Way of the New Religions," *Japanese Journal of Religious Studies* 22:3–4 (1995): 446. It is interesting to note that the sculpture was unveiled in mid-1986. Chronologically, this occurred after a former Rochester student had written to Yasutani's heir, Yamada Kōun, in December 1985 asking about Kapleau's credentials; Yamada had responded in January 1986 with a widely circulated public letter that discredited Kapleau and his community (447). Did the appearance of the Universal Buddha—a stark refutation of authoritarian claims on Zen, particularly those of ethnic privilege—later that same year arise directly from these events? Unfortunately, both Kapleau and Fillion are deceased, and the documentary record is too fragmentary to retrieve the exact dates when the statue was conceived, commissioned, or reached a stage where it could no longer be remolded in reaction to outside events.

39. Kenneth Kraft, "Recent Developments in North American Zen," in *Zen: Tradition and Transition*, ed. Kenneth Kraft (New York: Grove Press, 1988), 195.

40. Richard von Sturmer and Joseph Sorrentino, *Images from the Center: Daily Life at an American Zen Center* (Rochester, NY: Rochester Zen Center, 1998), 15.

41. Christopher Taylor, interview.

42. Fernandez, *American Zen*.

43. Von Sturmer and Sorrentino, *Images from the Center*, 12. The phrase "hears the cries of the world" alludes to Kannon Bosatsu, the *bodhisattva* of compassion. Thus, von Sturmer suggests that this is a "bodhisattvic garden" (the name of the essay) that actively communicates the *dharma* and helps suffering beings achieve enlightenment.

44. Fernandez, *American Zen*.

45. Nitschke, *Japanese Gardens*, 57. Though not specifically Buddhist in origin, the *Sakutei-ki* was often consulted by designers working on temple gardens.

46. Norris Brock Johnson, "The Garden in Zuisen Temple, Kamakura, Japan: Design Form and Phylogenetic Meaning," *Journal of Garden History* 10:4 (1990): 214–36.

Contributors

Michael C. Brannigan (PhD, Philosophy, MA, Religious Studies, University of Leuven, Belgium) is the Pfaff Endowed Chair in Ethics and Moral Values at the College of Saint Rose in Albany, New York. He is also Adjunct Full Professor of Medical Ethics at the Alden March Bioethics Institute in Albany Medical College. Prior to his recent appointment, he was Vice President for Clinical and Organizational Ethics at the Center for Practical Bioethics in Kansas City, Missouri. His specialty lies in ethics, medical ethics, Asian philosophy, and intercultural studies. Along with numerous articles, his books include *The Pulse of Wisdom: The Philosophies of India, China, and Japan; Striking a Balance: A Primer on Traditional Asian Values; Healthcare Ethics in a Diverse Society* (coauthored); and *Ethical Issues in Human Cloning* (ed.) His two most recent books are *Cross-Cultural Biotechnology* and *Ethics Across Cultures.*

Roger Corless (1938–2007) received his PhD in Buddhist Studies at the University of Wisconsin–Madison in 1973, and in that year joined the Department of Religion at Duke University. He retired from Duke in 2000. He was a prolific scholar, publishing three monographs—two titles in 1981 and one in 1989. He also published over one hundred articles, chapters in books, and encyclopedia entries. His chapter in this volume is one of his last essays.

David L. Dupree is a retired corporate executive and the literary executor of Roger Corless. David received his BA from the University of Delaware and his MBA from the Wharton School of Business. He is the founder of THE CORLESS, a nonprofit foundation providing scholarships for graduate students.

Rita M. Gross is Professor Emerita of Comparative Studies in Religion at the University of Wisconsin–Eau Claire. She is also a Buddhist *dharma* teacher, who teaches in several lineages of Tibetan Buddhism. Her best known books are *Buddhism After Patriarchy: A Feminist History, Analysis, and Reconstruction of Buddhism* and *Feminism and*

Religion: An Introduction. Her book *A Garland of Feminist Reflections* was published in 2009 by the University of California Press.

Carl T. Jackson is Professor of History at the University of Texas at El Paso. He has served as a Fulbright Lecturer at the Osaka University, Japan. Besides numerous scholarly articles, he has published monographs in 1981 and 1994.

John Kitterman teaches American literature, film, and theory courses at Ferrum College, where he is Associate Professor of English. Most of his research has been in contemporary American and African American culture. His most recent publications have been on Edgar Allan Poe and on the film *Brokeback Mountain.*

Ellen Pearlman is affiliated with nine *UTNE Magazine* awards for independent publishing and is one of the founders of both *The Brooklyn Rail* and *Tricycle Magazine.* A Breadloaf Writer's Conference Scholar, recommended by the late poet Allen Ginsberg, she was also awarded an Asian Cultural Council Grant to investigate Tibetan sacred dance in nomadic Eastern Tibet and to create a documentary film on the subject as a result of her work on *Tibetan Sacred Dance,* the first book in the English language on the subject. Winner of a Canadian Banff Mountain Culture Grant, a Banff Canadian Center Writer's residency, and four Vermont Studio Center President's Fellowships, she was a finalist for the Andy Warhol/Creative Capital Arts Writers Grant, and a recipient of the Prince Claus Trust Grant to go to Ulan Bator, Mongolia. Ellen has also received a black belt in Taijitsu (Ninja) under the auspices of Black Belt Hall of Fame Ninja Master Shidoshi Steven Hayes. She splits her time between Brooklyn, New York; and Beijing, China.

Lori Pierce is Assistant Professor of American Studies at DePaul University in Chicago, Illinois. She has previously contributed articles on Buddhism in the United States to *Buddhist Women on the Edge* (North Atlantic Books, 1996); *Innovative Buddhist Women* (Curzon Press, 2000); *The Encyclopedia of Religion and American Culture* (ABC-Clio, 2003); and *The Encyclopedia of Women and Religion in North America* (Indiana University Press, 2006).

Charles S. Prebish holds the Charles Redd Chair in Religious Studies at Utah State University. He came to Utah State University following more than thirty-five years on the faculty of the Pennsylvania

State University. He has published nineteen books and more than fifty scholarly articles and chapters. Dr. Prebish was cofounder of the Buddhism Section of the American Academy of Religion. He has also served as editor of the *Journal of Global Buddhism* and *Critical Review of Books in Religion*. In 2005, he was honored with a festschrift volume by his colleagues titled *Buddhist Studies from India to America: Essays in Honor of Charles S. Prebish.*

David L. Smith is Professor in the Department of Philosophy and Religion at Central Michigan University. His principal areas of research and publication are modern religious thought, American Transcendentalism, and religion and film.

Gary Storhoff has published widely on American, African American, and Ethnic American literature. He is the author of *Understanding Charles Johnson* (2004). He is currently at work on a book on William Faulkner and family systems theory.

Thomas A. Tweed is the Shive, Lindsay, and Gray Professor of Religious Studies at the University of Texas at Austin. His publications include *The American Encounter with Buddhism, 1844–1912: Victorian Culture and the Limits of Dissent* (1992), *Asian Religions in America: A Documentary History* (1999), and *Crossing and Dwelling: A Theory of Religion* (2006).

John Whalen-Bridge is Associate Professor of English at the National University of Singapore. He is the author of *Political Fiction and the American Self* (University of Illinois Press, 1998), and he is currently working on *Dharma Bums Progress*, a study of "engaged aesthetics" in the work of Gary Snyder, Maxine Hong Kingston, and Charles Johnson.

Judy D. Whipps is Chair of Liberal Studies and Associate Professor of Philosophy at Grand Valley State University. Her recent publications include *Jane Addams's Writings on Peace*, a four-volume collection of Addams's writings on peace (2003). She has also written "Jane Addams's Social Thought as a Model for a Pragmatist-Feminist Communitarianism" (*Hypatia*, 2004), "The Feminist Pacifism of Emily Greene Balch, Nobel Peace Laureate" (*NWSA Journal*, 2006), and essays on Lucy Sprague Mitchell, Jessie Taft, and Emily Greene Balch in *American Women Philosophers.*

Jeff Wilson is Assistant Professor of Religious Studies and East Asian Studies at Renison University College, University of Waterloo. He is the founding chair of the Buddhism in the West program unit at the American Academy of Religion and author of *Mourning the Unborn Dead: A Buddhist Ritual Comes to America* (Oxford University Press, 2009).

Index

Abortion, 6, 83–100

Addams, Jane, 6–7, 101, 120, 121n7; biography of, 107–09; Hull House, founding of, 103–04, 115–16; feminism of, 119

Aesthetics, 9, 28, 34, 49, 58, 106, 136, 195–200

Analogue Consciousness (subject-SUBJECT consciousness), 8, 191–93; see also Hay, Harry

Anatman (*see* Self and no-self doctrine)

Arendt, Hannah, 102, 120n3

Aristotle, 102

Avidya (Ignorance), 75, 186

Batchelor, Stephen, 33

Baudrillard, Jean, *Symbolic Exchange and Death*, 135–38; "Simulacra and Simulations," 141, 144, 146n26

Beat Movement, The, 2, 21, 46, 59, 64; see also Kerouac, Jack; Ginsberg, Allen; Snyder, Gary

Bioethics, 5–6, 69–82

Blake, William, 65, 167

Bodhisattva, 103, 109–10, 120n4, 152, 190, 208n43

Buddha, The (the historical Buddha: Siddhartha Gautama, Sanskrit; Siddhattha Gotama, Pali; c. 563 BCE–483 BCE), 1, 93, 102–03, 107, 110, 117–18, 160–61, 178; appearance of, 192; "Buddha mind" and, 131, 144; teachings of, 3, 5, 16, 108, 119, 125, 151–54; worldview of, 184–85, 189–90; see also Universal Buddha

Buddhism: abortion and, 83–100; American Pragmatism and, 101–23; Beats and, 21, 46, 57, 59; contemporary ethics and, 69–82, 83–100, 101–24; contemporary popularity of, 1–2; feminism and, 5, 6, 83–100, 104, 117, 119; postmodernism and, 38, 66, 125–47; science and 33, 43; sexuality and, 83–100, 152–54, 188–93, 193n7, 194n9; source of religious identity and, 1, 4, 8, 151–66, 167–82

Buddhist Churches of America (BCA), 156, 162, 171, 180n5; see also Jodo Shinshu Buddhism, Pure Land Buddhism, Shin Buddhism

Burma, 121

Carus, Paul, 30, 41–43, 54n12; see also Open Court, The

Celibacy, 92–95, 152, 189–90, 194

China, 3, 5, 55, 173, 189, 206

Christianity, 8, 20, 32, 52, 129, 156, 192; as alternative to Buddhism for Hawai'i Japanese, 169–79; view towards homosexuality of, 183–90

Co-inherence, 187–88

Coleman, James William, *The New Buddhism*, 4, 158

Compassion (*karuna*), 1, 6, 31, 69, 118, 154; abortion and, 86–89; Engaged Buddhism and, 101, 108, 110–13, 114–15, 119

Conze, Edward, 16, 33

Critical Buddhism, 193n3